# BUCKINGHAMSHIRE

# THE BUCKINGHAMSHIRE DOMESDAY

ALECTO HISTORICAL EDITIONS
LONDON
1988

ISBN for Buckinghamshire volumes: 0 948459 22 0
ISBN for this volume: 0 948459 86 7 ✓



Printed in England

ALECTO HISTORICAL EDITIONS
46 Kelso Place, London W8 5QG, England

# CONTENTS

# PREFACE

THIS is the third volume of the Alecto County Edition of Domesday Book to be published. In the manuscript eleven folios constitute the section for Buckinghamshire which comes thirteenth in the order of counties, though the spacing and style of the main scribe's writing show that it was written fairly early in the programme in which the thirty counties were inscribed. These folios are well-written and neatly laid out, despite the wrong chapter-numbering in the text which does not correspond with the numbers in the initial list of tenants-in-chief on folio 143, a relatively common error in the manuscript.

Of the people mentioned in the Buckinghamshire section, Domesday Book allows us a few rather more vivid glimpses than are usually found in its laconic entries. For example, folio 148v bears one of the very rare instances in which there is an explicit record of the plight and state of mind of one of the countless English landowners who were summarily dispossessed after the Conquest. In the time of King Edward, we are told, one Æthelric held a manor in Marsh Gibbon: now, twenty years later, he is obliged to lease his former property from the Norman owner, William fitzAnsculf, and is still living there 'in heaviness and misery'. Another hint of happier times before the Normans came is to be found opposite, on the next folio 149, in the entry for Oakley. Here Godric the sheriff is stated to have granted a small parcel of land to the skilful Ælfgyth 'the maid', so long as he retained his office and she continued to teach his daughter embroidery in gold thread.

Normally each part of this series will contain a large-scale map limited to the county in question, but in this case Buckinghamshire is mapped with Oxfordshire and Berkshire since the three shires combined together make a convenient and economical rectangle.

Throughout this edition the names and extent of the counties are those which obtained prior to the restructuring of the counties in 1974. Since their traditional boundaries had remained virtually unchanged since the time of the Domesday Survey, there seemed little purpose in following recent, arbitrary innovations which have neither historical justification nor useful function in this context. Buckinghamshire has been fortunate to escape these alterations, apart from an abrupt departure from its southern boundary along the Thames in order to effect the transference to Berkshire of the district around Slough. In this volume and in the associated county map this region, which contains the Domesday settlements of Eton, Datchet, Ditton, Horton, Wraysbury and Upton, is restored to its rightful county as was the situation for a thousand years or more.

The three volumes that constitute each part of the County Edition are designed to be mutually supportive and are separated in this way for the reader's convenience. For instance, it is desirable for the facsimile folios to be present in one book and the parallel translations in another so that both can be consulted side by side. For the same reason the key to the symbols employed in the translations for Great Domesday's marginal notes and signs (Appendix I), and the list of abbreviations found in the manuscript (Appendix II) are best incorporated in the third volume, *Domesday Book Studies*, so that they, too, can be used in conjunction with the folios of translations and facsimile to which they refer. A fourth separate element is the large-scale county map which is provided as a loose-leaf folded sheet in order to be spread out near at hand if required.

Besides the book containing the facsimile folios and the maps, the division of text into two further self-contained volumes reflects the character and scope of their contents. *Domesday Book Studies* (which is common to the entire County Edition) is a book of essays on topics concerning Domesday Book in general, while this volume contains all matter specific to the locality in question. The translations are put at the end, unusually after the indices, where they are easiest to find and where their pages can be matched with the facsimile of the manuscript by the same folio numbers without disrupting the pagination of the rest of this book.

In a project so closely bound up with local history, place-name identification will constitute a salient feature affecting all its aspects, especially in the translations, indices and maps where their occurrences must always be consistent. By chance, the present publication was first set in motion towards the end of a period when the place-names recorded in Domesday Book had come under particular scrutiny, but not always with unanimously accepted results. The only recourse was to log every mention of a place-name onto a card-index, enter into it all dissident opinion, and then to submit this organised body of raw material to an editor appointed for his or her special knowledge of a given county. The editor for the Buckinghamshire place-names was T. D. Cain, who also established their position on the map.

Those responsible for the making of the facsimile and for the production of this volume are noticed in the acknowledgements printed in the accompanying *Domesday Book Studies*, though special mention should be made of Westerham Press for the complex task of setting the translations to match the Latin text of the manuscript with such success. The database for the manipulation of the place- and personal names has been developed at the same printing-house under the personal supervision of their managing director, James Brennan. The design and typography for this, as for the rest of the work, is by Ian Mortimer, I. M. Imprimit, London.

Our thanks are due especially to Elaine Shaughnessy who has controlled the editing of this volume overall, to Basil Harley for guiding the diverse elements through the press, to Brian Martin for overseeing production at Westerham Press, and also to the following for their diligence in the accomplishment of its various parts:

County introduction: copy-editing, Tanya Schmoller.

Bibliography: Dr David Bates, for rearranging his *Domesday Bibliography* already published; editing, Suzanne Bosworth, Patricia Gibson.

Indices: Jenny Page for keying-in the material for the database from which both Indices are derived; Douglas Matthews for the compilation of the Index of Persons; and Cyril Simsa for editing both Indices.

Translation: initial standardisation, Eric Hemming, Paul Francis, Stephen Wilson; copy-preparation at Oxford University Press, George Tulloch; editing, Alexander Rumble, Christine Shaw, Caroline Thorn; type-setting at Westerham Press, Clive Logsdon.

Map: assistance with the design, Tom Phillips; compilation and editing, Tom Cain, Des Seal, Cyril Simsa; delineation of the hundred boundaries, Frank Thorn; overseeing production at Cook Hammond and Kell Ltd., Jackie Hoy.

Finally, at Alecto, for the myriad incidental activities that such a project requires, we must thank Emma Bird, Sarah Burton, Henrietta Pearson and Emma Wells-Cole.

Ann Williams, *Editor-in-Chief*

R. W. H. Erskine, *General Editor*

The following is a list of abbreviations which are used throughout this edition. References to publications are given in their abbreviated form if they occur in the county bibliography.

| | |
|---|---|
| *AntJ* | *Antiquaries Journal* |
| *ArchJ* | *Archaeological Journal* |
| *ASE* | *Anglo-Saxon England* |
| BAR | British Archaeological Reports |
| BL | British Library |
| *CA* | *Current Archaeology* |
| DB | Domesday Book |
| *EconHR* | *Economic History Review* |
| EETS | Early English Text Society |
| *EHR* | *English Historical Review* |
| EPNS | English Place-Name Society |
| Exon | Exeter Domesday Book |
| GDB | Great Domesday Book |
| HMSO | Her Majesty's Stationery Office |
| *JBAA* | *Journal of the British Archaeological Association* |
| *JMH* | *Journal of Medieval History* |
| LDB | Little Domesday Book |
| *MA* | *Medieval Archaeology* |
| MS, MSS | Manuscript(s) |
| *MS* | *Mediaeval Studies* |
| NGR | National Grid Reference |
| *N&Q* | *Notes and Queries* |
| *PBA* | *Proceedings of the British Academy* |
| PRO | Public Record Office |
| *TRHS* | *Transactions of the Royal Historical Society* |
| *VCH* | *The Victoria Histories of the Counties of England* |

# INTRODUCTION

# AN INTRODUCTION TO THE BUCKINGHAMSHIRE DOMESDAY

J. BRADBURY

It is a pleasant task to introduce this new major version of the section of Domesday Book which deals with the county of Buckinghamshire. The first pleasure is in knowing that however fallible the introduction, the new photographic record of Domesday Book is likely to retain importance and usefulness for scholars over many years to come.

In the eighteenth century, Abraham Farley made a transcription of Domesday Book, which in the following century was expanded by the addition of other documents relating to Domesday, an index, and an introduction by Sir Henry Ellis.[1] In the 1860s, county editions were made by the photozincographic method, the volume for Buckinghamshire being published in 1862.[2] In this century, the *Victoria County Histories* have provided translations of Domesday for many counties, Buckinghamshire being an early example.[3] In our own day, the publishers Phillimore have also provided a set of county volumes, using the old Farley text in its specially designed type, together with a translation.[4] In truth, the versions of Domesday have been few because it is such an enormous compilation, hence the importance of providing this present photographic record. Whatever scholarly arguments might rage around hides and hundreds, place-names and social labels, the text in its original form must remain the basis for study. At the same time as the Alecto edition is being produced, there are two major university projects to place Domesday on computer: at Santa Barbara in California, and at Hull.[5] The nine-hundredth anniversary of the great work has indeed provided a feast for future scholars to digest.

This introduction was begun in the first gloomy days of January 1986, the anniversary year of this monument to the vision and determination of William the Conqueror, and to the skill and application of his servants and subjects. Any attempt to recapture their aims, methods and activities is bound to be incomplete. Apart from Domesday Book itself, there is so little to assist our efforts: a few subsidiary texts, and a few scraps of information in chronicles and charters. In the end our attention has to focus on the interpretation of the main text.

The Buckinghamshire section is not one of the more hotly debated sections of Domesday Book. In some ways it is a typical and average Domesday county, on the small side and not especially rich, not at the top or bottom of any table. It also lacks the supporting documents that some counties possess. There is no record of any secondary inquisition, nothing in the style of Exon Domesday for the west, or of the *Inquisitio Eliensis* and the *Inquisitio Comitatus Cantabrigiensis* for the east, nor are there any surviving surveys that include Buckinghamshire. We must depend entirely upon Great or Exchequer Domesday, the greatest of all the Domesday materials. The lack of secondary materials does not however leave Buckinghamshire without interest. Domesday was compiled county by county, and even within the same circuit methods and information can vary for neighbouring counties. It is now recognized in terms of the construction of Domesday that 'the basic unit of the enquiry was the county'.[6] As a result it is necessary to study each county individually as a prelude to generalization. Even a 'typical' and 'average' county has its peculiarities in Domesday, and there are many unique features in the Buckinghamshire folios.

Another pleasure in producing this introduction has been the opportunity to return to childhood scenes. My father and his family for generations back were Bucks folk, assisting the population

[1] A. Farley, *Domesday Book; seu liber censualis Willelmi primi regis Angliae*. . ., 2 vols. (London, 1783); Sir Henry Ellis, *Domesday Book: seu libri censualis*. . . (London, 1816).
[2] James (director), *Domesday Book*.
[3] *VCH Buckinghamshire*, i (1905).
[4] Morris (ed.), *Domesday Book: Buckinghamshire*.
[5] J. Palmer, 'Domesday Book and the Computer', *Domesday Book: A Reassessment*, ed. P. H. Sawyer (London, 1985), 164–74.
[6] P. H. Sawyer, 'Domesday Studies since 1886', ibid. 1–4, esp. p.3.

spread in and around High Wycombe, many of them closely associated with its furniture-making industry. Some of my happiest childhood memories are of walks through the Buckinghamshire countryside, through orchards and fields which do not, alas, all now survive, and beside streams which, more happily, still do flow. The countryside of the Chilterns and the Wye valley, like so many other parts of the county, has a timeless feel which makes the reconstruction of the past that much easier. It is not so difficult to return to a time of villages, manors, open fields and agrarian activity in such surroundings. In some ways the Buckinghamshire of Domesday seems hardly more remote than that of childhood: a world that is gone but not entirely lost.

There has been pleasure too in reading and re-reading the histories of the county. It is not possible here to give a complete survey of the literature on Buckinghamshire, but the county has been fortunate in attracting the attention of some diligent and even great historians, many of whom have used Domesday Book as part of the evidence for their accounts. This past work must influence any modern discussion of the county's history.

Of the great early works on the county, mention must be made of Browne Willis's *opus* on what he called 'one of the least shires in England'.[1] It must be said that he was not a great Domesday scholar, and even dated the survey to 1080. Thomas Langley's work on the hundred of Desborough and the deanery of Wycombe was also of great importance in its day, but of limited assistance to the modern student.[2] In many ways a more useful quarry is the history of Buckinghamshire by George Lipscomb, published in four volumes in 1847.[3] G. H. Wyatt suggested that much of the groundwork was provided by Edward Cooke, the rector of Haversham, whose papers Lipscomb obtained.[4] Lipscomb was the rector's executor, and apparently expected much from Cooke's will but, receiving nothing, seized his papers instead. According to Wyatt, Lipscomb viewed the production of the history as a solution to his financial problems, in which case he must have been sadly disappointed, since only twenty-eight copies were sold to the gentlemen of Buckinghamshire, and only sixty-nine copies all told. Not all of this work had been published at Lipscomb's death. It is probably the case that however much was owed to the researches of the rector, we should not have the work at all were it not for the literary abilities and efforts of Lipscomb himself.

The early county histories have much discussion on the origin of the name of the shire. A review of this discussion gives something of the flavour of these period works. J. J. Sheahan in his book on the topography of Buckinghamshire in 1862 collected previous suggestions. Sir Henry Spelman had favoured the argument that the name derived from *buc*, the Old English for deer, whereas William Camden thought the origin was from beech. Lipscomb agreed with Lysons that it came from the word 'book' as in bookland. Sheahan himself argued for a derivation from a personal name, the imagined Anglo-Saxon 'proprietor' *Buck* which, one might add, seems still to be the favourite resort of place-name specialists when no other solution is forthcoming.[5] Such discussion has a delightfully antique tone, but it does not become us to be patronizing, especially when we remember that this discussion did not have the benefit of the county place-name volume, nor of modern place-name study. Even with such benefits we cannot certainly provide the answer to the origin of our county name. What can be said is that the county name derives from that of the borough upon which it was based. A. Mawer and F. M. Stenton support the personal name derivation, the suggestion that Buckingham is the settlement of the people of *Buck* or *Bucc*.[6]

The origins of many place-names remain doubtful, but we do have the assistance for Buckinghamshire of the work of Mawer and Stenton, a great work for browsing through, even if one feels

[1] B. Willis, *The History and Antiquities of the Town, Hundred and Deanery of Buckingham* (London, 1755), 1.

[2] T. Langley, *The History and Antiquities of the Hundred of Desborough and Deanery of Wycombe in Buckinghamshire* (London, 1797).

[3] Lipscomb, *History and Antiquities of the County of Buckinghamshire*.

[4] G. H. Wyatt, 'Lipscomb and his History of Bucks', *Records of Buckinghamshire* (abbr. *RB*), 19 (1972), 272–97.

[5] J. J. Sheahan, *History and Topography of Buckinghamshire* (London, 1862), quotes Camden and Spelman, 22–3. Lipscomb's discussion in *History and Antiquities of the County of Buckinghamshire*, pp.i–ii.

[6] Mawer and Stenton, *Place-Names of Buckinghamshire* (abbr. *PNBU*).

at times that their suggestions are no more certain than those previously quoted. Perhaps because of its alphabetical position, whenever national projects are envisaged based on counties, Buckinghamshire tends to be at or near the head of the list. This was true of the place-name volume, the first county volume to appear. At the time this no doubt seemed an honour and was of great value, but for later students it has the disadvantage of leaving us with a volume produced when such study was at an early stage. The place-name volume for Buckinghamshire is probably more in need of revision than those of most other counties.

The *Victoria County History* is another great monument to the work of local historians. Again, the Buckinghamshire volumes were among the earliest published, but the county was fortunate in being one where the scholar responsible for the commentary on Domesday Book was J. H. Round.[1] It has been suggested that all Round's work was limited to local history. He never produced a book that was a coherent whole, only collected papers. But he was one of the most remarkable men ever to undertake the study of history: an irascible individual whose words in print must have been much feared by his contemporary historians. How fortunate we should feel ourselves in being able to criticize the great man without the expectation of a salvo in return. An amusing paper by Edmund King has shown the faults and peculiarities of Round, as a man and as an historian, but he was a great scholar whose work retains importance today when much of the writing of his contemporaries is forgotten. His work was based on encyclopaedic knowledge and a razor-sharp intellect, and we do well to ponder his ideas with respect.[2]

One other reference should be made to a work from another day, that of F. H. Baring. His studies of Domesday Book employed much material from Buckinghamshire, including detailed statistics of Domesday figures. It is true that some of his ideas will be challenged in this introduction, in particular his suggestion that the movements of the army of William the Conqueror can be traced through a study of the Domesday figures for 'waste'. He himself admitted that some of his totals for hidage in the county were incomplete, but his work is still of great value to us.[3]

For the most part recent scholars who have examined the history of the county have been more concerned with periods other than that of the Normans. There are however a number of works with valuable comment on Domesday, including the history of High Wycombe by L. J. Ashford, the works on Sherington and the area beyond it by A. C. Chibnall, on the hilltop villages of the Chilterns by D. and J. Hay, and Michael Reed's volume on the Buckinghamshire landscape.[4]

All modern students owe an enormous debt to the work of previous scholars, not least to Sir Henry Ellis, F. W. Maitland, R. R. Darlington, V. H. Galbraith, R. Lennard and R. Welldon Finn.[5] Domesday has attracted many of the greatest medievalists in every age. Maitland forecast in 1897 that in a hundred years there would be maps of vills and other details not then prepared, since 'many men from over all England will have come within King William's spell, will have bowed themselves to him and become that man's men'.[6] We are not far away from the century, but we are some way still from the fulfilment of his hope.

It must be recognized that in any county study nowadays it is necessary to contemplate the ideas put forward in recent times as part of the Domesday 'industry' by such scholars as Henry Loyn,

[1] Round, *VCH Buckinghamshire*, i. 207–29.

[2] E. King, 'John Horace Round and the *Calendar of Documents Preserved in France*', *Anglo-Norman Studies* (abbr. *ANS*), 4 (1981), 93–103. See also W. R. Powell, 'John Horace Round, the County Historian: the *Victoria County Histories* and the Essex Archaeological Society', *Essex Archaeology and History*, 12 (1981), 25–38.

[3] Baring, *Domesday Tables*; *idem*, Note on 'The Hidation of Buckinghamshire'; *idem*, 'Conqueror's Footprints in Domesday'; *idem*, 'Hidation of Some Southern Counties'.

[4] Ashford, *History of the Borough of High Wycombe*; Chibnall, *Sherington: Fiefs and Fields*; *idem*, *Beyond Sherington*; Hay and Hay, *Hilltop Villages of the Chilterns*; Reed, *Buckinghamshire Landscape*; G. H. Fowler and J. G. Jenkins, *Early Buckinghamshire Charters* (Bedford, 1939).

[5] H. Ellis, *A General Introduction to Domesday Book*, 2 vols. (London, 1833); F. W. Maitland, *Domesday Book and Beyond* (Cambridge, 1897; repr. 1907); R. R. Darlington, *The Norman Conquest* (London, 1963); V. H. Galbraith, *Domesday Book: its Place in Administrative History* (Oxford, 1974); V. H. Galbraith, *The Making of Domesday Book* (Oxford, 1961); R. Lennard, *Rural England 1086–1135* (Oxford, 1959); R. Welldon Finn, *The Norman Conquest and its Effects on the Economy* (London, 1971); R. Welldon Finn, *An Introduction to Domesday Book* (London, 1961).

[6] Maitland, *Domesday Book and Beyond*, 520.

Edmund King, Sally Harvey, Cyril Hart and Peter Sawyer.[1] Above all, for county historians, there is available now all the material resulting from H. C. Darby's great project on the geography of Domesday, including the study of Buckinghamshire by E. M. J. Campbell.[2]

No survey of the literature on the Buckinghamshire Domesday would be complete without reference to the efforts of all those contributors to the *Records of Buckinghamshire*, which began publication in 1854. Over the years scholars have made valuable additions to the study of place-names, boundaries, charters, hundreds and many other matters relevant to Domesday. In particular it would be churlish, in the modern rather than the eleventh-century sense, to omit acknowledgement to such as A. H. J. Baines, A. M. Davies and G. R. Elvey. It would also be appropriate here to record thanks to Dr David Bates who provided a bibliography for Buckinghamshire as a part of his broader work on the Domesday bibliography.

## The Methods Employed in this Study

One last matter of introduction remains. Any discussion about Domesday Book is bound to rely considerably on figures and calculations, on the interpretation of statistics. The figures quoted here depend on a new totalling of the figures for Buckinghamshire. These have been produced by setting up a small database for Domesday Buckinghamshire on a home computer. It has been done on an index-card style of database, with thirty entries for each holding. It will soon be realized from a comparison with previous attempts of this kind, that rock-hard certainty cannot be expected for the results. Baring was brave enough to admit the errors in his own calculations.[3] Maitland was being critical of himself rather than others when he suggested that 'for unmethodical habits and faulty arithmetic no excuse is possible'. He quite rightly thought that 'two men not unskilled in Domesday might add up the number of hides in a county and arrive at different results', and longed for the results that would be obtained by 'careful and leisurely computers'.[4] Maitland of course had in mind the human variety of computer, and would be disappointed perhaps by the results arrived at by the electronic kind. We may doubt that even the results obtained by two different men using computers will be alike; the reason is that the Domesday material has to be interpreted before it can be entered on computer. The entries are too varied to allow simple additions, even within one county. For example, in Buckinghamshire, woodland is generally reckoned by the number of pigs it would support, but in some vills it is reckoned in a cash value. It is not possible to equate the two valuations and make one total. Problems of this kind are numerous in Domesday.

We must accept that no calculation from Domesday can be perfect, and that decisions must be arrived at in making the additions with which others will quarrel. In the calculations used here, certain decisions have been made, and it is thought best to detail them.

In the first place the entries were made by holding. The Phillimore volume has been used as the basis for this, being the most recent version of Domesday Buckinghamshire, and its interpretation of the hundreds to which the holdings belong has been followed. Interpretation is necessary here, since the rubrics for the county are clearly incomplete and sometimes erroneous.[5] Those holdings which Domesday includes in the county folios have been kept, even though geographically and in modern times they fall within other counties. Similarly holdings which lie within the modern county, but in Domesday are recorded elsewhere, have been excluded.

[1] E. King, 'Domesday Studies', *History*, 58 (1973), 403–9. See also H. R. Loyn, 'Domesday Book', *ANS* 1 (1978), 121–30; S. P. J. Harvey, 'Recent Domesday Studies', *EHR* 95 (1980), 121–33; S. P. J. Harvey, 'Domesday Book and its Predecessors', *EHR* 86 (1971), 753–73; S. P. J. Harvey, 'Domesday Book and Anglo-Norman Governance', *TRHS* 25 (1975), 175–93; S. P. J. Harvey, 'Taxation and the Ploughland in Domesday Book', *Domesday Book: A Reassessment*, ed. Sawyer, 86–103; C. Hart, *The Hidation of Cambridgeshire*, Dept. of Eng. Local Hist. Occasional Papers, 2nd ser., 6 (Leicester, 1974); C. Hart, *The Hidation of Northamptonshire*, Dept. of Eng. Local Hist. Occasional Papers, 2nd ser., 3 (Leicester, 1970); Sawyer (ed.), *Domesday Book: A Reassessment*.

[2] H. C. Darby, *Domesday England* (Cambridge, 1977); H. C. Darby and G. R. Versey, *Domesday Gazetteer* (Cambridge,1975); Darby and Campbell (eds.), *Domesday Geography*.

[3] Baring, 'Hidation of Buckinghamshire', 199.

[4] Maitland, *Domesday Book and Beyond*, 407.

[5] A more detailed discussion of the hundred heads in the Buckinghamshire folios, and their reconstruction in the text, may be found in F. R. Thorn, 'The Hundreds of Buckinghamshire', pp.37–41 below. Not all the conclusions reached in that article accord with those of the present author.

Secondly, a plough-team is taken to consist of eight oxen. This is a common assumption, though in some areas it has been argued that the team may be smaller. There seems no reason to doubt the traditional eight-ox plough as the figure for Buckinghamshire. This assumption is necessary in order to add an entry of, say, two oxen to the figure for plough-teams.

Third, the Domesday labels for social groups are retained. It is important to record this for the sokemen, since in the Phillimore version *sochemannus* is translated as 'freeman'.

Fourth, where values are given in irreconcilable form, for example woodland in pigs and cash, the main form of valuation is taken for the major total (in this case pigs) and no attempt is made to include the variant types. This inevitably means that the total is not complete, but seems better than producing an imagined relationship. This problem occurs in the valuation of pasture, commonly in plough-teams, but sometimes in money; of mills, commonly in money, but sometimes in eels; and of fisheries, commonly in eels, but sometimes in money.

Fifth and finally, the total valuation figures used for holdings are those recorded as such in Domesday. In other words, any sources of income mentioned in the entries are taken as being included within this total. Even with cash valuations there are problems, since not all the figures are given in normal pounds, shillings and pence. We have accepted that the ora was the Scandinavian *ora* of sixteen pence though this could be disputed since the ora was sometimes equivalent to twenty pence. The silver mark is taken as thirteen shillings and four pence, which is generally accepted. It is also clear that money assayed and weighed, or *in albo argento* ('blanched silver'), had greater value than money counted 'by tale' or *ad numerum*. The former allowed for coinage that had been worn, and meant that a greater number of coins had to be paid. We have decided, however, since there is not agreement on the allowance to be made, to keep to the figures given in Domesday. Again this will mean that our totals are short, but is thought to be better than a possibly incorrect adjustment.

However carefully we make our interpretations and allowances, there are too many variables to expect perfection. How, for example, does one deal with the entry: 'and (. . .) villans have one and a half ploughs',[1] where the blank left for the number of villans has not been filled in. Our solution has been to count this as two villans since the intended number was clearly plural and two is the least possible. One entry, for Grendon Underwood, has an unclear figure for the number of slaves, which could be three or four. In this case we have accepted the suggestion of four. In short, we make no claim to completely correct figures. When the work at Santa Barbara and at Hull is complete, no doubt we shall obtain more accurate figures than these, but even then we may not expect absolute accuracy. The most that can be said is that by making our own calculations, we have come to realize the uncertainty of such figures as well as the variety and imperfections of the Domesday text itself.

TABLE 1: Categories of Domesday information used by the author

| | |
|---|---|
| Hides | Meadow, measured in plough-teams |
| Land for x ploughs | Woodland, measured in pigs |
| Hides of demesne land | Pasture, measured in plough-teams |
| Lords' ploughs | Mills, and their value in money |
| Other ploughs | Fisheries, and their value in eels |
| Villans | Value of the holding TRE |
| Bordars, cottars, slaves, free men, sokemen, burgesses | Value of the holding TRW |
| 'More ploughs possible' | Value of the holding 'when received', if given |

The categories of information are listed in Table 1. Totals for the same categories have been computed for each hundred within the county, and for each vill within the hundred. For the vill totals, all holdings under the same name have been added together, if within the same hundred,

[1] GDB 149v (Leckhampstead). Compare also GDB 148 (Haversham) where no numeral has been given in the phrase 'in demesne are hides'.

even where modern divisions seem to be suggested by the separate holdings. Thus the various holdings in High and West Wycombe are all totalled together, since in Domesday although there are different holdings they are not given separate vill names but are all called *Wicumbe*. On the other hand, where Domesday does indicate a separate vill, as for example with Burnham and East Burnham, then these have been treated as separate.

Calculations under these same headings have also been made for the fiefs given in Domesday for the county, that is, the lands of each tenant-in-chief. It was thought unprofitable to attempt this for the Old English holders, where no Domesday list is given, and where the format of Domesday is too diverse to untangle easily. Similarly it has not been attempted for the post-Conquest under-tenants, on the grounds that their identity is too uncertain, as between, for example, the host of men called Robert and Roger.

In addition to the computer calculations, this introduction relies on mapped information based on those calculations. This also caused problems, in that some vills have not been identified, and others have only been tentatively located. It is also impossible in most cases to be sure of the Domesday boundaries, though some exciting work has been done on this by, for example, A. H. J. Baines on the early charters,[1] and G. R. Elvey on the vill of Amersham.[2] It will never be possible to reconstruct all the vills, and no attempt has been made to do this. The maps were therefore based on parish boundaries, which although not the same as vill boundaries, do give a rough guide.[3] Vills which did not become parishes have been inserted in their correct geographical position, without any attempt at realistic boundaries. The purpose was not to obtain an exact boundary map of vills, but to be able to view the distribution of Domesday values not only from hundred to hundred, but within the hundred from vill to vill.

These vill maps have also been used to give the distribution of Domesday landholders and overlords, and of previous, that is Old English, holders and overlords. Domesday is less informative about the Old English situation, but does give a rough guide to the powerful landholders in the county before the Norman Conquest. At a rough calculation there were 300 maps for the hundreds, for example, one for Ashendon Hundred to show hidage; and another 300 or so for the vills within each hundred, such as the one to show the woodland valuations for the vills in the hundred of Yardley. These maps have made possible the comments in this introduction on the distribution of valuations through the county, and within the hundreds. It would not be a practical proposition to print such a quantity of maps, and these working sketches should be distinguished from the carefully prepared map produced especially for this edition.

## The Early History of the County

Buckinghamshire was a recently created shire in 1086, with no previous history as a separate political unit as, for example, had the county of Sussex which had once been a kingdom. In some ways Buckinghamshire seems to have had little political significance before its creation: lightly populated, without great or sought-after resources, a difficult area to traverse because of its woodland. K. R. Davis has said that in the seventh century the Chilterns were still a 'wilderness'.[4] The county tended to be on the fringes of great events, and outside the knowledge of most chroniclers. For the most part the early Saxon history of Buckinghamshire is conjecture spiced by

[1] Articles by A. H. J. Baines in *Records of Buckinghamshire*: 'The Boundaries of Over Winchendon', 19 (1972), 169–73; 'The Boundaries of Wotton Underwood', 21 (1979), 141–53; 'The Olney Charter of 979', 21 (1979), 154–84; 'The Winslow Charter of 792 and the Boundaries of Granborough', 22 (1980), 1–18; 'Hasley: a Domesday Manor Restored', 22 (1980), 53–72; 'Turville, Radenore and the Chiltern Feld', 23 (1981), 4–22; 'The Boundaries of Monks Risborough', 23 (1981), 76–101; 'The Chetwode-Hillesden Charter of 949', 24 (1982), 1–33; 'The Lady Elgiva, St Æthelwold and the Linslade Charter of 966', 25 (1983), 110–38.

[2] G. R. Elvey, 'Buckinghamshire in 1086', with a map by M. A. Lloyd.

[3] C. R. Humphrey-Smith, *The Phillimore Atlas and Index of Parish Registers* (Chichester, 1984).

[4] K. R. Davis, *Britons and Saxons: the Chiltern Region, 400–700* (Chichester, 1982). Reviewed by A. H. J. Baines in *RB* 23 (1981), 130–1.

one or two facts. There is more evidence from archaeology than from written sources, and little enough from either.

The Anglo-Saxons may have arrived in the area earlier than was once thought, but probably without settling in great numbers. Some pagan Saxon burials suggest a fifth-century start. One of the few facts recorded in the Anglo-Saxon Chronicle is that the West Saxon Cuthwulf defeated the Britons at the unidentified *Bedcanford* in 571, and then captured four settlements (*tunas*), of which Aylesbury was one.[1] It was once thought that Lenborough was another of the four, but this has now been discounted. There has been some conjecture over why this area needed to be captured. It has been suggested either that the Britons had regained ground in the region after their victory at *Mons Badonicus*, or that they had survived through the early Saxon period, particularly in Bernwood Forest. Reed suggests that the name of the Chilterns may itself even be Celtic, though it became a Saxon tribal name recorded in the Tribal Hidage.[2] Several local historians have accepted a late British survival, co-existing with the early Saxon settlers. For example, J. Chenevix-Trench has argued that Britons remained in the region between the *Cilternsætan* to the north-west and the Middle Saxons to the south-east. He claims that the distribution of slaves in Domesday supports the conclusion that this was 'the last refuge of independent Britons in south-east England'. The idea is not impossible, but the evidence is slight, and, as we shall see, the slavery distribution-pattern is not as clear as Chenevix-Trench believed. He also conjectures that the line between the Chiltern hundreds and those of Aylesbury marked an ancient frontier between the *Cilternsætan* and the Middle Saxons. This again is a tempting proposition and not unlikely, since the survival of boundaries is known to be long-lived, but is also without supporting evidence.[3]

At some point the region fell under the sway of Mercia. This probably occurred in the seventh century, although there is no evidence beyond our knowledge that it had indeed happened, which is demonstrated by the controlling role taken by Mercian kings in the granting of land, as recorded in a number of charters. For example in the late eighth century Offa, King of Mercia, issued a charter disposing of Winslow.[4] The Scandinavian invasions that destroyed Mercia certainly affected Buckinghamshire, but to what degree is uncertain. Scandinavian place-names survive, though few in number, and could in any case represent later settlement. Turville, Owlswick, Ravenstone and Turweston have been considered Scandinavian, and Fingest and Skirmett are said to contain Scandinavian elements.[5] In addition there are a few records of Scandinavian personal names and field-names. There is precious little other evidence. An interesting suggestion is that Thurferth the *hold* had built up a personal power-base in the region of Buckinghamshire, so that Edward the Elder took over an already created political unit when he conquered the east midlands.[6]

The reconquest was accomplished in the second decade of the tenth century. In 905 or 906, Edward the Elder made peace with the Danes of East Anglia and Northumbria at Tiddenfoot on the boundary between Buckinghamshire and Bedfordshire.[7] One consequence of this was to allow Danes to settle in English Mercia, and it has been suggested that the Scandinavian names associated with the Chilterns could have resulted from such a settlement. In 909–10 the peace was broken, and Edward the Elder began his reconquest, a process which necessitated the building of a fortress at Buckingham in 914 against the Danes of Northamptonshire and Bedfordshire. Edward 'went to Buckingham with his army and stayed there four weeks, and made both the boroughs, on each side of the river, before he went away'.[8] The need for a stronghold was emphasized by a number of Danish raids in the years that followed, for example in 917, when they advanced into the area between Bernwood Forest and Aylesbury. Buckingham's claim to importance depended first on its

[1] C. Plummer, *Two of the Saxon Chronicles Parallel*, i (Oxford, 1892), 19, *s.a.* 571.

[2] Reed, *Buckinghamshire Landscape*, 79.

[3] J. Chenevix-Trench, 'Coleshill and the Settlements of the Chilterns', *RB* 19 (1972), 241–58, esp. p.248. Compare Baines, 'Wotton Underwood', 148.

[4] Baines, 'Winslow Charter', 1–18.

[5] Baines, 'Turville', 4–7; Chenevix-Trench, 'Coleshill', 252; Baines, 'Monks Risborough', 82; Reed, *Buckinghamshire Landscape*, 77.

[6] Suggestion of T. C. Cain.

[7] D. Whitelock *et al.* (eds.), *The Anglo-Saxon Chronicle: A Revised Translation* (London, 1961), 60, *s.aa.* 905–6, gives Tiddingford; Baines, 'Monks Risborough', 81, insists on Tiddenfoot.

[8] Whitelock *et al.* (eds.), *Anglo-Saxon Chronicle*, 64, *s.a.* 914.

significance as a military site overlooking the Upper Ouse. The organization of a garrison for the *burh* and the maintenance of its walls probably explains the creation of the county and the initial imposition of hidage. Sixteen men were normally required for every twenty-two yards of wall. The wall of Buckingham has never been fully examined, but in the Burghal Hidage Buckingham is assessed at 1,600 hides, which has been taken to indicate that the wall may have been one and a quarter miles long.[1] The creation of the shire probably occurred soon after the building of Buckingham in the early tenth century, but there is no mention of it in records until 1016. By that time Buckingham had developed as a *burh*. The *witan* met there in 934, and by 956 it possessed a mint.

The influence of Mercia in Buckinghamshire was not yet ended. In 957 Eadwig lost control of the region. It was this king who had disgraced himself at his coronation banquet by leaving the feast in order to enjoy the favours not only of his wife but also of his mother-in-law, and was found wallowing 'as if in a vile sty' between the two of them. No doubt he deserved the Mercian revolt that broke out against him, and which led to a partition of his lands, the area north of the Thames, including Buckinghamshire, going to his brother Edgar. Royal holdings were always important in the county, and Edgar's were increased after the death of Eadwig in 959 by gifts from the latter's widow Ælfgifu, which included estates at Wing and Marsworth.[2]

During the Danish wars of Æthelred II's reign, Buckinghamshire was disturbed by the movement of armies through the shire. In 1009 Thorkell's army lived off the land on either side of the Thames, and retreated via the Chilterns, and in the following year the Danes reappeared on the Ouse.[3] But during the eleventh century disturbances became fewer, and Buckinghamshire lost its 'frontier' significance. By 1086 Buckingham had developed as a smallish borough, with fifty-three burgesses recorded, of whom twenty-six or more were men of the barons of the shire and paid rents to them. The role of burgesses is not entirely clear. They may have acted as a garrison, but equally they may already have had commercial significance. At Hereford the burgesses were also warriors, and it may be that the appearance of *cnihts* in some boroughs has a military significance. There was a castle at Buckingham, but it does not appear in Domesday. Willis assumed, probably correctly, that it was built by Walter Giffard on the site of Edward the Elder's fortress, and its existence is remembered in the later place-names of Castle Farm and Castle Hill. One should not exaggerate the social position of burgesses in this period. In other places they were ranked with the villans. The information on Buckingham in Domesday, as Round pointed out, is comparable with the survey of a royal manor, and the burgesses fill the space which in the manor survey was filled by the villans.[4] The burgesses were clearly not the only residents in the borough, but Domesday gives no indication of others. We can assume from such an omission that for tax purposes it was the burgess who mattered in the borough.

Buckingham is the only place in the county which is stated to be a borough in Domesday. There are two other possible candidates. Newport Pagnell contained burgesses, though we are not told how many. The name of the town may indicate that it began life as a market (*port*). Aylesbury possessed a toll worth ten pounds, and in 571 it is referred to in the Chronicle as one of four *tunas*, but this may not mean it was urban. Round argued that Aylesbury's population was greater than that of Buckingham, and it has been postulated that it might have been a borough.[5] But since we cannot know the total population of Buckingham, and since Aylesbury may well be one of those Buckinghamshire estates where a central manor represented a multiple estate, the argument cannot be sustained. Domesday does not explicitly treat either Newport or Aylesbury as boroughs, and it would be unsafe to assume that they were.[6] We are also told that Princes Risborough supported a burgess at Oxford, and this is the extent of 'urban' information in the Buckinghamshire Domesday. Apart from Buckingham, all the settlements in the county appear to be manorial and agricultural.

[1] Reed, *Buckinghamshire Landscape*, 78.
[2] Baines, 'Lady Elgiva', 112.
[3] Whitelock *et al.* (eds.), *Anglo-Saxon Chronicle*, 90, *s.aa.* 1009–10.
[4] Round in *VCH Buckinghamshire*, i. 221.
[5] M. Farley, 'Aylesbury – a Defended Town', *RB* 19 (1974), 23; Maitland, *Domesday Book and Beyond*, 430; Round in *VCH Buckinghamshire*, i. 222.
[6] Newport Pagnell, however, is marked as a borough on the associated map as the mention of burgesses there puts it in this category.

According to Round, even Buckingham was 'quasi-rural'.[1] Altogether, from twenty-three of the burgesses, the king obtained sixty-six pence, and twenty-six burgesses were worth thirty-one shillings to their respective lords. Presumably the houses in the borough belonged to these lords such as Hugh, Earl of Chester, and the Bishop of Coutances, and the burgesses paid a rent. In short Buckingham was a small and not very wealthy borough. Although the county had been established in order to maintain the borough, by 1086 Buckingham lacked any great military significance. Buckinghamshire was agrarian, not heavily populated, with some large estates around manorial centres, but with few signs of urban development.

## Buckinghamshire in the Eleventh Century

We may now begin our examination of rural Domesday Buckinghamshire. In order to do so, we need to establish the limits of the county in the eleventh century. The accompanying map indicates how although a considerable number of minor changes have affected the boundaries since 1086, the general outline of the Domesday shire is very similar to that of the modern county up to the reorganization of borders in 1974. The details of Domesday settlement sites which have either become a part of Buckinghamshire or have been lost to adjacent counties since 1086 are to be found in the boxes bordering the map. In this introduction, all statements and figures relate to the county as it was at Domesday.

The landscape of Domesday Buckinghamshire is still recognizable in the twentieth century, though our own time seems to be doing its best to smother views that have existed from then till now. There is a contrast between the fertility of the north and the less populated Chilterns in the south. The north is clay, with gentle hills and flowing streams, the south is chalk, making for more dramatic hills and woodland. There is another wooded region around Newport Pagnell in the far north of the county. The county extends about fifty miles from north to south, and about twenty miles from east to west at its widest point. In early days the valleys of the Hamble, Wye and Misbourne attracted settlers, the hills above them attracted fortifications. The Thames and its tributaries, the Thame, Ouse, Chess and Gade, offered fish. They possessed good meadow land in 1086, which was mowed and used for hay and grazing.[2] Roman roads that crossed Buckinghamshire were on lines followed by modern roads: Watling Street has become in part the A5, Akeman Street the A41, the Icknield Way the A4010. Especially where the country was more difficult, as through the Chilterns, the river valleys and the roads that followed them dictated historical development. Domesday gives some indication of which areas remained inaccessible. The figures for woodland, in Buckinghamshire usually valued by the number of pigs that could be supported, give us a fair idea of woodland distribution in the eleventh century. The hundred of Cottesloe returned no woodland at all, possibly because of an omission in the returns; there is good reason, in any case for treating Cottesloe as an exception among the hundreds. It seems that the returns for Cottesloe were made separately and in a slightly different form, possibly in haste. All the Chiltern hundreds have high returns for woodland: Desborough 4,620 pigs, Burnham 5,530, Stoke 3,016. The hundreds to the immediate north of these, Risborough, Aylesbury and Yardley, also have high figures, suggesting that all of the south of the county was quite heavily wooded in 1086. Most of the northern hundreds have low returns, suggesting light woodland, with the exception of the two most northerly boundary hundreds of 'Stotfold' at 3,720 pigs, and Bunsty at 3,335.

Analysis of the vill returns for woodland mainly reinforces the hundred picture. It seems likely that the returns do not represent real numbers of pigs, but are round estimates of the number that an area of woodland might support, usually given in tens and hundreds. There are a few exceptions to this rule, such as Ellesborough in Aylesbury, reckoned at 205 pigs.[3] We can but wonder whether

[1] Round in *VCH Buckinghamshire*, i. 221.
[2] Reed, *Buckinghamshire Landscape*, esp. ch.2, pp.53–87.
[3] The irregularity of the figure for Ellesborough results from the return for the holding held by Ralph of William fitzAnsculf, where the woodland is calculated at 105 pigs (f.148v).

this represents an actual count. Measurement in pigs was of course a realistic calculation of value, since pigs would normally be fed on acorns and beech-mast.

Some vills had very large assessments, which may represent important areas for pig-keeping, as well as large stretches of woodland. Wendover in Aylesbury was reckoned at 2,000 pigs, Hanslope in Bunsty at 1,000. This may point to the north-west rather than the north-east as being the wooded part. In the south, Chesham in Burnham has 1,650 pigs, Chalfont[1] in Burnham 1,200, Wycombe[2] in Desborough 1,500, and Marlow in Desborough 1,250. The hundred of Risborough, though small, has two vills in Bledlow and Princes Risborough with 1,000 pigs each.

Apart from Cottesloe, with no woodland, it is interesting that the main part of Ixhill has but a modest return, while the detached part with four vills has no woodland at all. Mursley, whose southern border meets with Cottesloe, has a block of eight vills in the south of the hundred which has no woodland, and 'Seckley', also bordering on Cottesloe, has a block of twelve vills, one of which returns 100 pigs, the rest none at all. Although Yardley has 2,225 pigs, the part immediately to the east of Cottesloe contains four vills bordering on Cottesloe and all returning *nil*. It does seem unlikely that there was no woodland at all in Cottesloe, yet the surrounding areas seem equally devoid of woodland and pigs, and Cottesloe may well have been low in this respect. The northern part of Stone has only one vill out of seven with any return for woodland. In other words, virtually all the woodland in Stone was in the southern detached section of Missenden,[3] emphasizing further that the central part of Buckinghamshire was lightly wooded, and the whole southern area was well wooded. One minor but interesting side-effect of the woodland is the existence of eyries of hawks. The reference to men living in the woods at Newport Pagnell is fascinating but also puzzling. Clearly they owed dues to the manor and so appear in Domesday. It is one of several hints that the Domesday population may be larger than at first appears. We do not know how many of these men there were, nor the nature of their living or status, but they seem to be outside the usual manorial organization.[4]

We can learn a little of the eleventh-century landscape from other sources. Charters from the period before 1086 occasionally refer to landmarks in their boundary clauses. One of the most remarkable was the Black Hedge, the great hedge that divided the two Risboroughs.[5] Part of it still survives, and as it is first mentioned in an Old English charter, it obviously also marked the Domesday landscape. The mention of trees, rivers, marshes and other natural features in such charters fills out for us the barer information in Domesday.

## Place-Names in Buckinghamshire

Charters also provide additional information with regard to the place-names in Domesday. We must take as our guide the volume for the county edited by Mawer and Stenton, together with some work on the hundreds by O. S. Anderson, and some illuminating articles in the *Records of Buckinghamshire*. The study of place-names is fascinating, but a minefield for the amateur. As mentioned earlier, we have a problem in the county which arises from the early date of its place-name volume.

Names in the county are mainly of Old English origin with a sprinkling of Celtic survivals, and some Scandinavian and Norman additions. They suggest an original English settlement in an area that was not heavily populated. The Celtic survivals are few, and not always certain. Wendover in Aylesbury, which appears as *Wendovre* in Domesday and *Wændofran* in a 970 charter, does seem to be a perfect Celtic survival, meaning clear streams and in correct plural form.[6] Chalfont in Burnham,

[1] Includes both Chalfont St Giles and Chalfont St Peter.
[2] Includes both High Wycombe and West Wycombe.
[3] Includes both Great Missenden and Little Missenden.
[4] Hawks at Chalfont St Peter, f.144, and at Chalfont St Giles, f.152, probably referring to the same eyrie. Men in the woods at Newport Pagnell, f.148v.
[5] Baines, 'Monks Risborough', 76, 83–5.
[6] Davis, *Britons and Saxons*, 154; Baines, 'Monks Risborough', 92; Mawer and Stenton, *PNBU*, 157.

which appears in Domesday as *Celfunte* and *Celfunde*, is to be found in a charter of 949 as *Ceadeles funtan*. This is taken to mean Ceadel's spring, and Mawer and Stenton suggest that the personal name Ceadel is Celtic. Iver has been put forward as another Celtic possibility from the word *yfre* meaning slope. Mawer and Stenton quote in support reference to 'a somewhat eccentric canon of Windsor' who pronounced the name as 'Iv-ver'.[1] Some Celtic elements are also preserved in hybrid names together with English elements, suggesting a name taken over by the English from an imperfectly understood British name. This would seem to be the case with those place-names that simply repeat a meaning in the two languages, such as Chetwode which adds the English word 'wood' to the Celtic word with the same meaning, or Brickhill which means 'hill-hill'. Brill, which appears as *Brunhelle* in Domesday, is a similar combination.[2]

The fact that most of the county place-names are English suggests strongly that the English settlement was the dominant one in the region. Many of the Buckinghamshire names derive from common English elements, such as *-ham* and *-ton*. Thus Denham in Stoke, *Daneham* in Domesday, is thought to derive from *denn-ham* meaning a valley settlement, or Amersham in Burnham, *Elmodes-ham* in Domesday, which is interpreted as 'Ealhmod's' or 'Ealhmund's settlement'. The alternative Domesday form, *Elnodesham*, would mean 'Ælfnoth's' or 'Æthelnoth's settlement'. The *-ton* ending similarly means a settlement, possibly an enclosed one. It is to be found, for example, in Addington in 'Mow', *Eddintone* in Domesday, interpreted as 'Æddi's settlement'. There are many other common English endings. One of the more interesting, since it suggests something of the making of the settlement, is *-leah* meaning a clearing, as found, for example, in Akeley in 'Stotfold', *Achelei* in Domesday, interpreted as 'Acca's', or perhaps 'Aki's clearing'.[3]

The first elements in the place-names often give additional information about the settlement, as we have already seen in the examples quoted above. Claydon, which appears in Domesday as *Claidone* and *Claindone*, means a clayey hill. Crafton in Cottesloe, *Croustone* in Domesday, is interpreted by Mawer and Stenton as coming from *croh-tun*, which they translate as 'saffron farm'. Ditton in Stoke, *Ditone* in Domesday, comes from *dic-tun* meaning 'dyke farm'. Eaton Leys in 'Seckley', *Etone* in Domesday, comes from *ea-tun* meaning a river settlement, differing from Eton in Stoke, *Ettone* in Domesday, deriving from *eg-tun* and signifying an island settlement. This last example nicely illustrates the problems and dangers of place-name interpretation, and the importance of discovering and using the earliest surviving forms. Other names that contain similar information are Gayhurst in Bunsty meaning 'goat's wood', Granborough in Waddesdon meaning 'green hill', Hollingdon in Cottesloe meaning 'hollow valley', Horton in Stoke and Horton in Yardley[4] both meaning 'muddy settlement', Horwood in Mursley meaning 'muddy wood', Moreton[5] in 'Stotfold' meaning 'swampy settlement', Radclive in Stone meaning 'red cliff', Shipton in Ashendon meaning 'sheep hill', and Whitchurch in Cottesloe meaning 'white church' or perhaps 'stone church'.[6]

Often the first element is thought to contain a personal name, and these can cause the greatest problems in interpretation. They are usually of otherwise unknown individuals. Accepting that the interpretations are correct, they may be the names of the leaders of the early English settlement. One such name is Chicheley, taken as Cicca's *leah*, meaning 'Cicca's clearing'. The name might be a form of Cissa, as in Cissa's chester or Chichester in Sussex. Taplow in Burnham, *Thapeslau* in Domesday, comes from Tæppa's *hlaw* meaning 'Tæppa's barrow'. There is a fine group of grave-goods in the British Museum which was excavated from this barrow, clearly the possessions of a chieftain who was perhaps called Tæppa. There must often be doubt over the interpretation. Can we be certain, for example, that Gawcott in 'Rowley' comes from *gafol*-cottage (a cottage paying tax) when the first element is remarkably similar to the English name Chaua which may be preserved in the Domesday spelling of the place as *Chauescote*?[7]

[1] Mawer and Stenton, *PNBU*, 219, 240.

[2] Mawer and Stenton, *PNBU*, 62, 30–2, 118.

[3] Mawer and Stenton, *PNBU*, 109, 235, 209–11, 51–2, 40–1.

[4] Identified in the accompanying translation as Horton (near Stoke) and Horton (in Ivinghoe) respectively.

[5] Identified in the accompanying translation as Maids Moreton.

[6] Mawer and Stenton, *PNBU*, 53, 87, 244, 19, 236, together with Morris (ed.), *Domesday Book: Buckinghamshire*, n.29,2; Mawer and Stenton, *PNBU*, 5, 134, 84, 239, 97, 68, 45, 46, 75, 86.

[7] Mawer and Stenton, *PNBU*, 33, 232, 60–1; GDB 144.

There are a few place-names that appear to be Scandinavian, though whether they are sufficient in number to merit any theory of Scandinavian settlement must be doubtful. Turweston in 'Stotfold', *Turveston* in Domesday, is 'Thorulf's settlement', containing a Scandinavian personal name. It is now thought that Turville in Desborough, though *Tilleberie* in Domesday, is the *Thyrefeld* of a 796 charter, and means 'Thyri's plain'.[1] If 796 is correct, however, this would pre-date the Scandinavian settlement. Chenevix-Trench has suggested that Coleshill derives from the Scandinavian personal name Kollungr.[2] Scandinavian elements have also been suggested for Skirmett and Fingest.[3]

Finally we should mention that there are several county place-names in which a Norman element has been added to the previous form, such as Stoke Mandeville and Drayton Parslow, from the Mandeville and Passelewe families respectively. Marsh Gibbon, which had simply been called Marsh in the eleventh century, preserves the name of the family known to have been associated with it in the twelfth century. Towersey in Ixhill, which had simply been *Eie* ('island') in Domesday, likewise preserves the name of the Tours family.[4]

There are also a few places in Domesday Buckinghamshire which have proved difficult to identify. Some have been solved, some have been approximately located, others remain uncertain. The Domesday version of the name has often been an important factor in the attempts at identification. One example is *Dileherst* in Burnham. The second element in the name means 'wood', and the first element appears to be a personal name, Dill, and the whole may be interpreted as 'Dill's wood'. The same personal name appears in *Dillepoe*, 'Dill's pool', which, according to the Close Roll of 1244, lay in Chippenham, and *Dileherst* may therefore have lain in the same vill.[5] Round made a rare mistake, though an understandable one, in believing that *Dileherst* was Tylers Green, from the 1316 form *Tygelhurst*.[6]

Another problematic name is *Haseleie* in Rowley, from *hæsel-leah*, probably meaning 'hazel-clearing'.[7] This has been located by A. H. J. Baines in Radclive, from the appearance of the name in thirteenth-century documents. In a charter of Luffield Priory, Ellias de *Hesele* and his wife hold half of a croft in Thornborough and probably took their surname from this vill. Baines prefers the form 'Hasley', though in this edition the name 'Haseley' has been adopted and the settlement has been located in the nearby parish of Thornton. *Lesa* in Ixhill has been identified with Nashway, which appears in later records in similar forms, such as *Esses*.[8] *Sortelai* in Ashendon has been located in or near Shipton Lee,[9] and it has been suggested that the *-lai* ending might be the 'Lee' in Shipton Lee. The name means 'short-clearing' and was probably given to contrast it with Shipton Lee itself; both were held by Alsige in Domesday Book. *Wandene* in Aylesbury might be an error for *Handene*, Little Hampden, but this remains uncertain.[10] There must also be a continuing doubt over *Hanechedene*, which Round in the *VCH* volume identified with Whinch Bottom; but more recently Fowler and Elvey have suggested it represents Radnage, for which the form *Eaningadene* is found in an Old English charter.[11]

As mentioned earlier, it seems mistaken to assume that modern villages existed as separate entities in the eleventh century, unless Domesday gives them separate names. The existence of more than one holding is not sufficient proof, since many Domesday manors contained several

[1] Mawer and Stenton, *PNBU*, 49–50, 196; Baines, 'Turville', 4–7, 16.

[2] Chenevix-Trench, 'Coleshill', 252.

[3] Reed, *Buckinghamshire Landscape*, 77.

[4] Mawer and Stenton, *PNBU*, 156, 66–7, and Morris (ed.), *Domesday Book: Buckinghamshire*, n.40,1; Mawer and Stenton, *PNBU*, 54, 128–9, and Morris (ed.), *Domesday Book: Buckinghamshire*, n.39,2.

[5] The accompanying translation uses the form 'Dilehurst' (in Taplow).

[6] Round in *VCH Buckinghamshire*, i. 235; Jenkins, *History of the Parish of Penn*, 5–6; Mawer and Stenton, *PNBU*, 232; G. R. Elvey, 'Buckinghamshire in 1086', 359; Morris (ed.), *Domesday Book: Buckinghamshire*, n.4,14.

[7] G. R. Elvey, 'Buckinghamshire in 1086', 359; Baines, 'Hasley', 53–72; Mawer and Stenton, *PNBU*, 64; Morris (ed.), *Domesday Book: Buckinghamshire*, n.41,7; G. R. Elvey, (ed.), *Luffield Priory Charters*, ii, Northamptonshire Record Soc. 26 (1973), no. 711F, p.347.

[8] G. R. Elvey, 'Buckinghamshire in 1086', 359; *idem*, *Luffield Priory Charters*, ii. no.764, p.409.

[9] Mawer and Stenton, *PNBU*, 111; Morris (ed.), *Domesday Book: Buckinghamshire*, n.23,11.

[10] Round in *VCH Buckinghamshire*, i. 276; Mawer and Stenton, *PNBU*, 157; Morris (ed.), *Domesday Book: Buckinghamshire*, n.57,10; G. R. Elvey, 'Buckinghamshire in 1086', 360; P. Gardner, 'The Palace of Minos', *Antiquity*, 5 (1931), 320, n.3.

[11] Mawer and Stenton, *PNBU*, 203, n.1; Morris (ed.), *Domesday Book: Buckinghamshire*, n.4,20; G. R. Elvey, 'Buckinghamshire in 1086', 344–5.

settlements. Only occasionally does Domesday show the existence of separate units, as in the case of Great Kimble and *parva* or 'Little' Kimble, and Burnham and East Burnham.[1]

The hundred-names are also of interest, and give information about their organization and assemblies. A number of the Buckinghamshire hundreds are named after a settlement within the hundred which was almost certainly the meeting-place for the hundred court, Aylesbury and Ashendon are examples of this. Sometimes the hundred-name seems to derive from a meeting-place which was not a settlement, as for example that of 'Rowley', meaning 'rough hill'. There is a hill in the area, 370 feet in height, where several tracks meet and which would seem to have been the assembly point.[2]

## The Making of the Buckinghamshire Domesday

William the Conqueror met his council at Gloucester at Christmas 1085. One can still stand in the hall in the cathedral where the decision was taken to proceed with the survey we know as Domesday. It was seemingly completed within a year. Even though we may now accept that Domesday depended to some extent on previously existing surveys and lists, it was still a gigantic task, surprising in its depth and detail. Interpretations of related documents give us a guide to the methods of the survey. The *Inquisitio Eliensis* shows the kind of information which the commissioners were required to obtain. The *Inquisitio Comitatus Cantabrigiensis* and Exon Domesday give knowledge of the stages of the inquisition, from hastily organized local and county material to Great Domesday Book itself. In this final version, as we can see by comparison with Exon, details were trimmed and arrangement improved, and the whole thing was framed within the feudal holdings of tenants-in-chief.[3]

Commissioners were given circuits with which to deal. Some of their information they received in written returns, some was collected locally and probably checked in the hundred courts. It appears likely that the early stages of writing up the collected information were also performed within the local circuit. The determination of which shires lay within a given circuit depends chiefly on the comparison of the contents of Domesday, to see which counties are closest in method. Buckinghamshire is thought to have been in the same circuit as Middlesex and Hertfordshire, and some historians suggest that Cambridgeshire and Bedfordshire lay in this circuit also. However, C. Stephenson was probably correct in believing that 'the primary circuit was the single shire'.[4] The only group of commissioners known are those for Worcestershire. It is interesting that they included none of the great holders in that county, but did in fact contain three who were important in Buckinghamshire: Remigius, Bishop of Lincoln, Henry de Ferrers, and Walter Giffard.

Within the shire, the survey followed a pattern common to some other counties, but worth commenting on in detail. We may assume that the final version was an assembly of different documents, which included a list of tenants-in-chief, information on the borough of Buckingham, a schedule of the lands of the king, and others describing the holdings of the tenants-in-chief. In our circuit the lands of Queen Matilda follow after the holdings of the leading barons, though elsewhere they are made a sub-section of the lands of the king.

That the borough evidence was collected separately seems practically certain. In several cases in other counties, space was left on the first of the county folios. Some borough returns were never supplied, such as those for Winchester and London which were never described in Domesday Book, though it was almost certainly intended that they should have been. In most other counties,

[1] Kimble appears as *Chenebella* (f.147), and as *parva Chenebelle* (f.151). Burnham appears as *Burneham* (f.151), and *Esburneham* (f.145v).

[2] Hundred-names in Mawer and Stenton, *PNBU*, and in O. S. Anderson, *The English Hundred-Names: The South-Eastern Counties* (abbr. *EHNSE*) (Lund, Leipzig, 1939), 1–15. For a full discussion, see Thorn, 'Hundreds of Buckinghamshire', pp.37–41 below.

[3] For a more detailed discussion of the making of Domesday Book, see H. R. Loyn, 'A General Introduction to Domesday Book', *Domesday Book Studies*, eds. A. Williams and R. W. H. Erskine (London, 1987), 3–7.

[4] Welldon Finn, *Introduction to Domesday Book*, 38; C. Stephenson, 'Notes on the Composition and Interpretation of Domesday Book', *Speculum*, 22 (1947), 1–15.

including Buckinghamshire, the borough information comes at the start of the county entry. It is also to be noted that the style of the Buckingham entry differs from that for the other holdings. There is, for example, a different form of recording ploughlands for the borough as *terra est* x *carucarum*, 'there is land for *x* ploughs'. Probably the sheriff was responsible for producing separate information on the borough.[1]

The information on the king's lands also appears to have been drawn up separately from the rest of the county material. Income from royal possessions was bound to have a different significance for central government than income from other lands. The distinct treatment of royal land seems one more argument for seeing the purpose of Domesday as primarily fiscal. One may also suspect either the use of pre-existing statistics on royal lands, or else a separate collection of evidence. The most obvious pointer is that although for the holdings of the tenants-in-chief the order of hundreds follows a more or less set pattern, the hundred order for royal lands is somewhat different.

For some other counties, notably Cambridgeshire, the evidence of related documents suggests that information may first have been collected by hundred and vill, and then reorganized into fiefs. This would fit well with a geld system depending on the hundred being modified into a tax system dependent upon fiefs. Buckinghamshire contains what may be a remarkable piece of evidence about the collection of such materials as the Domesday survey. This is the entry for Stoke Mandeville in Aylesbury, in which we are told that the surrounding hundreds had sokemen owing court to Aylesbury, and having to make payments.[2] They were, it says, *in circuitu Elesberie*. Clearly this refers to pre-Conquest times. This can be translated as the hundreds 'which lie round Aylesbury', but could also mean 'the hundreds in the circuit of Aylesbury'. Even more remarkable is the fact that eight hundreds surround the boundary of Aylesbury, and, if taken with Stoke, make up the southern half of the county. When we list these, and then examine the hundred order for the tenants-in-chief's holdings, we discover that these neighbouring hundreds, together with Aylesbury itself, are always grouped together so that they form half of the eighteen hundreds of the county.[3] The remaining hundreds form the northern half of the county, and may represent another larger administrative unit. Thus, Buckinghamshire may have been divided at the time of Domesday into two already-recognized administrative districts, one of which was the Aylesbury circuit, containing Aylesbury, Stone, Risborough, Burnham, Desborough, Ixhill, Ashendon, Waddesdon, and probably also Stoke. The northern district then included Yardley, Mursley, 'Stotfold', 'Rowley', 'Mow', 'Seckley', Bunsty, Moulsoe and probably also Cottesloe.

The other notable fact about the hundred order is that the common pattern usually associates those hundreds that came to be grouped together as 'triple-hundreds' in the hundred returns of the thirteenth century. For a more detailed discussion of this see the article by F. R. Thorn below.

## The Nature of the Buckinghamshire Information

The Buckinghamshire entries are fairly typical of Domesday as a whole. Let us examine an ordinary entry, and consider the facts that we are given, in order to see what a typical entry contains, and also in what ways the Buckinghamshire information varies from that for other counties. The following is an entry for Chesham in the hundred of Burnham:

> In Chesham the Bishop of Bayeux himself holds 1½ hides. There is land for 3 ploughs. In demesne is 1 hide, and there is 1 plough, and 2 villans with 3 bordars have 2 ploughs. There are

[1] The usual form is *terra est* x *carucis*; Buckingham has *terra est octo carucarum*.

[2] 'This manor lies with the (lands of) Aylesbury church . . . From the eight hundreds which lie in the circuit of Aylesbury, each Freeman (*sochemannus*) who has one hide or more pays one load of corn to this church.': Morris (ed.), *Domesday Book: Buckinghamshire*, 3a,1. Translated in *VCH Buckinghamshire*, i. 233, and in this edition as 'which lie round Aylesbury'.

[3] For another interpretation of the phrase *in circuitu Elesberie*, see Thorn, 'Hundreds of Buckinghamshire', p.38 below.

2 slaves, and 2 mills rendering 3*s*., (and) meadow for 3 ploughs. It is and always was worth 60*s*. This manor 2 sokemen held: one a man of Earl Leofwine, the other a man of Earl Harold, and they could sell.[1]

This holding is part of the fief headed 'The Land of the Bishop of Bayeux'. The current bishop was William the Conqueror's half-brother, Odo, who, because of his activities against the king was in prison in 1086. Within the vill of Chesham there were no less than five holdings altogether, of which two (including that quoted above) were held by the Bishop of Bayeux. The totals given here therefore relate only to a portion of the whole vill. This particular small estate was assessed at one and a half hides. Most Domesday holdings are assessed in hides, though some, mainly in the north and east, are reckoned in carucates. Some have taken the hide to be an estimate of area, normally 120 acres, and sometimes this equation seems to work. We shall need to investigate at greater length the origin and significance of the hide, but for now let it suffice to say that although the hide may have started as an areal measurement, it was probably never of a uniform size. Long before Domesday it had been used as the unit for fiscal and military assessment, and may indeed have originated as such. The various hidage documents, only one of which includes the region of Buckinghamshire, make it clear that the hidage attached to a region did not remain stable through the centuries.[2] By the time of Domesday, as practically all historians are now agreed, the hide did not represent a precise area but had become a unit of assessment, rather like the modern rateable value of property: an assessment related to size and actual value but with independent fiscal significance. Thus a Domesday holding would be assessed at so many hides, and when the geld tax was levied, at so many shillings on the hide (say two shillings), the holder must pay according to how many hides he had: ten shillings for a five-hide estate, three shillings for this holding in Chesham.

The second piece of information in our entry is that there is land for three ploughs, or perhaps we should say plough-teams. The meaning is not entirely clear. The Buckinghamshire entries are invariably in the form as here: *terra est* x *carucis*. This is probably an assessment of value rather than a statement of agricultural fact, though in many cases, including this one, the total of ploughs equals the number for which there is land: the lord has one plough-team, and the peasants have two. This may be a literal description of the actual plough-teams in use, but it may also be that every single item in Domesday is an assessment rather than agrarian reality. We are inclined to think that in Buckinghamshire the references to ploughs represent actuality. This seems to be confirmed by the entries that say 'there is land for *x* ploughs: they are there', giving the impression of an assessment made in advance and followed by a check on what exists. Sometimes there are more, and sometimes less, than the expected figure – so it is clear that 'the land for *x* ploughs' is not based on an addition of actual existing ploughs.

Domesday then tells us of the peasants on the holding. Probably we are given the heads of households, those responsible for performing the service and paying the rent. On this fairly small holding at Chesham, there are two villans and three bordars. Villans and bordars are the main peasant groups in Domesday: the villan being the typical villager of some standing, holding lands of his own, but also owing services to the lord and therefore unfree. The bordar is probably a cottager, holding a smaller amount of land, perhaps five acres against the villan's half-virgate or so. In Norman England the main peasant groups are increasing in size, absorbing into their ranks free men from above and slaves from below. Although other counties have a variety of social groups, there are very few apart from villans and bordars in Buckinghamshire. There is a handful of cottars, all attached to the Church of Buckingham, but far fewer than in the counties of Hertfordshire and Middlesex which were in the same circuit. It is puzzling why they do not appear in Buckinghamshire more frequently. Bordars and cottars had much in common, appearing to be groups of

[1] GDB 144.

[2] The main documents are the Tribal Hidage, in W. de G. Birch, *Cartularium Saxonicum: A Collection of Charters Relating to Anglo-Saxon History*, i (London, 1885), no.297; the Burghal Hidage, in A. J. Robertson (ed.), *Anglo-Saxon Charters* (Cambridge, 1956), 246; the County Hidage, figures given in Maitland, *Domesday Book and Beyond*, 456; the Northamptonshire Geld Roll, in Robertson (ed.), *Anglo-Saxon Charters*, 230.

cottagers distinguished by larger or smaller holdings. Probably in Buckinghamshire they were generally lumped together. It may be that really small cottagers were not significant in the county. One other category of peasant is represented by the four boors (*buri*) mentioned in these folios. They are probably to be equated with the peasants described as *geburas* and *coliberti* who appear elsewhere. Boors appear in only six counties in Domesday Book and are clearly of low rank, not very different from slaves.

Domesday then gives a variety of additional information relating to the resources of the holding, presumably including the main elements that could provide income. Across the county there was a good deal of variety in this section. It is clear from both Exon Domesday and Little Domesday that original returns included more information than was finally used. For Buckinghamshire we have only Great Domesday Book itself, the final and most abbreviated version. Even here it is clear that the scribe was working from information that varied a good deal, not only in the kind of resources which were detailed, but also in the way that those resources were valued. Mills, as in this Chesham holding, were generally valued in cash, but sometimes they were reckoned by numbers of eels, presumably to be supplied from the mill-pool, while one owed a render of malt. This section of Domesday might include values of fisheries, woodland, meadow and pasture. The Chesham holding has enough meadow to support three plough-teams. This, it will be noted, is the number of teams listed for the holding, suggesting that it has sufficient for its own needs.

A typical entry will then give the value of the holding, probably the overall value, the kind of figure it might be worth if rented. Clifton Reynes in Moulsoe is an example where Domesday tells us that the value given is indeed the total value. Sometimes the value suggests a render, that is an actual rent paid and always given in terms of money. Buckinghamshire is quite unusual for the frequency with which values are given for three dates: 'then', that is before Edward the Confessor's death; 'now', at the time of the Domesday survey; and the less usual figure for an intermediate time, 'when King William gave it'. This latter category depends upon the relevance here of the three valuations to be given for manors described in the *Inquisitio Eliensis*.[1] The Chesham entry is in a common form where the value has not changed: *valet et valuit semper*, 'it is and always was worth', in this case, sixty shillings. Cheddington has a variant form: *valet et valuit lx solidi TRE c solidi*, 'it is and was worth sixty shillings; in the time of King Edward, a hundred shillings'. Leckhampstead in 'Stotfold' has another form: *valet xxx solidi. Quomodo recepit xx solidi. TRE xxx solidi*, 'it is worth thirty shillings; when received twenty shillings; in the time of King Edward thirty shillings'.

Finally the entry tells us the history of the holding by naming the pre-Conquest holder, and sometimes his lord. Domesday will already have given the name of the holder in 1086: if he was a mesne-tenant, his lord's name is implicit in the position of the entry within that lord's fief. In many entries we receive a laconic but telling contribution to the story of the real effect of the Norman Conquest. The Chesham holding was previously in the hands of two sokemen, respectively men of Earl Leofwine and Earl Harold (the latter, as usual in Domesday, is recognized only as Earl of Wessex, not as King of England). Sokemen were generally linked with free men, and the distinction is sometimes hard to see. In general they were both free landholders, the free men usually greater than the sokemen in possessions and rights. What Domesday so often does not tell us, except by omission, is the fate of these previous holders. What happened to these men at Chesham? Had they been killed? Have they now become villans? Certainly they are no longer holding freely.

One last comment on the nature of the Buckinghamshire information should be made, for it is one of the counties which frequently has a marginal 'M' inscribed against a holding. This is also found in Middlesex, though rarely in Hertfordshire. There has been dispute over the significance of the 'M' to the extent that we cannot be certain of its meaning or purpose. Probably it is an abbreviation for 'manor', for the entry for Chesham has this 'M' both in the margin and within the text, where it is certainly an abbreviation for 'manor'. The most likely explanation is that the mark

[1] Loyn, 'Domesday Book', 123; Record Commission, *Domesday Book*, iv (London, 1816), 495–528, questions on 495, 497.

had some fiscal significance, denoting the holding responsible for the collection of taxes for a vill or region.[1]

The Buckinghamshire entries frequently refer to a holding *pro uno manerio* ('for one manor'). Since these are sometimes holdings within a divided vill, 'manor' can clearly mean something less than a vill, presumably simply a holding that was responsible for its own tax. Baring has pointed out that the phrase only appears in eleven of the hundreds, again suggesting a distinction as to how the information was collected.[2] The seven hundreds which do not use this form are all in what we have called the Aylesbury circuit: the two triple-hundreds of Risborough and the Chilterns, and Ixhill.

## The Hundreds

The hundred was an essential part of Anglo-Saxon administration, a unit for finance and for justice.[3] Hundreds were established in the tenth century, and possibly each had originally one hundred hides. There were, however, one-and-a-half hundreds and double-hundreds, and it may be that these had always existed. The Buckinghamshire hundreds seem to have been created soon after Edward the Elder had founded the borough of Buckingham. Vills of course existed when the hundreds were made, and could not be uniformly distributed, but there must have been some standard. One possibility is that a hundred would normally have about ten vills within it, a double-hundred twenty vills and so on. Allowing for occasional changes in landholding arrangements and the status of vills, most Buckinghamshire hundreds have around ten or fifteen vills to a hundred. H. R. Loyn has pointed out that the hundreds of Wessex are less uniform than others and may be more ancient, suggesting that areas such as Buckinghamshire owe the later imposition of more uniform hundreds to the historical domination of Wessex.[4]

In the Old English period, the hundred courts were the usual local assembly, and their usefulness continued into the fourteenth century at least. They were probably established by Edward the Elder. It has been suggested that meetings of three hundreds were not uncommon,[5] and possibly the Buckinghamshire hundreds were, for some purposes, grouped in threes from early times. The first certain evidence for this grouping belongs, however, to the thirteenth century. Such associations of hundreds are well known: there was a famous triple-hundred at 'Oswaldslow' in Worcestershire, while according to the *Leges Henrici Primi* 300 hides made a ship-soke.

Often hundreds were associated with royal manors, and these seem to occur in Buckinghamshire at Aylesbury, Princes Risborough, and possibly Brill. H. M. Cam suggested that in origin the hundred was a district depending on a king's *tun*. A. M. Davies has conjectured that the hundreds might have pre-dated the shire, but later withdrew the idea for which he had made an interesting if unconvincing argument.[6]

The significance of hundreds in 1086 is apparent from Domesday, in that all the holdings though arranged by counties and in fiefs are related to their hundreds. At some stage the hundred had produced the evidence which the Domesday clerks used and had also verified the facts. We can sometimes see this process under way in Buckinghamshire when the testimony of the men of the hundred is recorded.[7]

How the information from the hundreds was then used we can only conjecture. The strongest probability is that evidence was taken or collected for each hundred in turn, and that the material

[1] For a more detailed treatment of the 'M' marginal annotation, see C. Thorn, 'Marginal Notes and Signs in Domesday Book', *Domesday Book Studies*, eds. Williams and Erskine, 123–4.

[2] Baring, *Domesday Tables*, 140.

[3] Anderson, *EHNSE*, 1–15; H. R. Loyn, 'The Hundred in the Tenth and Early Eleventh Century', *British Government and Administration*, eds. H. Hearder and H. R. Loyn (Cardiff, 1974), 1–15; H. M. Cam, 'Manerium cum Hundredo: the Hundred and the Hundredal Manor', *EHR* 47 (1932), 353–76; Davies, 'Ancient Hundreds of Buckinghamshire'; *idem*, 'Hundreds of Buckinghamshire and Oxfordshire'.

[4] Loyn, 'The Hundred', 2.

[5] Ibid. 11.

[6] Cam, 'Manerium cum Hundredo', 362, 369; Davies, 'Ancient Hundreds of Buckinghamshire', 118; *idem*, 'Hundreds of Buckinghamshire and Oxfordshire', 231.

[7] See for example f.144v (West Wycombe): 'This land a man of Archbishop Stigand held; he could not sell or give it away from West Wycombe, his manor, as the hundred testifies'. See also ff.148v, 149, 151v.

was then reorganized under tenants-in-chief. For Buckinghamshire this comes after the material on the borough in the following order: the king; the ecclesiastical holders beginning with the Archbishop of Canterbury; the main male landholders, beginning with the Conqueror's half-brother Robert, Count of Mortain; then the female landholders, of whom there are only three: Queen Matilda, the Countess Judith, and Azelina wife of Ralph Taillebois. The list concludes with 'The Land of the king's thegns and almsmen'.

## Assessments and Valuations: Hides

One of the most difficult aspects of Domesday to interpret is the information on measurements, valuations and assessments. We have seen something of this by examining the unusual features of the Buckinghamshire material, but there is a need to look at each valuation and assessment in turn, whether common or uncommon, and attempt to see what it tells us about the county.

The first of these assessment figures, and one of the most difficult, is the hidage. We may sympathize with Maitland's complaint: 'however unwilling we may be to face this dreary old question, we cannot escape it', or with Baring's: 'the hide is grown somewhat tiresome'.[1] One is tempted to add that if it was true for Baring at the beginning of the century, how much more true is it for us today. It is, however, a vital area for our understanding of Domesday and of the Old English governmental system. It is clear that hidage assessment was old by the time of Domesday: 'lost in the mists of antiquity', according to Hart.[2] It may go back to the seventh or even the sixth century, and is certainly mentioned by Bede.

The precise meaning of the word is not clear, but it has associations in Old English with words relating to the household, and Bede's 'land of one family' is probably the best definition we have. Hart's modern rendering is the 'value of the entire agricultural package farmed by a single family'.[3] The hide was used as an assessment unit for taxation and other burdens, including military service. Hart argues for an imposition of hidage in Cambridgeshire in 917 by Edward the Elder, and a reduction in 942 by Edmund. He suggests that in some areas the first hidage was obliterated by Danish domination.[4] The existence of earlier hidage lists, with very much greater hidage figures than those of Domesday, strongly suggests that the assessment was revised on more than one occasion, generally in a downward direction: that is, land that may once have been assessed at a hundred hides might be reassessed at, say, eighty hides. This kind of revision, which does not seem to have been uniform, makes it unprofitable to try to transform Domesday hidages into measured areas. Even if the hide began as a measured area—which is by no means certain—by 1086 the original link has been lost. The revisions were almost certainly done on some local basis, presumably through shire and hundred, and variations in redistribution occurred at this level.

The hide was also used, at least occasionally, in multiple groups. A unit of five hides had some significance in levying military service, exemplified by the frequent if not universal demand of the service of one man from five hides. Evidence in the *Inquisitio Comitatus Cantabrigiensis* and in the Berkshire Domesday shows this.[5] The continuation through into the Norman period of estates made up of five hides, or of multiples of five, is also indicative of this. Buckinghamshire certainly has a large number of such estates.

With regard to hidage, there is one earlier document that does refer to the Buckinghamshire area. Hart places the Tribal Hidage as early as the sixth century, though most have thought it later.[6] It

[1] Maitland, *Domesday Book and Beyond*, 357; Baring, 'Hidation of Some Southern Counties', 290.

[2] Hart, *Hidation of Northamptonshire*, 9.

[3] B. Colgrave and R. A. B. Mynors (eds.), *Bede's Ecclesiastical History of the English People* (Oxford, 1969), 374: *terram lxxxvii familiarum*, cf. pp.72, 162, 222, 336, 520. Bede, p.382, refers to this as 'the English way of reckoning' (*aestimationem Anglorum*). Compare B. Colgrave (ed.), *The Life of Bishop Wilfrid by Eddius Stephanus* (Cambridge, 1927), 82–3, translates *lxxxvii mansionum* as 'eighty-seven hides'; Hart, *Hidation of Cambridgeshire*, 11.

[4] Hart, *Hidation of Cambridgeshire*, 36.

[5] Round in *VCH Buckinghamshire*, i. 207–8; E. John, *Land Tenure in Early England* (Leicester, 2nd edn., 1964), 80, 148; GDB 56; N. Hooper, 'Anglo-Saxon Warfare on the Eve of the Conquest: a Brief Summary', *ANS* 1 (1978), 88; Welldon Finn, *Introduction to Domesday Book*, 266.

[6] Hart, *Hidation of Northamptonshire*, 45.

gives hidage figures in large round numbers for certain tribal regions. One such region is that of the *Cilternsætan*, obviously connected with the Chiltern region. The area covered by this group has been much discussed, but no precise conclusion can be reached. The assessment given is 4,000 hides, and whatever juggling one does with the area, there must have been a reduction of this assessment by Domesday. In Northamptonshire, where the documentation is fuller, Hart shows a direct relationship at an early stage between the number of hundreds, thirty-two, and the number of the hides, 32,000, together with a more or less logical reduction by the time of Domesday. We need not agree with all of Hart's reasons and conclusions, but this general idea of a connection between hidage and hundreds plus a series of downward revisions seems acceptable. The County Hidage, generally dated to the eleventh century (though Hart places it earlier) does not cover Buckinghamshire, but again supports the idea of a downward revision of hidage.[1] These reductions were not necessarily always universal and uniform. There is a good case to be made for some individual reassessments, perhaps for deserving poverty, or as a royal favour, or to benefit the crown itself. Royal estates seem generally to be given a low rate. The church might also be the recipient of beneficial hidation. Wing in Buckinghamshire, which Ælfgifu bequeathed to King Edgar, seems to have benefited in this way.[2]

The revisions meant that by the Norman Conquest there was need for a new and fairer assessment. In addition to individual valuations, there clearly were a number of national redistributions. Several historians have suggested that the method for this, having decided on the reduction, was to pass this down to the shire, from the shire to the hundred, and from the hundred to the vill, sometimes at a uniform rate, sometimes in a more elaborate manner. Then, too, we should not assume that reductions were necessarily meant to be permanent. If granted for temporary disability, caused, for example, by famine or raids, the previous assessment might well be restored. Almost certainly hides in demesne were exempted at an early stage. Crown 'inland' seems not even to have been hidated, only the 'warland', that is the land worked by the peasants, was hidated. It may be that demesne hides were recorded because, though not liable to geld, they were liable to other burdens. After 1066 baronial demesnes seem also to have received geld exemption. Welldon Finn poses another question: what happened to land brought under the plough after the hidage assessment? He thinks that the formula which includes carucates in demesne as well as hides might be a result of this.[3] Such estates are found in Buckinghamshire at Turweston, Hanslope, Newport Pagnell and Tickford End. All these complications over the centuries were bound to result in inequalities and anomalies. The need for a full-scale investigation into the situation was pressing, and supports Sally Harvey's argument that Domesday was accompanied by a reassessment.[4]

The hidage figures for Buckinghamshire are given in three forms. The first is '*a* holds *x* hides', as for example at Ilmer in Ixhill: *tenet Robertus de episcopo quatuor hidas* ('Robert holds four hides from the bishop'). The second form is '*a* defends itself for *x* hides', as at Hughenden in Desborough: *Huchedene pro x hidis se defendit* ('Hughenden defends itself for ten hides'). The third and more unusual form is '*a* holds *x* hides for one manor', as at Shalstone in 'Stotfold': *tenet Robertus de Roberto iiii hidas pro uno manerio* ('Robert holds four hides of Robert for one manor'). There is also a variant of the second example in the form '*a* always defends itself for *x* hides', as at Brill in Ixhill: *pro viginti hidis se defendit semper* ('Brill always defends itself for twenty hides'). This formula appears in five instances, four of which are royal vills, while the fifth belongs to the church, and had previously been Queen Edith's. This suggests some separate version of returns for royal properties. An even greater oddity is the entry for Oakley in Ixhill, held by Robert d'Oilly, which 'defends itself for five hides and three virgates', and then adds 'these five hides and three virgates are eight hides'. This is difficult to explain, but does point to the figures being assessments rather than measurements.[5]

[1] Hart, *Hidation of Northamptonshire*, 9–10, 14.

[2] Baines, 'Lady Elgiva', 135.

[3] Welldon Finn, *Introduction to Domesday Book*, 261; Hart, *Hidation of Northamptonshire*, 31.

[4] Harvey, 'Taxation and the Ploughland'.

[5] GDB 144v(x2), 149v, 143v, 149; but see also Robertson (ed.), *Anglo-Saxon Charters*, no.111, pp.208–9: 'Bp Ealdred (of Worcester) grants to Wulfgeat 1½ hides in the manor of Ditchford . . . and at the king's summons he should discharge the obligations on these 1½ hides at the rate of one'. That is, the holding is assessed at 1½ hides for the bishop's service but only 1 hide for the king's service. The date is between A.D. 1051 and 1053.

Buckinghamshire is often mentioned as a county that is obviously divided into five-hide units. E. M. J. Campbell calculated that eighty-six of the 206 estates were five- or ten-hide units, twenty-eight were in multiples of these, and two were at two and a half hides, totalling 116. He concludes: 'the five-hide principle is readily apparent in over one-half of the Buckinghamshire villages'.[1]

In fact, it is only by 'corrections' that Buckinghamshire can be made to look like an aggregation of neat five-hide units. It can readily be agreed that the starting-point of hidage was some round figure, which the shire distributed, if not evenly then at least logically, between the hundreds. There may also have been, as elsewhere, three-quarter hundreds, one-and-a-half hundreds and double-hundreds. Even so, it is not easy to demonstrate from Domesday what were the original allocations. If we allow five hides in either direction for the Domesday hidage figures, there are seven hundreds that come out at one hundred hides, three at one and a half hundred hides, but eight that are not close to either figure. If one looks at the vills within hundreds, the same sort of partial neatness is true (see Table 2).

TABLE 2: Hidage by hundreds (to nearest quarter-hide, or virgate)

| Hundred | Hides in 5-multiples | Approximately 5-multiples | Others | Total of hides in hundred |
|---|---|---|---|---|
| Ashendon | 9 | – | 4 | 112¼ |
| Aylesbury | 6 | 1 | 6 | 150¾ |
| Bunsty | 7 | 3 | – | 97½ |
| Burnham | 2 | 1 | 6 | 104¼ |
| Cottesloe | 9 | 2 | 5 | 140 |
| Desborough | 7 | 1 | 5 | 148 |
| Ixhill | 8 | 3 | 4 | 121 |
| Moulsoe | 5 | 4 | 2 | 113 |
| 'Mow' | 6 | 1 | 2 | 127 |
| Mursley | 6 | 1 | 6 | 112½ |
| Risborough | 3 | 1 | – | 99¼ |
| 'Rowley' | 7 | 1 | 3 | 101 |
| 'Seckley' | 11 | 1 | 3 | 138½ |
| Stoke | 6 | – | 3 | 95½ |
| Stone | 3 | 2 | 3 | 150 |
| 'Stotfold' | 6 | 2 | 7 | 98½ |
| Waddesdon | 4 | 1 | 2 | 96¼ |
| Yardley | 3 | 2 | 5 | 124½ |

Total for the county: 2,129¾ hides

There can be no certain conclusions about the hidation of Buckinghamshire, but we may suggest that it was hidated early from the evidence of the Tribal Hidage, and that it was probably affected to some degree by Scandinavian control and later Scandinavian settlement, leaving remnants of carucation in demesne carucates, and perhaps also in the six-hide vills. Buckinghamshire must have been hidated at some time subsequent to Edward the Elder's success in 915, and probably not long afterwards. The regularity of the appearance of five-hide multiple units does indeed suggest some deliberate imposition in units of five, perhaps even from the beginning. The number of vills which do not fit the pattern are, however, sufficient to make one believe that considerable revision had occurred since any imposition based on five-hide units had been made.

The hidage totals for each hundred are given in the right column of Table 2 and add up to just under 2,130 hides for the whole county. However, as Baring said: 'no two computations of any set of Domesday figures for a county have ever exactly agreed'.[2] His own total was 2,128 hides, which he 'corrected' to 2,160, though in his hidation article he gives 2,078 hides. Darby gives 2,210 hides; Campbell has the elaborate figure of 2,125 hides, 3¾ virgates and 3 acres less 5 feet, 'corrected' to 2,100; Maitland makes it 2,074 hides.[3]

[1] Darby and Campbell (eds.), *Domesday Geography*, 146.
[2] Baring, *Domesday Tables*, p.xv.
[3] Baring, *Domesday Tables*, 132; Darby, *Domesday England*, 336; Darby and Campbell (eds.), *Domesday Geography*, 149; Maitland, *Domesday Book and Beyond*, 400.

## Assessments and Valuations: Ploughlands

That hidage and ploughland figures were related is supported by twelfth-century commentators who saw the two as being the same thing. Thus Henry of Huntingdon referred to 'hides, that is to say, ploughlands' (*hidae id est jugera*), and Orderic Vitalis to 'ploughlands which are called hides in English' (*carucatas quas Anglice hidas vocant*).[1] We have already argued that ploughlands are figures of assessment rather than of agricultural reality, that it is land which can maintain so many ploughs rather than land that does employ given numbers, though the two may sometimes coincide. In Buckinghamshire, as in Bedfordshire and Middlesex, the common form is: 'there is land for *x* ploughs', and often to this is added 'and they are there'. Thus at Leckhampstead in 'Stotfold': *terra est i caruca et ibi est* ('there is land for one plough, and it is there'). Or sometimes we are told they are not there, as at Milton Keynes in Moulsoe: *terra est una caruca sed non est ibi* ('there is land for one plough, but it is not there'). On other occasions we are informed that there is land for so many ploughs, some are there, but so many more are possible: for example, at Maids Moreton in 'Stotfold' there is land for two ploughs, one and a half are there, and another half is possible; or at Shipton Lee, where 'two others are possible' (*et aliae ii possunt esse*). At times there are actually more ploughs than are estimated. For example, a second holding at Milton Keynes has land for ten ploughs, and not only possessed ten and a half teams, but is said to be capable of having one half more. All this makes it plain that the ploughland figure has been assessed in advance, probably on the basis suggested in Exon Domesday, that so many ploughs 'can till this land'.[2]

Assessment by ploughs was, after all, not a new phenomenon, appearing at other places and other times with some regularity. In England we find it in the seventh-century code of Æthelberht of Kent, with a tax on every plough.[3] We can take it that the ploughland figures were an assessment, probably used to levy services other than the geld, and so were necessary in addition to hidage figures. What we cannot be clear about is whether or not they pre-dated the hidage assessment. Most historians have argued that they are an earlier assessment: Hart dating them from a much earlier period, Maitland dating them as figures from Edward the Confessor's reign. Sally Harvey, on the other hand, suggests that they represent a new assessment under the Conqueror, made at the time of Domesday, though in some areas relying on earlier assessments.[4] Conclusion on this is not easy, since both assessments were probably revised at intervals.

The ploughland figures for the county are less regular than those for the hidage, which would probably fit with an older and somewhat altered assessment. For a start there is greater range in the figures, from sixty-two for Risborough, which was presumably given a favourable assessment, to Desborough at 207½. On the whole, we are inclined to the view that the two sets of figures should be treated separately in the county, and that they represent two quite different assessments made on a different basis.

It is not easy to see how the ploughland figures were distributed. Historians who see them as virtually the same as hides must expect the distribution method to be similar. Two hundreds, Desborough and Cottesloe, are near to 200 ploughlands; three hundreds, Bunsty, Aylesbury and 'Seckley' are near to 150; two hundreds, Waddesdon and 'Rowley', are near to 100, but for the most part they are not close enough for it to be truly significant, and the other eleven hundreds are at intermediate figures. This seems to support the conclusions that if there was any original regular distribution, it was distant, and, more probably, that ploughland assessment was done in a different manner from the hidage and was perhaps judged locally on an agricultural basis.

If there is any significance in the distribution of ploughland figures for individual vills, it is that there are more six-ploughland units than there were six-hide units, and fewer five-ploughland units than six-hide units. This could be taken to suggest older and possibly Danish influence, but the

[1] Harvey, 'Anglo-Norman Governance', 188–9; Henry of Huntingdon, *Historia Anglorum*, ed. T. Arnold, Rolls Ser. 74 (1879), 207; M. Chibnall (ed.), *The Ecclesiastical History of Orderic Vitalis*, iv (Oxford, 1973), 172.

[2] GDB 147v, 148, 147v, 151, 153; Darby, *Domesday England*, 116.

[3] Harvey, 'Anglo-Norman Governance', 189.

[4] Hart, *Hidation of Northamptonshire*, 25; Maitland, *Domesday Book and Beyond*, 421; Harvey, 'Taxation and the Ploughland', 103.

variety is so great that it seems doubtful that five- and six-unit figures with regard to ploughlands are anything more than coincidence. Aylesbury, with twelve vills has only one with a five-ploughland unit, Risborough has no five-ploughland units in its four vills, both Waddesdon and Yardley have one five-ploughland unit and three six-plough units. For the total figures, see Table 3. Again, we find disagreements with other additions: Campbell's total for the county was 2,244 ploughlands and Baring's 2,293.[1]

A very tentative conclusion is that the ploughland figures for Buckinghamshire are earlier than the hidage figures, and more affected by a previous Danish carucation. This would then imply that the Domesday hidage for Buckinghamshire had been revised at some time closer to Domesday. The relative prevalence of six-ploughland figures may suggest either greater Danish influence, or Danish settlement. All the hundreds where five-ploughland figures dominate are in the west: 'Rowley', Ashendon, Ixhill and Desborough. In other words, if it is the result of Danish influence, then that has had more effect in the east of the county where one might expect it. The one thing with which all can agree is Sally Harvey's comment, that the ploughland 'still requires much work'.

The distribution of actual ploughs we shall consider when looking at the social and economic situation. Suffice it to say here, that, as suggested, they seem to represent figures of actual ploughs in use by lords and peasants. The plough totals for the county are: ploughlands, 2,264½; lords' ploughs, 688½; other ploughs, 1,366½; total ploughs, 2,055; more ploughs possible, 258¾.

TABLE 3: Ploughlands in Buckinghamshire by hundred

| | | | | | |
|---|---|---|---|---|---|
| Ashendon | 112½ | Ixhill | 138 | 'Seckley' | 159¼ |
| Aylesbury | 155½ | Moulsoe | 118½ | Stoke | 109 |
| Bunsty | 115½ | 'Mow' | 124½ | Stone | 124½ |
| Burnham | 153 | Mursley | 108¾ | 'Stotfold' | 112 |
| Cottesloe | 191½ | Risborough | 62 | Waddesdon | 97 |
| Desborough | 207½ | 'Rowley' | 93 | Yardley | 82½ |

Total for the county: 2,264½

## ASSESSMENTS AND VALUATIONS: VALUES

The remaining area of assessment that needs to be examined is that of the total valuations for the holdings. Each holding is given a value, which we have suggested may be taken as roughly equivalent to its rentable value, and is sometimes almost certainly an actual rental. It probably does represent a total value, including the other sources of income listed for the holding. In four cases of Buckinghamshire holdings, at Aylesbury, Taplow, Wendover and Hambleden, we are specifically told that it is the total value, for example, *in totis valentiis*, or *in totis redditionibus per annum*.[2] Lennard has shown how frequently in Domesday as a whole values equal rents, and the Buckinghamshire evidence seems to support his case. He argued that a large number of manors were let out at farm, that is, passed on by the landholder to another person, to exploit under an arrangement whereby the 'farmer' (*firmarius*) would pay a fixed annual sum in return.[3] Any holder with numerous estates would have to employ some such system. In Buckinghamshire valuations are generally given for the time of Edward the Confessor, for the time of the Domesday survey, and for an intermediate time, probably that at which the Conqueror appointed or confirmed the holder. The latter figure is not always given, so it is misleading to compare totals of all three periods, as the intermediate one is bound to be smaller. It can, of course, be instructive to compare where all three figures are given. The actual overall totals for the county are: value TRE, £1,878. 18*s*.; value between, £1,321. 17*s*.; value in 1086, £1,920. 6*s*. 3*d*.

[1] Darby and Campbell (eds.), *Domesday Geography*, 154; Maitland, *Domesday Book and Beyond*, 400; Darby, *Domesday England*, 336.

[2] GDB 143 (Aylesbury), 143v (Wendover), 144 (Taplow), 152v (Hambleden).

[3] Lennard, *Rural England*, for example, ch.5, pp.105–41, as on p.124.

Where all three figures are given, the general pattern is of a slight reduction in value at the intermediate point, and a slight increase over both previous valuations for the 1086 figure, though this pattern is by no means universal. Many estates are given exactly the same value for all three times, and others drop in value. One major difficulty is the intermittent use of the intermediate valuation, our lack of knowledge about its exact meaning and about its timing. Nor do we know if the intermediate valuation depended on an earlier assessment, as the TRE figure presumably does, or if the value was requested in the course of the Domesday survey. If the latter was the case and the holders themselves estimated that value, it might reveal a desire to exhibit their own efficiency or to show that the present value was unjustifiably high. We certainly cannot take it for a fact that the intermediate figure represents great devastation caused by the Conquest, though some loss of value through this might be a factor.

The examination of values for individual vills is of interest. Some vills are clearly prosperous, and retain their value throughout all three periods. In Ashendon Hundred, Winchendon[1] is always the most valuable vill, twice the value of any other. Valuations do, of course, have a relation to size. Any vill of great value is bound also to be of fair size, giving some indication of the local significance of certain settlements. This can be particularly helpful where vills did not develop into parishes, and boundaries are difficult to establish. Thus the valuation of Pollicott[2] in Ashendon is high enough to suggest fair size, and means that land later in the parishes of Ashendon, Winchendon and Chearsley was almost certainly part of the Domesday vill of Pollicott.

In the hundred of Aylesbury, Aylesbury itself and Wendover are the two major vills, valued respectively at £1,320 and £800. They also demonstrate the potentially misleading nature of the intermediate value, given as *nil* for Aylesbury and only £20 for Wendover, presumably because of omission rather than some catastrophic drop in value. The relative values of Bierton and Broughton must mean that a great deal of the later parish of Bierton was at Domesday contained within the vill of Broughton.

In Bunsty, Hanslope is the only highly valued vill, whereas in Burnham there are four vills of high value, at Chesham, Amersham, Chalfont and Burnham itself. All the Burnham high-value vills drop greatly at the intermediate point, and none of them have risen above the TRE figure by 1086. In Cottesloe, Wing is the outstandingly valuable vill. In Desborough there are high values for Wycombe, Marlow and Hambleden, all covering a large area, and probably representing the type of estate with a central vill and satellite settlements. In Ixhill, Brill and Long Crendon stand out, while Brickhill[3] is the main vill in Moulsoe. In 'Mow' there are several vills of modest value, of which Steeple Claydon is greatest by 1086, but none are very high. Winslow is the main vill in Mursley, but it is only modest. In Risborough, Bledlow and Monks Risborough have high valuations. Princes Risborough is a royal vill, valued moderately TRE at £200, against £400 for Bledlow and £320 for Monks Risborough. At the intermediate date the values are Bledlow £240, Monks Risborough £100, and Princes Risborough *nil*. By 1086, however, Princes Risborough has outstripped the others, standing at £938. 13*s*. 4*d*., against £440 for Bledlow and £320 for Monks Risborough. If the answer is not omission, it may be that the valuations represent a real value to the Crown, that at the intermediate point the Crown held directly, but by 1086 was expecting a high rental. The rental aspect of the payments should remind us that the figures do not necessarily show the real wealth of a vill, that some may be undervalued and others let out at exorbitant rents.

'Rowley', with a royal interest, is also exceptional. The highest TRE valuation is for Buckingham with Bourton, but in the intermediate period this goes down from £340 to a modest £120, and is only £30. 3*s*. 8*d*. in 1086. There is clearly little uniformity in the valuation figures. Some must have benefited from privileged treatment.

In 'Seckley', the main vills are Newport Pagnell and Wolverton. At Domesday it is noticeable, here as elsewhere, that totals seem to reflect a duodecimal system, almost certainly related to currency. Thus two 'Seckley' vills are valued at £120 and two at £240. In Stoke, there are three vills

[1] Includes both Lower Winchendon and Upper Winchendon.

[2] Identified in the accompanying translation as (Lower or Upper) Pollicott.

[3] Includes both Bow Brickhill and (Great or Little) Brickhill.

TRE at £120, and two at £240, others as fractions at £80 and £40, leaving only two vills outside this pattern. Wraysbury is the highest valued vill TRE but by 1086 has given place to Iver. In Stone, Haddenham is twice as valuable as any other vill. 'Stotfold' vills are all modest. In Waddesdon, Claydon[1] and Waddesdon stand out, and in Yardley, Marsworth and Ivinghoe.

## Economy of Buckinghamshire in 1086

Domesday Book is a great source of social and economic information, and from it can be formed some view of the eleventh-century economy and of social structure both before and after the Conquest. Buckinghamshire was economically important, without being a major area for any particular product. It was largely agricultural, its economy depending on its natural resources. Although Buckinghamshire has some important routes passing through it, both north to south and east to west, this brought no great benefit to the eleventh-century county, since the termini were elsewhere. No great passing trade or market centre developed, though both occurred on a modest scale. The most notable mention of more distant contact is in the entry for Princes Risborough, which possessed an interest in a salt-worker from Droitwich in Worcestershire: presumably he produced salt for the Buckinghamshire vill. Most economic resources in the county spring from local possessions: from the soil, the woodlands, the rivers, the pasture and the meadow. Assessment figures, though not representing agricultural reality, do give some indication of the spread of ploughlands, pigs and woodland, and tell us something of the importance of oxen and pigs to the economy. The returns for woodland already examined (pp.9–10, above), indicate large numbers of pigs within the county, especially in the Chilterns and in the north.

The river valleys also had economic significance: they provided the routes, sometimes through otherwise difficult country; they often meant fertile soil for agriculture and good grass; they also meant fish. Domesday refers to all of these directly or indirectly. The high figures for ploughs in some of the riverside vills indicate good soil and flourishing agriculture. Although the figures for meadow and pasture are recorded erratically, those that are returned show the significance of the rivers. If one follows the route of the Thames along the southern boundary of the county, one finds that in Desborough every vill has recorded meadow: Fawley for two teams, Hambleden eight, Medmenham ten, Marlow thirty-six, and Wooburn six. The three Burnham vills on the river are all small but all have meadow: Taplow for one team, Dorney three, and Boveney three. Similarly, in Stoke, the figures for meadow in the river vills are: Eton two teams, Datchet five, and Wraysbury five. Buckinghamshire on the whole was well provided with meadow, though one area that lacked it was the north part of Desborough, away from the river.

Domesday Buckinghamshire gives both numbers and values of fisheries. There are relatively few fisheries, but they do not lack interest. Again, of course, they follow the rivers, and the Thames completely dominates all others so far as this resource is concerned. Of twenty-seven fisheries in the county, only three were in the hundreds not bordering the Thames. Again the Chiltern hundreds are the significant ones; Desborough having six fisheries, Burnham five, and Stoke thirteen.

The fisheries in Buckinghamshire were usually valued in eels, though it must be doubted whether this implied an actual render. It was probably an estimate of value comparable with woodland valued in pigs. Three hundreds outside the Chilterns had one fishery each: Ixhill valued at only 100 eels, Moulsoe at 125, and Stone, the only important one, at 1,000 eels. They are swamped by the Chiltern total of 9,500 eels: 4,800 from Desborough, 3,000 from Burnham, and 1,700 from Stoke. Twelve hundreds had no fisheries at all. The northern fisheries were at Shabbington in Ixhill on the Thame, Clifton Reynes in Moulsoe on the Ouse, and at Upton in Stone[2] whose boundaries are uncertain but probably extended to the Thame. The southern fisheries depended on the Wye and the Colne as well as the Thames. Sometimes eels are recorded as the value of mills, presumably

[1] The Claydons of Waddesdon Hundred include both Middle Claydon and (Botolph or East) Claydon.

[2] Identified in the accompanying translation as Upton (in Dinton).

implying the value of the mill-pond. The most unusual fishery entry is for Iver, which possessed four fisheries, valued at 1,500 eels, which also had to provide fish every Friday for the work done by the reeve of the vill.

The mills of Domesday are all water-mills, the windmill not yet having been introduced into western Europe. Mills were more common than fisheries and more evenly distributed. This suggests that major income from fisheries was rare and depended on a large river, while the possession of a mill was common provided there was reasonable running water to drive it. Thirty-eight per cent of settlements in the county had mills. Although twelve hundreds possessed no fisheries, no hundred was without at least one mill, though there were two with only one each, in Waddesdon at Waddesdon itself, and in Ashendon at Lower Winchendon. There were naturally more mills in the areas through which the greater rivers ran, and again the Chilterns predominate with fifty mills out of 135 in the county. It should be noted that in Burnham the Misbourne was more important for mills than the Thames, and in Desborough the Wye. The other two hundreds with a large number of mills were Aylesbury with twelve and 'Seckley' with thirteen. Indeed the thirty mills in the three north-eastern hundreds of Bunsty, 'Seckley' and Moulsoe had a total value of £377, almost as high as the total for the Chiltern hundreds of £464. Sometimes mills were valued in money: for example, the mill on the land held by Hugh of Walter Giffard was valued at 20*s.*, which suggests an actual rent. Sometimes also a mill was valued in a mixture of eels and money, for example that at Lower Winchendon which rendered 20*s.* and eighty eels.[1] Mills were clearly valuable possessions, grinding the corn; generally it seems they were rented to a man of some, if modest, local standing. Their numbers do give some indication of the volume of corn grown in the county and used for bread.

There have been attempts to establish the amount of arable land under cultivation in the twelfth century. This has been calculated at being more than the amount under cultivation in the twentieth century; but it is based on relating Domesday assessments to actual acreage, and we have seen how uncertain and uneven any such relationship is. Nevertheless, the impression is one of a large area under the plough. Even the Chilterns have a considerable number of ploughs, and were far from being completely covered with woods. Certainly a large area had to be cultivated in order to cope with an economy more or less based on local self-sufficiency. Maitland has calculated that the English, a people thought by the Pope to drink much beer, needed at least one-third of their arable as 'beer-land', to produce crops for the favourite national beverage.[2]

Domesday hints at some other economic resources of the county. Sometimes the woodland render was in iron rather than pigs. This was the case at Bledlow, Wing and Chesham, former royal manors which had belonged to Ælfgifu, wife of King Eadwig, suggesting a payment in kind.[3] Bledlow also made another unusual render for its mill, of twenty-four loads of malt.[4] It is one of only two places in Domesday to owe loads of malt. The county probably also possessed some stud farms, as it certainly did later, when Princes Risborough was a royal stud. In the Black Prince's day, records were kept of its everyday working, even naming some of the stallions, such as Grisel King. It was a royal stud under Edward II, and the manor had belonged at various times to Harold II, William I, and Henry III. It has been suggested that the ancient place-name of its neighbour, Horsenden, might refer to animals kept in the park between the two. More certainly Stotfold actually means a horse-stud.[5] The wetlands under the Icknield Way were suitable both for horses and deer. By the fourteenth century there were fifty-two parks in Buckinghamshire in the four forests of Windsor, Bernwood, Whittlewood and Salcey. In Domesday there were parks at Long Crendon and at Oakley, both in Bernwood. That at Crendon was said to be for the woodland

[1] GDB 147v (Leckhampstead), 147 (Lower Winchendon).

[2] For example, Reed, *Buckinghamshire Landscape*, 86; Maitland, *Domesday Book and Beyond*, 435–6, gives 165,000 acres for 1895, and 269,000 for 1086. Maitland, 439–41, on beer-land, quotes *Multum biberunt de cereuisia Anglicana*.

[3] GDB 146(x2), 150v; Baines, 'Lady Elgiva', 115.

[4] GDB 146. The only other render of malt in Domesday Book was at Yockleton in Shropshire (f.255v). See also Lennard, *Rural England*, 283.

[5] F. H. Pavry and G. M. Knocker, 'The Mount, Princes Risborough', *RB* 16 (1957–8), 131–78; F. F. Parsons, 'Some Additional Notes on the Name of Risborough', *RB* 13 (1934–40), 470–2; Anderson, *EHNSE*, 2.

animals. At Oakley it was said there would have been woodland for 200 pigs, were it not for the king's park in which it lies.[1]

Other resources included a vineyard at Iver, reckoned at the continental measure of two arpents, suggesting Norman introduction. This was one of the forty or so vineyards recorded in Domesday but the only one in Buckinghamshire. Finally it might be noted that the woodland, besides supporting pigs and producing iron, could also provide wood for houses, fencing and fuel.[2]

## Eleventh-Century Society

For all the detail that Domesday gives us, the picture of society it presents is full of puzzles and uncertainties. Since its information on urban society is very sketchy, the overall image we receive is that of a largely rural society, dominated by king and magnates. Organization was principally manorial, though some Domesday vills seem to have been multiple estates covering a broad area. Brill, which had previously been a royal hunting-lodge, was one such example.[3] Sometimes the magnates resided on one of their own manors, and generally reserved the produce of at least one usually wealthy manor for their own personal use. Most manors though, would be passed on for direct exploitation to vassals or to persons who held them 'at farm' (*firmarii*).

The vill at Amersham with its five separate holdings has been brilliantly reconstructed by G. R. Elvey. As for Chalfont, E. M. Elvey suggests it was not an agricultural unit at all, consisting rather of separate hamlets 'united only in being under one lord'.[4] In social terms it means that the magnates may have been less evident in the county than they appear in Domesday, especially if they had far-flung holdings, of which the more significant were in other counties. It was the man on the spot who must often have seemed to matter most to the peasants, whether he be overlord, vassal, *firmarius*, or bailiff.[5]

Detail is given of the other residents: from free men and sokemen, to villans, bordars, cottars, slaves and boors. In essence, these are the people who laboured on the land in order to live. Through them Domesday gives some view of the structure of society. We may, for example, accept a rough hierarchy based upon the order in which Domesday lists the residents. Free men and sokemen are almost invariably treated separately from the others, and were socially superior to ordinary peasants. The Frenchman (*francigenus*) at Weston Underwood[6] was probably both French and free. Although some of these free groups may have owed services, and although some were clearly less wealthy than others, they had rights denied to the peasants. In Buckinghamshire, as elsewhere, the free group had clearly suffered from the effects of the Norman Conquest. Many who had been landholders before the Conquest were so no more. By Domesday, Buckinghamshire has only twenty-two free men and sokemen, grouped in the later triple-hundreds of Newport and Aylesbury, and perhaps indicating the urban pretensions of these settlements.[7] A typical reference is in Horsenden in Risborough where Ralph held six hides and three virgates of the Count of Mortain. Previously three sokemen possessed this manor with the right to sell. Often what happened to such men is a mystery. Some presumably stayed on as subtenants or as villans, but usually we can only guess whether they are numbered among the 1086 residents. At Horsenden, for example, in 1086 there are seven villans and one bordar, but we cannot know if the three Old English sokemen are among them. The entry for Wendover strikes a note of caution, since we find two sokemen with one and a half hides who were not there before 1066. Similarly at Weston Turville, under Roger, there are men who did not belong to Leofwine before 1066. Just as Domesday does not

[1] L. M. Cantor and J. Hatherly, 'The Medieval Parks of Buckinghamshire', *RB* 20 (1977), 431–47, esp. pp.432–3. References to parks at Long Crendon (f.147) and Oakley (f.149). References to horses at High Wycombe (f.149) and at Dorney (f.149v).

[2] Darby, *Domesday England*, 275; Welldon Finn, *Introduction to Domesday Book*, 202. Vineyard at Iver (f.149). Wood for fences at Great Kimble (f.147), and (Botolph or East) Claydon (f.148). References to iron at (Great and Little) Hampden (f.148v), Aston Clinton (f.150v), Chesham (f.150v) and Burnham (f.151).

[3] Reed, *Buckinghamshire Landscape*, 74.

[4] G. R. Elvey, 'Buckinghamshire in 1086'; E. M. Elvey, 'Abbot of Missenden's Estates in Chalfont St Peter', 20–40, esp. p.21.

[5] Lennard, *Rural England*, 105.

[6] GDB 145v.

[7] Darby, *Domesday England*, 65; the totals of free men and sokemen are: Aylesbury 3, Bunsty 8, Moulsoe 5, Risborough 1, 'Seckley' 3, Stone 2.

tell us what happened to men who were on their manors in 1066 but gone by 1086, so it does not inform us of the previous whereabouts of men who were not residents in 1066 but had arrived by 1086.[1]

According to Baring, north Buckinghamshire has no sokemen, unlike Northamptonshire and Bedfordshire, but there are numerous thegns with small holdings who seem equivalent in status to sokemen.[2] Four of the eight thegns at Woughton on the Green shared half a hide, though half a hide each or even a whole hide was more common. At Tickford End there were five thegns TRE, and there are five sokemen in 1086.[3] There must be a strong inclination to believe that the label and rank is all that has changed. The decline of sokemen in society was a common eleventh-century phenomenon. In Cambridgeshire numbers dropped from 900 to 177, in Bedfordshire from 700 to 90, and in Hertfordshire from 250 to 43. In Middlesex and Surrey they practically disappeared, and the same is true of Buckinghamshire. The 1086 sokemen in Buckinghamshire are indeed among the few recorded outside the Danelaw, and their presence reinforces the view of some earlier Danish settlement in the region.[4]

The peasant population of Buckinghamshire in Domesday is not unusual. It consists of the normal groups in the expected pattern. The greater part consists of villans, with bordars as the second most numerous class. One notable fact is the near omission of any lesser cottager group. The only ten cottars in the county are tied to the hundred of 'Rowley', on the estate of the Church of Buckingham.[5] Cottars appear in nine other Domesday counties. Maitland thought that perhaps what distinguished cottars was that they lacked their own arable land.[6] There are a few other minor groups, such as 'the men who dwell in the woods' at Newport Pagnell. Seemingly they pay a rent for the privilege of being there, but how many they were, what they did and what they paid individually is unknown.[7] Craftsmen are barely mentioned in Buckinghamshire, though at Ibstone there was a smith. Caldecote possessed two 'vavasours', presumably feudal underlings, but why they should be mentioned for this vill only is unclear.[8]

If we allow fifty-three burgesses in Buckingham, the total population of the county in Domesday is 5,155. The hundreds with notably high populations are Desborough with 455, 'Seckley' with 392, and Moulsoe with 369. High groupings appear in the Chiltern hundreds with 455, 277 and 198, totalling 930, and Newport triple-hundred with 1,081. But generally the population is quite evenly distributed according to the size of the hundreds.

Most of the population consists of villans and bordars. The total villan population is 2,900, and there are two interesting points about their distribution. Firstly, in the hundred of Risborough there is a close relationship between the number of villans and the number of hides. In all the assessment figures, Risborough has an unusual place: assessed at almost exactly a hundred hides ($99\frac{1}{4}$), it possessed 101 villans. As for the vills: Monks Risborough had 30 hides and 32 villans; Princes Risborough 30 hides and 30 villans; Horsenden $9\frac{1}{4}$ hides and 7 villans; Bledlow 30 hides and 32 villans. The relationship seems too close to be merely coincidental, but is apparently peculiar to this hundred. A second odd fact is that several hundreds seem to be arranged in pairs in respect of numbers of villans. Is this imagination playing too much with numbers? There are, for example, the neighbouring hundreds of Waddesdon and Mursley each with 132 villans; 'Stotfold' with 81 and 'Rowley' with 80; 'Mow' with 163 and Ashendon with 162; Stone and Aylesbury with 178 each; 'Seckley' with 225 and Cottesloe with 222. It is certainly difficult to see the logical explanation for this correspondence, but it leaves a suspicion, first, that at some early stage of assessment hidage may have been based on villan family holdings; and second, that villan numbers might also be an assessment. But if any clear pattern once existed, it seems too well obscured by 1086 for it ever to be unravelled.

In general villan numbers are evenly distributed throughout the county. Some vills have large numbers of villans among their population; for example Waddesdon has 50, Wing 51, Wycombe

[1] GDB 146 (Horsenden), 143v (Wendover), 144 (Weston Turville).
[2] Baring, *Domesday Tables*, 136.
[3] GDB 146v, 149.
[4] Darby, *Domesday England*, 63–5.
[5] GDB 143.
[6] Maitland, *Domesday Book and Beyond*, 40.
[7] GDB 148v.
[8] GDB 152v (Ibstone), 146v (Caldecote).

67, Marlow 63, Hambleden 50, Long Crendon 52 and Steeple Claydon 50. There must be a suspicion that high numbers often disguise a multiple settlement gelding at one central manor.

The social position of the villan was that of the respectable, fairly well-off villager. In the *Quadripartitus* of Henry I's time villans were equated with Old English *ceorls*, meaning all the non-noble free. Maitland showed the link between the villan and the Old English *tunesman*, or man of the vill, and Lennard with the Old English boor, who normally held a virgate, noting, for example, the 51 villans in Middlesex with one virgate each. Quite often a villan held more, often a hide, and commonly more than the bordar.[1] It appears that a villan could become a thegn if he possessed five hides of land.

Numbers of bordars in the county follow a similar pattern. The highest hundred populations are in Moulsoe with 127, and Desborough with 106. There are usually fewer bordars than villans. The 2,900 villans make up 56 per cent of the Domesday population, the 1,318 bordars, 25 per cent. There are large numbers of bordars in certain vills. Stoke Mandeville has 22, Lavendon with only 13 villans has 34 bordars, Wing has 20, Marlow 39, and Clifton Reynes 20. There are also 846 slaves who make only 16 per cent of the population, though this seems to be higher than in other areas. Much has been made of the numbers of slaves. It has been suggested that high numbers may represent some survival of British groups within the county. Unfortunately the distribution map by hundreds does not support this, except insofar as 'Seckley' in the north-east has a number almost twice as great as any other hundred at 92. Table 4 gives all the figures to show this distribution.[2] It will be seen that the only high number of slaves is in the north-east, which would seem to relate more to Scandinavian influence than Celtic survival. The only really low figure is once again for Risborough, though it is a small hundred. The general spread does not favour any particular regional significance.

TABLE 4: Slave totals by hundred grouped in the later triple-hundreds

| Triple-hundred | Member-hundreds with totals | Triple-hundred total |
|---|---|---|
| Ashendon | Ashendon 40, Ixhill 58, Waddesdon 34 | 132 |
| Aylesbury | Aylesbury 42, Stone 63, Risborough 17 | 122 |
| Buckingham | 'Mow' 51, 'Rowley' 46, 'Stotfold' 37 | 134 |
| Chilterns | Burnham 41, Desborough 58, Stoke 25 | 124 |
| Cottesloe* | Cottesloe 46, Mursley 46, Yardley 47 | 139 |
| Newport | Bunsty 53, Moulsoe 50, 'Seckley' 92 | 195 |

* This triple-hundred has a remarkably even distribution

If these figures are then analysed by vills, we find that vills with large numbers are Aston Clinton with 13, Weston Turville 12, Chesham 14, Wycombe 15, Brickhill 12, Buckingham with Bourton 12, Haddenham 15, Lower Hartwell 12, Eaton Leys 12, and Waddesdon 17. Vills with low numbers for their size are, Wendover *nil*, Wing *nil*, Denham *nil*, Missenden 2, and Stowe *nil*.

It may be noted that vills with large numbers of slaves are often near the borders of the county, possibly reflecting a link between warfare and enslavement. Low numbers, on the other hand, probably speak of enlightened landholders. At Wendover, for example, we know that in her will Ælfgifu had freed her slaves.[3] Maitland suggested that the Domesday slave could be compared with the pre-Conquest *theow*, as shown by the equation of the two in the twelfth-century *Quadripartitus*. He also pointed out there were degrees of servility.[4] Norfolk, for example, has *liberi villani* (free villans).[5] The role of the enigmatic *buri* is probably somewhere between that of the slave and the cottar, probably tied to the soil as were the *coliberti*.[6] Slaves in the period of Domesday do not appear to have been kept in barracks, but to have had their own dwellings. Some slaves were employed as swineherds, though it may be coincidence that at Marsworth there were eight slaves and 800 pigs.

[1] Maitland, *Domesday Book and Beyond*, 30, 59; Lennard, *Rural England*, 367.

[2] See p.7, n.3 above. The figures for slaves do not include the four *buri* in Desborough, but their inclusion would not alter the general conclusions there reached.

[3] Baines, 'Lady Elgiva', 116.

[4] Maitland, *Domesday Book and Beyond*, 30, 43.

[5] Ibid. 45.

[6] Darby, *Domesday England*, 77; Maitland, *Domesday Book and Beyond*, 28, 36; Welldon Finn, *Introduction to Domesday Book*, 122.

Slaves were also used as ploughmen. A slave was valued at about 20*s*., and was therefore worth looking after, but there were no penalties for ill-treatment of slaves. They could, however, possess property, earn money during their own time and purchase their freedom.[1]

In turning to the landholders, it is important to remember that in the eleventh century all tenure, except the king's, was dependent. In the Norman period the vassal holds of the lord as in the pre-Conquest period the man held under the lord. Landholding is a legal contract, and feudalism a legal agreement about the terms on which land is held. Rights in land may be very complex, and Domesday does not reveal all the subtleties, particularly of the pre-Conquest situation.

Before the Conquest there was a handful of great landholders whose direct interest in Buckinghamshire was probably no greater than that of their Norman successors. Buckinghamshire has important information on the role of Old English thegns. They are not for the most part great men. In Berkshire the royal thegn is described as *miles regis*, 'the king's soldier'. In order to become a thegn, a *ceorl* was said to need five hides, a church, a kitchen, a house in the *burh*, and office in the king's hall. The laws of Cnut suggest that a king's thegn had high social rank, but the label was a broad one, and other men had their thegns. In Welldon Finn's view this broad use makes thegn 'a somewhat meaningless word'. Campbell suggests that there were two grades of thegn in Buckinghamshire.[2] In the north thegns were small men, often with less than a virgate, hardly to be distinguished from sokemen. There had been large numbers of them before the Conquest, for example, at Woughton, Moulsoe, Chicheley and Lavendon. In one case we have a group of thegns represented by Alli, described as *senior*.[3] It might be conjectured whether these groups of thegns have any connection with the laws of Athelstan concerning free men acting in groups of ten and under a senior.[4] The *Rectitudines* has the following social labels: thegn, *geneat*, cottar and *gebur*, suggesting that if not necessarily a great man, the thegn nevertheless had a recognized social status three ranks above the slave. The Berkshire reference to *tainus vel miles regis* indicates that at the time of the survey the thegn still had a military function.[5]

Buckinghamshire also has landholding housecarls (*huscarls*). One of these, Burgheard, is called both a housecarl and a thegn; and Ulf, who is a housecarl in Buckinghamshire, is probably to be identified with the thegn of the same name in Gloucestershire and Cambridgeshire. Azur son of Toti, described both as a housecarl and a thegn, also appears as a man of Queen Edith, with men of his own. 'Housecarl' seems to have a more immediate social implication than thegn in the eleventh century, probably arising from a more definite military function in the period. The Buckinghamshire housecarls are Alli, with lands in Lavendon and Clifton Reynes and his own man called Hunmann; Burgheard with lands in 'Seckley'; Healfdene with lands in Bunsty, who also occurs as a man of Harold Godwineson, and had land in Northamptonshire; Azur son of Toti; Ulf, who also held in Gloucestershire and Cambridgeshire; Thorir; and Goldnir with lands in Moulsoe. In Buckinghamshire the term thegn applies to a broad band of free landholders, housecarl to a small group of men of high social standing.[6]

## THE CHURCH

Although the Church is an important landholder in the county, it does not dominate to the degree found elsewhere, and there is relatively little information on either churches or churchmen. One result of the Conquest was the granting of land to Norman and French churches, and since the county lacked any great monasteries of its own, a good deal was made over to foreign houses. The abbots of Saint-Pierre-de-la-Couture, for example, kept a priory at Woolstone on land given to them by Walter Giffard. Land at Crafton and Marsh Gibbon was given to the church of Saint-Nicolas at

[1] GDB 149v (Marsworth); Welldon Finn, *Introduction to Domesday Book*, 119.

[2] Welldon Finn, *Introduction to Domesday Book*, 140; Darby and Campbell (eds.), *Domesday Geography*, 157.

[3] GDB 152v.

[4] Loyn, 'The Hundred', 5.

[5] Lennard, *Rural England*, 364; Welldon Finn, *Introduction to Domesday Book*, 127; Maitland, *Domesday Book and Beyond*, 163.

[6] GDB 146v, 147, 149, 152, 152v, 150, 152(x2), 146v. See also Round in *VCH Buckinghamshire*, i. 19; N. Hooper, 'The Housecarls in England in the Eleventh Century', *ANS* 7 (1984), 161–76.

Angers. The Count of Mortain granted lands and the advowson of the church of Bledlow to the Abbey of Grestain, itself recently founded near Honfleur by his father Herluin who had been given Herleva (the unmarried mother of the Conqueror) for his wife. Ilbert de Lacy granted the manor of Tingewick to La Trinité-du-Mont at Rouen.[1]

Some great houses outside the county had lands within it, including the abbots of Westminster, and St Albans, the abbess of Barking and the monks of Christ Church, Canterbury. They were among the few to continue in possession after the Conquest. The payments of sokemen around Aylesbury to the church have already been noticed (see p.14, above). Under Remigius, Bishop of Lincoln, a sokeman with one hide rendered a load of grain to the church as well, but Domesday tells us this was not continued after the Conquest.[2] Sources other than Domesday reveal that the monks of Canterbury received money payments from Halton and Monks Risborough, and that at Haddenham the Bishop of Rochester instructed his reeve, the monk William from Rochester, to take over Aston in Gloucestershire for the house and render a farm of eight days a year. This monkish stewardship was something the church would soon come to frown upon, the practice being forbidden at the 1102 council in London.[3] There is a brief mention of the pre-Conquest minster of St Firmin at North Crawley, and the county has at least five Saxon churches, some known from other sources, like that built by Swærting in Wycombe. Probably this county like others had minsters in the pre-Conquest period that lost their significance afterwards.[4] Priestly holdings seem generally to have been small and on a level with peasant holdings, perhaps just a little larger than the average. In Essex priests were ranked with the villans, and in Middlesex priests' holdings were between half a virgate and a hide. The eleventh century is still an age of proprietary churches, from which owners expected an income paid by the priest.[5] One puzzle in the county entries are those persons referred to as *homines dei* ('men of God'). Probably Maitland is right to see them as laymen rather than priests.[6] Another interesting entry is that relating to Regenbald the priest, the 'classic case', according to Lennard, of a great pluralist. Round suggested that he was chancellor to Edward the Confessor as well as to the Conqueror. He held valuable churches in Somerset, Wiltshire, Berkshire and Gloucestershire besides his holdings in Buckinghamshire.[7]

Buckinghamshire would, in due course, have its own monastic houses, and became a more significant monastic area after, and perhaps as a result of, the Conquest. Benedictine houses were founded at Luffield, Bradwell and Snelshall; Cluniac priories at Tickford and Newport Pagnell; a Cistercian house at Biddlesden; and an Augustinian priory at Great Missenden.[8]

## The Effects of the Norman Conquest

It is clear in Buckinghamshire, as elsewhere, that one of the main effects of the Conquest was to depress the position of the Old English landholders, great and small. Sokemen almost disappear, there are not many free men, surviving English landholders are few, and wealthy ones fewer still. Some individuals held on to their lands in reduced circumstances. The most pathetic of these is Æthelric at Marsh Gibbon, where according to Domesday he had held land freely before the Conquest, but was now in 1086 holding of William fitzAnsculf 'in heaviness and misery'. Darby suggests he was probably holding as a *firmarius*. He is one of those who have only survived by

[1] Guilloreau, 'Possessions des Abbayes Mancelles et Angevines en Angleterre', esp. pp.16, 17; A. Young, 'Bledlow, I', *RB* 17 (1964), 266–76, esp. p.268; Round in *VCH Buckinghamshire*, i. 212; Wightman, *Lacy Family in England and Normandy*, 11.

[2] See p.14, n.2 above; and Welldon Finn, *Introduction to Domesday Book*, 197.

[3] Lennard, *Rural England*, 121, 156–7, 159; Kissan, 'Lanfranc's Alleged Division of Lands'; Baines, 'Monks Risborough', 76.

[4] GDB 149; C. Hohler, 'St Osyth and Aylesbury', *RB* 18 (1966), 61; Lennard, *Rural England*, 295; M. Farley, 'Burials in Aylesbury and the Early History of the Town', *RB* 21 (1979), 116–21, esp. pp.119, 121; Lennard, *Rural England*, 300–1.

[5] Lennard, *Rural England*, 312–4, 321–2.

[6] GDB 145(x2), 150v; Maitland, *Domesday Book and Beyond*, 281. In the accompanying translation the phrase *homo dei* is treated as a byname, and translated as 'God's man'.

[7] Regenbald appears in Bucks. on f.146. See also Lennard, *Rural England*, 317.

[8] Sister Elspeth of the Community of All Saints, 'The Religious Houses of Buckinghamshire', *VCH Buckinghamshire*, i. 346–96.

accepting harsh terms, but perhaps was a little luckier than the free man at Benfleet in Essex who we are told was 'made one of the villans'.[1]

The building of castles was generally seen as a heavy burden resulting from the Conquest, but it has left little mark in Buckinghamshire. As we have seen (p.8, above), little is known of the castle in the borough. The most interesting Domesday evidence on this score is the information that two armed men at Drayton Parslow owed castle-guard at Windsor.[2] The increased use of land for hunting is another burden of the Conquest. In Domesday there are two parks in the county, at Long Crendon and Oakley, but by the fourteenth century there were no less than fifty-two.[3]

The appointment of sheriffs is a sign of the direction of the political wind. Several references to sheriffs appear in Domesday. Among the sheriffs of Buckinghamshire are Ansculf de Picquigny, the only known non-Norman sheriff of William I who had held the shrievalty of Surrey also; and Ralph Taillebois who had been sheriff in Hertfordshire and Bedfordshire and probably Buckinghamshire too, to judge from his acquisitions for the king's manor at Wendover. Ralph also exchanged lands in Princes Risborough and Ellesborough, and erected a mill at Farnham Royal on the land of Bertram de Verdun. Henry de Ferrers also took action as sheriff to increase the royal demesne. These hints give one the practicalities of oppression and power imposed by the Conquest. One of the most fascinating of all the titbits of information supplied by Domesday relates to the sheriff Godric, who seemingly took over parts of the royal demesne for his own use and that of his friends. He used half a hide of this land to pay a woman for teaching his daughter embroidery. These references show power and the abuse of power, but also remind us that Domesday was being used to investigate these abuses. Sheriffs had obviously been given a good deal of licence within their counties, but they were not beyond the reach of royal control and the king was prepared to use the hundred court to assert this. At Princes Risborough and Aylesbury there are mentions of sokemen serving the sheriff.[4]

The degree of force behind the Conquest is apparent at times in the manner of the change of landholding, though none of the Buckinghamshire sheriffs has quite the notoriety of Urse d'Abetot who was cursed for digging up a graveyard for the castle at Worcester. Ansculf de Picquigny as sheriff had taken over three virgates at Bradwell. The Bishop of Coutances at Drayton Parslow had taken land from Ralph Taillebois for his own men. The men of the hundred said that land at Clifton Reynes had been taken without the king's knowledge. There are also some signs of pressing circumstances, such as the land at Simpson which had been mortgaged by William Bonvalet. Lennard points out that many of the *firmarii* were native English, and suggests that Norman lords had driven hard bargains with them, letting at excessive rents as was probably the case with Æthelric of Marsh Gibbon mentioned above. As the Anglo-Saxon Chronicle says, 'the king sold his land on very hard terms, as hard as he could', and would not worry 'how sinfully the reeves got it from poor men, nor how many unlawful things they did'.[5]

Probably the greatest effect of the Norman Conquest was the full-scale introduction of feudalism, with all the legal significance for landholding and personal relationships that it entailed. The development of feudalism in England is in many ways still a vexed question. Undoubtedly in pre-Conquest England there had been some developments parallel to Continental feudalism, but there also remained differences. By 1086 Buckinghamshire is clearly feudal, with estates arranged by fiefs as they had never been before. The form '*x* holds of *y*' almost certainly also reflects the existence of subinfeudation.[6]

Finally we come to the question of how far Old English Buckinghamshire differed from the county under the Normans. In general the pre-Conquest organization survived: the hundreds and

[1] For Æthelric, see GDB 148v; Welldon Finn, *Introduction to Domesday Book*, 147, 130; Darby, *Domesday England*, 213. For Benfleet, see LDB 1v.
[2] GDB 151v.
[3] See p.26, n.1 above.
[4] Ansculf de Picquigny, see GDB 148v; Round in *VCH Buckinghamshire*, i. 221; J. Green, 'The Sheriffs of William the Conqueror', *ANS* 5 (1982), 129–45, esp. pp.129, 134. Ralph Taillebois, see GDB 148v; Round in *VCH Buckinghamshire*, i. 220, 221; Green, 'Sheriffs of William the Conqueror', 134. Farnham, see GDB 151v. Henry de Ferrers, see Round in *VCH Buckinghamshire*, i. 221. Godric, see GDB 144, 152, 149; Round in *VCH Buckinghamshire*, i. 221. See also Round in *VCH Buckinghamshire*, i. 217; Welldon Finn, *Introduction to Domesday Book*, 30. Sokemen, see GDB 143v.
[5] GDB 148v, 151v, 145v, 149, 145, 148v. Whitelock *et al.* (eds.), *Anglo-Saxon Chronicle*, 163, E *s.aa.* 1086–7; Plummer, *Two of the Saxon Chronicles Parallel*, i. 218.
[6] Lennard, *Rural England*, 107.

vills remain and are the backbone of Domesday. There is no reason to believe that boundaries were seriously affected by the Conquest, nor that the Normans made any drastic change to the natural appearance of the county. The assessment in Domesday is in hides and ploughlands, even if revised, firmly grounded on Old English practice, and probably in Old English documents. There was no Norman economic revolution. Few of the resources in Domesday seem to be new, though the vineyard is probably an exception.[1] The social groups one meets, the free men, sokemen, villans, bordars, cottars, and slaves all have Old English labels and must generally be the descendants of Old English families.

And yet there has been change. It has been argued that the very march through the county of the Norman army in 1066 created the areas described as 'waste' found in Domesday. With increasing elaboration, Baring and his followers have tried to demonstrate the route the army took, and even how it was divided into sections of varying size, according to the degrees of 'waste'.[2] Much waste equals the passage of a large army, less waste that of a smaller detachment. Mark the 'waste' vills, draw lines to connect them and you have the route of the conquering army. Baring criticized E. A. Freeman's description of William's march straight to London, claiming that 'Domesday tells us a rather different story'.[3] He suggested that one force went north to the Thame, to Bledlow and Risborough; another eastwards to Slough. The force to the west of the Chilterns was to protect the flank and threaten London. The main body went through east Buckinghamshire from Stoke Mandeville to Tingewick and Lavendon; the right wing from Risborough to the east. Butler, elaborating, says 'a probing force crossed to the left bank of the Thames to survey the country north and west into southern Buckinghamshire', but 'after a foray north to Wooburn' withdrew to the south-east.[4] A. M. Davies saw Baring as 'the good fairy' who waved his wand and put everything in order.[5] But is it the right order? We do not intend to examine the variations of 'waste' to suggest other routes, but rather to question the validity of the whole process. One fears that the herculean efforts of Baring and his cohorts have themselves been wasted. There is only one reference in Domesday to waste being caused by an army,[6] and there are obviously many other factors, from natural disaster to change of land use. Even if armies did damage land, there is no knowing from Domesday which campaign was responsible. Then again, 'waste' could be a method of assessment. Judith Green's study of Danegeld shows that 'waste' was a means of writing off tax rather than necessarily describing physical reality.[7] Some 'waste' in Domesday is even valued.[8] It is surely taxing our sense of probabilities to believe that 'waste' by 1086 always reflects waste caused by an army in 1066, and even more so to believe that the degree of waste indicates the size of that 1066 army. Sometimes the failure of the 'waste' to correspond to simple routes has led to the most ridiculous conclusions and assumptions: diversions, raiding groups and so on. The logical solution is that it does not fit a simple route because it does not represent a route at all. The march of William's armies through Buckinghamshire is not supported by any chronicle evidence, and must be taken as sheer imagination. Nor should we assume that Domesday's 'waste' is even necessarily a consequence of the Conquest at all.

## Landholders TRE and TRW

There is one respect in which Domesday does show drastic change very definitely, and that is in the membership of the ruling group, both lay and ecclesiastical. This is no less true of Buckinghamshire

[1] See p.26, n.2 above.

[2] See Baring, *Domesday Tables*; *idem*, 'Conqueror's Footprints in Domesday'; Lemmon, 'Campaign of 1066', 116–22; Welldon Finn, *Norman Conquest*, 19; G. H. Fowler, 'The Devastation of Bedfordshire and the Neighbouring Counties in 1065 and 1066', *Archaeologia*, 72 (1922), 41–50; Butler, *1066: the Story of a Year*.

[3] Baring, 'Conqueror's Footprints in Domesday', 20.

[4] Butler, *1066: the Story of a Year*, 266, 273.

[5] Davies, 'Eleventh Century Buckinghamshire', 69.

[6] Welldon Finn, *Norman Conquest*, 27.

[7] J. Green, 'The Last Century of Danegeld', *EHR* 96 (1981), 241–58, esp. p.251.

[8] Half a hide at Chesham is stated to be waste, but is valued at 5*s*. (f.151v).

than it is of England as a whole. Our last project in this introduction is therefore to survey the landholding situation before and after the Conquest.

In both periods a small group of individuals held the bulk of the land, and were obviously the politically powerful men of the nation. For local significance, we clearly need to distinguish between those who were great men both in the land and in the county, those who were important men in the land with small estates in the county, and those who were modest men nationally with important estates in Buckinghamshire.

The royal presence in the county is important both before and after the Conquest. As so often, what we find is not a restructuring of estates, but a take-over by new people. In Domesday, ignoring the role of Harold II, King William takes over from King Edward as many other Norman and French lords did from English holders. If the English survived, it was nearly always at a lower level of society than before the Conquest, as the Anglo-Saxon Chronicle baldly puts it, they 'became his man's men'.[1] Before the Conquest the king was the only holder to have an interest, either directly or through his men, in every single hundred in the county. If one adds in the lands of Edward's queen Edith, the royal strength is reinforced, since she held land in as many as twelve of the eighteen hundreds.

Domesday also shows the power of the Old English earls. The suggestion that the Conquest altered the structure of landholding from old earldoms which were powerful compact areas into a scatter of possessions, is not reinforced by Domesday. Before as after the Conquest, great men held lands scattered over a wide area, though they might well have a particular power base. In Buckinghamshire the two major landholding earls were Harold Godwineson with land in fourteen of the hundreds, and Leofwine, his brother, with land in fifteen hundreds.

As has been pointed out above (pp.29–30), the church was not as dominant a landholder in Buckinghamshire as elsewhere, but church holdings were still considerable. The Bishop of Dorchester had lands in seven hundreds, the Archbishop of Canterbury in five, and valuable manors belonged to the abbots of St Albans and of St Peter's, Westminster.[2] There were a variety of lesser ecclesiastics holding before the Conquest, including Godwine the priest with several holdings, and Wulfmær, 'King Edward's priest' at Lower Hartwell. But this was yet another group to suffer with the Conquest, for Godwine retained only one small holding at Wavendon. There are a few small post-Conquest holdings, for example that of Gilbert the priest at Haddenham, and of Turstin the priest at Wingrave.

It has been noted that as well as Queen Edith, there are a number of Old English female landholders in the county, but their holdings are not extensive. One of note was the Countess Goda, King Edward's sister, with lands in Bunsty, 'Mow' and Stoke; her daughter-in-law, Countess Gytha, widow of Ralph, Earl of Hereford, held land in Bunsty and 'Mow'. One of the most interesting is 'that mysterious lady', Eddeva, Eadgifu (or possibly Edith) 'the Fair'.[3] Because Domesday does not list lands of the Old English main holders in the way that it does for the Normans, it is unfortunately not possible to be certain of the total of Eadgifu the Fair's holdings in the county, nor can we know that every Eadgifu is Eadgifu the Fair; it is a common name, and in Buckinghamshire we have Eadgifu the wife of Wulfweard in Ashendon and Ixhill, Eadgifu in Bunsty, as well as Eadgifu the Fair herself in Cottesloe.[4] At least we can agree that she was a major landholder in England. There are seventy-nine references to her altogether, thirty-eight as *pulchra*, and one as *bella*, and she also appears as *dives* and *faira*. Boyle has established that the lady of this name who also appears in Hertfordshire, Yorkshire and Lincolnshire is our same Buckinghamshire beauty.[5] She has never been satisfactorily identified, though several attempts have been made. Ellis suggested she might be the sister of Edwin and Morcar, but she was called Ealdgyth, and others have suggested Edith (Eadgyth) 'Swan-neck', Harold Godwineson's mistress. The latter is an

[1] Maitland, *Domesday Book and Beyond*, 520; Whitelock *et al.* (eds.), *Anglo-Saxon Chronicle*, 162; Plummer, *Two of the Saxon Chronicles Parallel*, i. 217.

[2] GDB 153, 151, 143v, 150.

[3] Maitland, *Domesday Book and Beyond*, 129; Boyle, 'Who was Eddeva?'.

[4] GDB 145, 147, 143, 144, 145(x2), 146v, 148v, 152(x2), 146.

[5] Boyle, 'Who was Eddeva?', 20.

interesting possibility. The lady in question might well be expected to possess beauty and lands and to be deprived of her proper place by the Normans in Domesday.[1]

Office-holders form an interesting group of pre-Conquest tenants. Godric the sheriff we have already met.[2] He had lands in Burnham, and may also be the Godric mentioned in Cottesloe, Desborough, Moulsoe and 'Stotfold'. Esger the staller had lands in nine hundreds, and other office-holders are Bondi the staller, Leofwine of Nuneham Courtenay (perhaps the same man as Leofwine the king's reeve), and two chamberlains, Ælfric and Wynsige.[3]

Few Old English landholders survived the Conquest as men of substance but Leofwine of Nuneham Courtenay was an exception. As so often, he may have been wealthier than we can show. It is not clear how often the many other Leofwines in Domesday may be identified with him. In Buckinghamshire he certainly held sixteen hides, and had lands also in neighbouring Oxfordshire. Other survivors included Godric Cratel and the miserable Æthelric, but by 1086 the English had become an 'insignificant element'.[4]

The change in landholding after the Norman Conquest was sweeping. Few revolutions have achieved greater change, for William truly 'gave away every man's land'.[5] Buckinghamshire confirms the idea that Norman holders were seen as the legal successors to Old English holders whom they replaced. Frequently lands descended *en bloc* to the successor. Thus Geoffrey de Mandeville succeeded to the estates of Esger the staller in eight counties including Bucks.[6] The fact that the lands of Healfdene the housecarl went to Winemar the Fleming may well be an example of lands going with function.

The royal strength was confirmed. So too, the greatest men, William's chief earls, are strongly represented. The church kept its estates. Men now hold 'of' rather than 'under' a lord, and feudalism is undoubtedly transforming the social structure of the county. The personnel was almost entirely changed, with a few relatively minor exceptions. By Domesday we may believe that in theory all men held directly or indirectly of the king. William retained valuable properties for himself, totalling 116¾ hides, valued at £4,498. 13*s.* 4*d.* His properties included the manors taken over from Harold at Princes Risborough, Swanbourne and Upton (in Slough). In addition Queen Matilda had thirty-five hides valued at £60.

Not surprisingly the Conqueror's two half-brothers had benefited enormously from the Norman triumph. Each had extensive lands in about twenty shires. Odo, Bishop of Bayeux, had lost his royal half-brother's good graces in 1082, but his possessions in Domesday show the favour he had earlier received. The Bishop had lands in fifteen of the eighteen hundreds, forty-four holdings totalling 226 hides valued at £3,412. 6*s.* 8*d.* Odo's full brother, Robert, Count of Mortain, had lands in thirteen hundreds consisting of thirty-eight holdings totalling almost 119½ hides which were valued at £112. 4*s.*

Apart from Odo and Robert, the tenants-in-chief with the most valuable holdings in the county were Mainou the Breton with eleven holdings amounting to *c.*106½ hides; Robert d'Oilly with seven holdings totalling 66¼ hides; William fitzAnsculf, son of the sheriff and founder of Tickford Priory, with thirty holdings of *c.*106½ hides; Miles Crispin with thirty holdings of 114¼ hides; and Walter Giffard with forty-nine holdings of just under 300 hides. All of these had lands valued at over £75, but Giffard's was the most valuable at £214. 2*s.* 6*d.* The family lands were at Longueville in Normandy. Giffard the elder had helped plan the Conquest and promised thirty ships and a hundred knights for it.[7] His son became the first Earl of Buckingham. The major holder with an ecclesiastical title was the Bishop of Coutances, though he is usually deemed to have held his lands in a lay capacity. In Buckinghamshire he possessed twenty-two holdings, at almost 101½ hides which were valued at £899. 1*s.* 10*d.*

[1] Boyle, 'Who was Eddeva?', 20–1.

[2] See p.31 above.

[3] GDB 143v, 146v, 151, 153(x2), 151(x2), 153.

[4] Morris (ed.), *Domesday Book: Buckinghamshire*, n.B, 13; GDB 152v, 153, 148v, and see p.31, n.1 above; Lennard, *Rural England*, 69.

[5] Whitelock *et al.* (eds.), *Anglo-Saxon Chronicle*, 146; Plummer, *Two of the Saxon Chronicles Parallel*, i. 200, *s.a.* 1067.

[6] Lennard, *Rural England*, 29.

[7] I. J. Sanders, *English Baronies* (Oxford, 1960), 34, 62; J. Parker, 'The Giffards', *RB* 7 (1897), 475–509, *RB* 8 (1900), 289–308; Lennard, *Rural England*, 33.

This group clearly make up the dominant political figures in the county. There were, however, other men equally great or greater in the world at large with lesser estates in Buckinghamshire. These included William de Warenne, Geoffrey de Mandeville, Henry de Ferrers (with land in fourteen counties), Hugh, Earl of Chester, Hugh de Bolbec, Roger d'Ivry the steward of Normandy, Robert de Tosny, William Peverel, Nigel d'Aubigny, and Ilbert de Lacy. Ilbert is a good example of a great lord with but one single manor in the county. W. E. Wightman suggests it may have been this isolation of his manor of Tingewick which inclined him to choose it as a gift to La Trinité-du-Mont in Rouen.[1]

Not all the new holders were Normans. Bretons, Flemings and a few Lotharingians also possessed lands in the county. Among the Bretons the most important was Mainou with lands valued at £78. The others were Joscelin the Breton, William and Ralph de Feugeres, Hervey the Breton, and Hascoit Musard. The Flemings were Winemar the Fleming, Walter the Fleming and Gilbert de Ghent. The Lotharingians were William fitzAnsculf and Ernulf de Hesdin. According to William of Malmesbury, Ernulf suffered from a disease that denied him the use of his hands, and was cured by balsam from St Aldhelm's tomb at Malmesbury. Ernulf was said to be skilled in agriculture and a good manager. He claimed he was wrongfully accused of involvement in the revolt of 1075, but still left England to go on the first Crusade and die in Antioch.[2]

Notable lesser holders included Regenbald the priest with his hide worth 10*s*. in Burnham; the cripple with one hide worth 20*s*. which he held in alms; Richard Engaine brother of William and a royal huntsman; William the chamberlain; and Hervey the legate at Ibstone. Earl Aubrey's name survives as a holder in 'Stotfold', though with the unusual use of the past tense to indicate that he had lost his lands by 1086.[3] In the Norman period there are still a number of female holders. Apart from Queen Matilda, we find Countess Judith, the niece of the Conqueror, with just over sixteen hides worth £10. 10*s*.; the Abbess of Barking; and an Eadgifu who holds land of the Bishop of Coutances in Bunsty.[4]

There is a little group of native English who have survived as landholders. They include Alsige with three holdings valued at £7. 10*s*.; Alric the cook with twenty hides at £16; Edward of Salisbury with about twenty-six hides at £23. 10*s*.; Godric Cratel with eight and a half hides at £5; and Swærting with almost seven hides at £3. Others with very small holdings include Godwine the beadle, Hearding, Ketil, Leofwine, and Leofwine Chava, possibly the same man as Leofwine Oaura. A better known survivor is Leofwine of Nuneham Courtenay, with five holdings of a little more than sixteen hides at £66.[5]

Among the undertenants, it is worth noting the two knights (*milites*) who held of Walter Giffard at Pollicott in Ashendon. There were also two knights holding of the Bishop of Coutances at Oving in Ashendon.[6] Following up a suggestion of David Crouch, that Roger the undertenant of the Bishop of Bayeux was probably Roger de Beaumont of that great and rising Norman family, we find that a Roger was subtenant of the bishop in seven hundreds. We cannot be certain that there are no other persons called Roger involved since it is a common name, but we may, for example suspect that it is one man who holds the three neighbouring vills of Chesham, Amersham and Chalfont St Peter in Burnham, which are treated consecutively in Domesday. A Roger also holds at Taplow in Burham; West Wycombe and Saunderton in Desborough; Drayton Parslow in Mursley; Horsenden in Risborough; Westbury in 'Stotfold';[7] Whaddon in Yardley;[8] and Weston Turville, Bedgrove and Bierton in Aylesbury—the last three also consecutive entries. The *antecessores* for

[1] Wightman, *Lacy Family in England and Normandy*, 59–60.

[2] Round in *VCH Buckinghamshire*, i. 215; Lennard, *Rural England*, 67, 69.

[3] Regenbald, see GDB 146, and p.30, n.7 above. Cripple, see GDB 153 as 'a certain bandy-legged man'. Richard Engaine, see GDB 151v, also at Lillingstone Lovell in Oxfordshire Domesday as a king's officer. William the chamberlain, see GDB 151. Hervey the legate, see GDB 152v. Earl Aubrey, see GDB 143v.

[4] Countess Judith, see GDB 152v. Abbess of Barking, see GDB 146. Eadgifu, see GDB 145.

[5] Alsige, see GDB 153. Alric the cook, see GDB 153. Edward of Salisbury, see GDB 150v. Godric Cratel, see GDB 153, and p.34, n.4 above. Swærting, see GDB 148v. Godwine the beadle, see GDB 153. Hearding, see GDB 153. Leofwine, see p.34, n.3 above. Leofwine of Nuneham Courtenay, see GDB 153; Morris (ed.), *Domesday Book: Buckinghamshire*, n.B,13, and p.34, n.4 above.

[6] GDB 147, 145.

[7] Identified in the accompanying translation as Westbury (near Brackley).

[8] Identified in the accompanying translation as Whaddon (in Slapton).

many of these holdings were Earl Leofwine and his man Ælfric Varus, which suggests that the estates passed to a single Roger. If only half of these references are to Roger de Beaumont, he would still emerge as a figure of importance. Undoubtedly Domesday conceals many important subtenants. Examination of later family holdings will, as with Roger, sometimes give the clue to the identity of the Domesday holder. One note of caution must be sounded, however, for in Buckinghamshire the bishop does have another Roger as his subtenant in at least one instance, no less a person than Roger d'Ivry in Stowe.[1]

Some of the families and fiefs in Domesday have a long subsequent history. The estates of Robert d'Oilly, who married the daughter of Vigot of Wallingford, together with those of Miles Crispin, who married Robert's daughter, made up the honour of Wallingford which would play such a vital role in the civil war of Stephen's reign. This estate owed its origins to the pre-Conquest lands of Beorhtric. Robert d'Oilly had a remarkably close association with Roger d'Ivry. The two were said to have sworn to be brothers and are often found sharing land. They divided the lands of Azur son of Toti between themselves, holding Stowe jointly of the Bishop of Bayeux, and they were joint founders of St George's chapel in Oxford Castle.[2] Robert d'Oilly was said to have acquired meadow outside Oxford from the Church of Abingdon for the use of his knights. But in a dream, a virgin took him to the meadow where two evil youths threw lighted hay in his face and set alight his beard. He immediately renounced his right to the rent, restored the land, gave £100 to the abbey's building fund, helped the poor, repaired churches in Oxford, and built a bridge!

The Giffards were perhaps the greatest Buckinghamshire family, eventually becoming earls of the shire. In Domesday Walter Giffard held 107 manors, forty-eight of which were in Buckinghamshire.[3] Walter Giffard I had been at Hastings, where he opted out of being the standard-bearer, preferring to fight perhaps, though claiming justly that he was of advanced age. Walter Giffard II became Earl of Buckingham in about 1093 and died in 1102. He is almost certainly the Domesday holder. By the time of Henry II, Walter Giffard III had ninety-eight knights *de vetero*, and one and a half *de novo*. The *caput* of the Buckinghamshire honour was at Long Crendon. Other families with interesting histories include the Bolbecs, whose heirs were to become Earls of Oxford, and the Mandevilles who would become Earls of Essex. There are also the fitzOthers, keepers of the forest of Windsor and constables of Windsor Castle, and the Peverels.[4]

## Conclusion

What then in the end does Domesday tell us about Buckinghamshire and the Norman Conquest? It shows us in detail the agrarian nature of the county, its prosperity dependent upon oxen and ploughs. Economically wealth was engendered also by fish from the rivers, and pigs living off the woodland. There was little to show of urban development, even in Buckingham itself. In social terms, we see some change brought about by the Norman Conquest, or at least during the eleventh century. Before the Conquest there were many smaller landholders, thegns and sokemen. After 1066 these lesser men, where they survived, did so in a lower social capacity and became more dependent on their lords. As for the greater men, those in control before 1066 had mostly gone by 1086. A few Old English holders survive in reduced circumstances, but most have been replaced by Norman and French lords. Buckinghamshire had not been of great military significance once the Danelaw disappeared as a separate political unit. The Norman Conquest sees the continued decline in importance of the county as any sort of frontier district. Buckinghamshire estates are drawn into honours whose military significance is elsewhere, such as Windsor and Wallingford. In conclusion we may say that the Norman Conquest had little effect on the county's economy, but a great deal on its social and on its political structure.

[1] GDB 144(x4), 144v(x3), 144, 144v, 144(x3), 144v.

[2] Round in *VCH Buckinghamshire*, i. 213–4; Lennard, *Rural England*, 65, 70–1.

[3] See p.34, n.7 above.

[4] See Sanders, *English Baronies*; G. E. Cokayne, *The Complete Peerage*, eds. V. Gibbs *et al.*, 13 vols. (London, 1910–59).

# HUNDREDS AND WAPENTAKES

## F. R. THORN

UNDER William I, as under the English kings, vills were grouped together for taxation, judicial and other obligations into 'hundreds' or, in former Danish areas, into 'wapentakes'. These administrative units, intermediate in size between the vill and the shire, and laid down before civil parishes came into existence, usually consisted of a single unified tract of territory (in 1086 varying widely between twenty and 300 hides in extent) which could belong to a variety of tenants-in-chief. Often a lord (particularly the king or a church) was paramount in a hundred; or the lordship of the hundred was attached to a particular manor by a system that was developed in the later medieval period. Some hundreds contained a single large manor only, and these and others had but a single tenant-in-chief. A few had isolated detachments and fewer still were ecclesiastical hundreds geographically scattered but owing suit to their church, however remote, and not to some local meeting-place. Vills were sometimes divided by hundred boundaries and the members of large manors were often in several different hundreds. Many of the hundred-names, if not replaced in 1086 by those of manors, refer to the meeting-places, 'moots', which were often at road-junctions, river-crossings, beside barrows or mounds, on hilltops or near isolated trees in a prominent position.

Hundreds cannot be described or mapped on the basis of Domesday Book alone, for the boundaries of estates and hundreds are never indicated, nor can every estate be allocated with certainty to a particular hundred, especially when it is mentioned in passing or is the dependency of some composite manor. The composition of hundreds can be partly restored from internal evidence by noting those places that fall directly beneath a hundred heading in the text and by identifying hundredal groupings which in many counties are inscribed in a standard sequence. However, the later history of the manor and of the hundred as well as geographical probability must also be employed and the hundredal rubrication itself examined, for it can be shown to be sometimes incorrect or deficient. The scribe's not infrequent errors are of only a few types and easily allowed for, and some restoration of missing headings can be made from the evidence of the text; but a decision sometimes has to be made to restore a hundred heading above a place from later evidence alone.

If these restorations are not made, Domesday will seem to allocate such a place to a different hundred, of which it will appear, owing to its geographical position, to be an improbable detachment. Allowance must be made for the fact that places lying close to the boundary of a hundred in 1086 may well be found in an adjacent hundred in the thirteenth-century surveys which are the first to show the composition of hundreds in detail.

Strictly speaking, it is impossible to map eleventh-century hundred boundaries. The hundred is the sum of exploited land and woodland, while 'waste', 'forest', moor and bog are either to be regarded as being outside the hundred, or the hundred boundary through them is ill-defined. Expansion of arable land, assarting, and drainage have all tended to change boundaries considerably. Compared with the number of vills surveyed in Domesday Book, charters with boundary clauses are few, their interpretation difficult and their relation to Domesday estates often indirect. Few estate maps survive from the Middle Ages and the first accurate hundred maps, dating from the early nineteenth century, are at the end of a process of change which may have left the 1086 pattern scarcely recognizable. But by using the evidence, whether certain, probable or supplemented, for the composition of the eleventh-century hundreds, lines can be drawn between manors—which may well contain more than one place and extend over more than one modern parish—according to the hundred in which they probably lay in 1086. In this way it is possible to recover something that approximates to eleventh-century topography and administrative divisions.[1]

### THE HUNDREDS OF BUCKINGHAMSHIRE

Buckinghamshire seems to have contained about 2,130 hides in 1086,[2] but this figure unfortunately cannot be compared with that of the eleventh-century County Hidage which does not include a total for Buckinghamshire, and it is well in excess of the 1,600 hides given in the Burghal Hidage of the early tenth

[1] Apart from works cited in individual articles in this series, documents and discussions concerning the hundredal system will be found in O. S. Anderson, *The English Hundred-Names* (abbr. *EHN*) (Lund, 1934); *Inquisitions and Assessments Relating to Feudal Aids with other Analogous Documents, Preserved in the Public Records Office A.D. 1284–1431* (abbr. *Feudal Aids*), 6 vols. (HMSO, London, 1899–1920); F. Liebermann, *Die Gesetze der Angelsachsen*, 3 vols. (Halle, 1903–16); H. R. Loyn, *The Governance of Anglo-Saxon England, 500–1087* (London, 1984); A. J. Robertson (ed.), *The Laws of the Kings of England from Edmund to Henry I* (Cambridge, 1925); F. M. Stenton, *Anglo-Saxon England* (3rd edn., Oxford, 1971).

[2] Baring, *Domesday Tables*, 132.

century.[1] It is possible that the original total was 2,400 as for adjacent Oxfordshire and Berkshire, but Domesday, apparently without omitting any hundreds, names only eighteen in the county, ranging in size between 100 and 150 hides.[2] The number of hundreds, their differences in size and their sometimes irregular shape suggests that Domesday does not describe the primordial arrangement, but records a state evolved from an earlier, simpler pattern.

There are a few incidental references to the 'men of the hundred' and to the work of the hundred courts in the compilation of the survey,[3] but, in contrast to Oxfordshire and Worcestershire, nothing is said about the interdependence or the overall pattern of hundreds in the county, although there is a fairly systematic hundredal rubrication as well as one remarkable render of corn to the church of Stoke Mandeville from 'the eight hundreds that lie around Aylesbury'.[4] Other such large groupings of hundreds—perhaps a very early arrangement—are known from elsewhere.[5]

There have been several modern studies of the Buckinghamshire hundreds,[6] but in contrast to Northamptonshire there are no documents close in date to Domesday Book that help to check what it says. They are scarcely needed, however, since the manuscript supplies an abundance of hundred heads and the hundreds are entered apparently by groups of three, in the same order in virtually every fief.[7] The order of these groups is as follows: Stone, Aylesbury, Risborough; Stoke, Burnham, Desborough; Ixhill, Ashendon, Waddesdon; Cottesloe, Yardley, Mursley; 'Stotfold', 'Rowley', 'Mow'; 'Seckley', Bunsty, Moulsoe.

Moreover, within each group the hundreds always occupy the same relative position when their lands are entered in a fief, although no fief contains land in every hundred. It will be apparent that each group of three forms a geographical entity, but that there is no particular topographical scheme in the succession of groups. Groupings of two or three hundreds are found in other counties where they usually depend on a single manor, often a royal one, and the pattern of the Buckinghamshire hundreds in 1086 strongly suggests that the structure of six groups of three hundreds set out in the *Nomina Villarum* of 1316[8] was already in existence in the eleventh century. There the hundreds are described respectively as the three hundreds belonging to Aylesbury, 'Chiltern', Ashendon, Cottesloe, Buckingham and Newport. Even by 1066, any form of dependence by these groups on royal manors (if it had ever been the case) had been effaced by the granting of royal land to laymen and churches.[9]

This standard sequence of hundreds is found in every chapter except Chapter 1, 'The Land of the King', and Chapter 57, ostensibly 'The Land of Leofwine of Nuneham' but in fact corresponding to the chapter entitled 'The Land of the King's Thegns' in other counties. The order of the king's land, probably emanating from a different survey, is irregular as in most other counties, whilst Chapter 57 is organized by subtenants not by hundred groups. Where, however, an individual holder (for example Leofwine of Nuneham Courtenay or Swærting) holds in more than one hundred in this chapter, the hundreds are entered in the expected order under each man. In one case the scribe had been influenced by the hundred heads that he had just entered (Ixhill in Chapter 39, then Mursley in Chapter 40), and repeated Ixhill and Mursley at the beginning of Chapter 41, the latter being an error for 'Stotfold'.[10] The hundredal rubrication is not perfect. There is occasional carelessness in the writing;[11] the Ixhill hundred heading seems to come one entry too

[1] F. W. Maitland, *Domesday Book and Beyond* (Cambridge, 1897), 503–5. On the Burghal Hidage, see D. Hill, 'The Burghal Hidage: the Establishment of a Text', *MA* 13 (1969), 84–92.

[2] Baring, *Domesday Tables*, 131. The minor adjustments needed do not affect the overall pattern.

[3] GDB 144v, 146, 148v, 149, 151v.

[4] GDB 143v. Aylesbury Hundred was touched by the hundreds of Cottesloe, Waddesdon, Stone, Risborough, Desborough, Burnham and Yardley, making eight in all. Closer than several of these was the hundred of Tring in Hertfordshire. *In circuitu* should not be pressed to mean more than *circum*, 'around, encircling', but for a more elaborate translation and interpretation, see J. Bradbury, 'An Introduction to the Buckinghamshire Domesday', p. 14 above.

[5] Eight hundreds are associated with Oundle (Northants) in the pre-Conquest period; the seven that encircled Cirencester (Glos.) and the six that lay around Basingstoke (Hants) are only attested later but may well be early. All perhaps date from a time when large tracts of territory (only subsequently hidated) were administered and controlled by a royal *tun*. In Buckinghamshire, Buckingham itself might have been the centre of another group. The whole of Oxfordshire is arranged in this way in DB and there are sporadic references to two or three hundreds dependent on or related to a manor: for example, three hundreds rendered to the manor of Much Cowarne in Herefordshire (f. 186), while Molland in Devon received the third penny of three hundreds (f. 101). There are further examples in Shropshire and Hampshire. The basic study is H. M. Cam, *Liberties and Communities in Medieval England: Collected Studies in Local Administration and Topography* (Cambridge, 1944; repr. London, 1963), 91–106.

[6] See Baring, *Domesday Tables*, 129–71; Davies, 'Ancient Hundreds of Buckinghamshire'; *idem*, 'Hundreds of Buckinghamshire and Oxfordshire'; J. H. Round in *VCH Buckinghamshire*, i (1905), 225–8; Darby and Campbell (eds.), *Domesday Geography*, 138–40.

[7] This phenomenon was studied by P.H. Sawyer, 'The "Original Returns" and Domesday Book', *EHR* 70 (1955), 177–97, esp. pp. 179–80. In Buckinghamshire even the same vills often appear in the same order in different fiefs; see Baring, *Domesday Tables*, 130.

[8] *Feudal Aids*, i (1899), 107–8.

[9] There were very few royal manors in Buckinghamshire in 1086 and also few in other hands that are likely to have been the royal *capita* of hundreds (possibly West Wycombe, East Burnham and Ivinghoe among them); thus the Buckinghamshire hundreds may always have been grouped into larger units depending on a handful of royal manors. On the dependence of the hundred on a manor, see Cam, *Liberties and Communities*, 64–90.

[10] This notion was peremptorily rejected by Round in *VCH Buckinghamshire*, i. 269, n. 1. But the later history of this *Westberie* shows that it was Westbury near Brackley and that it lay in 'Stotfold' Hundred and was not the Westbury in Shenley parish; moreover, the two holdings at Westbury (near Brackley) make a five-hide unit. See *Feudal Aids*, i. 79; Baring, *Domesday Tables*, 131; Davies, 'Ancient Hundreds of Buckinghamshire', 105; *idem*, 'Hundreds of Buckinghamshire and Oxfordshire', 246.

[11] The word 'hundred' was omitted after 'In Yardley' on f. 149v, while on f. 151 the hundred-name was at first erroneously put for the place-name. On f. 153 'In 'Stotfold' Hundred' was unnecessarily repeated in adjacent entries, presumably because this chapter was not arranged in order of hundreds but of subtenants.

late on f.150 when it rightly belongs before Aston Sandford,[1] while on f.151 the Burnham hundred heading may be one entry too early, belonging not with Eton but with Burnham itself.[2]

It is evident that, as in all other counties, some hundred headings are omitted, but restoration is made easy by this predictable sequence of hundreds. Only a few cases remain doubtful: for example, Hoggeston (f.148v) is in later times a member of Mursley Hundred, but to restore a Mursley heading would be to distort the normal sequence of hundreds. Though topographically awkward it has been assumed to lie in Waddesdon Hundred.[3] Altogether it has been felt necessary to supply nineteen headings to supplement the 185 already present in the text.[4]

The Buckinghamshire map in the accompanying volume gives primacy to what Domesday Book itself says. It does not start from a map of the later hundreds and look backwards, but begins from Domesday and only uses later evidence[5] as a check or to supply a lack in the survey. The composition of the 1086 hundreds is restored, as described in the introduction to this article, by beginning with places that the text shows to have certainly or probably lain in the hundred in 1086,[6] other places being restored from later evidence or geographical likelihood.[7] Hundred headings have been scrutinized for the commoner scribal errors and replaced mainly from internal evidence.[8] Hundred boundaries, checked against Bryant's map,[9] are drawn between vills on the basis of this reconstruction largely following parish boundaries. Estates or parishes not named in Domesday Book but subsumed under some other entry have been included following later evidence.[10]

The resulting pattern, typical of a southern English shire, comprises eighteen hundreds of fairly similar size. It contains no hundreds consisting of a single manor and no dispersed ecclesiastical estates forming a single disparate hundred, but it is made slightly unusual by its shape and the number of places detached from their hundreds. The shape is partly a matter of geography: on the wooded Chilterns, as in the five Oxfordshire 'Chiltern' hundreds dependent on Benson manor, the hundred boundaries, for want of natural demarcation, seem often to have followed important tracks, while in the northern area of the county major rivers such as the Thame, the Great Ouse, the Ray, the Ouzel (or Lovat) and a host of minor brooks seem for all or part of their length to have formed the hundred limits.

Detachments make the pattern complex. Beachampton and Thornton formed an isolated part of 'Rowley', and the Missendens (Great and Little), of Stone. Waddesdon and Ashendon, forming part of the same group of three hundreds, intersected each other, with Shipton Lee and Quainton,[11] which lay in Ashendon Hundred, nearly severing Waddesdon into two sections. The resulting corridor of Waddesdon Hundred isolated Oving from Ashendon Hundred, and Oving nearly cut off Hoggeston from Waddesdon.[12] Ixhill lay in two halves although perhaps once united by the presence of Haddenham which by 1086 lay in Stone Hundred.[13] As mapped, Drayton Beauchamp (including Cholesbury and Hawridge) is isolated from Yardley Hundred and was perhaps originally in Aylesbury, but still in the nineteenth century a few Buckinghamshire fields lying in the Hertfordshire parish of Tring Rural provided a link; the eleventh-century

[1] Assuming that this identification is correct.

[2] Eton is later in Stoke Hundred, but has here been mapped in Burnham. Better geographical sense could be made if the Waddesdon hundred head on f.145 governed the previous entry for Oving, but this vill was a detachment of Ashendon Hundred later as it appears to have been in 1086.

[3] This heading is restored by Morris (ed.), *Domesday Book: Buckinghamshire*, 17,9 (f.148v); see Davies, 'Hundreds of Buckinghamshire and Oxfordshire', 235. The problem is connected with that of Oving (see preceding note).

[4] Hundred heads have been restored as follows: Aylesbury above Aylesbury (f.143); Risborough above Princes Risborough (f.143v); Mursley above Swanbourne (f.143v); Stoke above Upton (in Slough) (f.143v); Ixhill above Brill (f.143v); Aylesbury above Halton (f.143v); Desborough above West Wycombe (f.143v); Aylesbury above Weston Turville (f.144); Moulsoe above (Great or Little) Brickhill (f.145); 'Stotfold' above Lamport (f.147v); 'Mow' above Edgcott (f.147v); 'Seckley' above Woolstone (f.147v); 'Mow' above Adstock (f.148); Bunsty above Tyringham (f.148v); Cottesloe above Creslow (f.150v); Moulsoe above Hardmead (f.150v); Desborough above Marlow (f.151); Ixhill above Aston Sandford (f.152); Ashendon above Quainton (f.152v). This reconstruction largely accords with Baring, *Domesday Tables*, 130, and Davies, 'Ancient Hundreds of Buckinghamshire', 105. J. Morris in Morris (ed.), *Domesday Book: Buckinghamshire*, places a Stone hundred heading above Upton (in Slough) on f.143v but his note to 1,5 makes it clear that Stoke Hundred is intended. His edition does not put a Cottesloe hundred head above Creslow (f.150v) although it lay in that hundred in 1334. He also, perhaps wrongly, restores a Mursley hundred head above Hoggeston (f.148v), as discussed in n.3 above; replaces the Burnham hundred heading above Eton (f.151) with Stoke Hundred (see n.2 above); and inserts a Stotfold hundred heading over Dadford (f.151v). This is not needed, however, as the previous heading, Mursley, above Westbury (in Shenley), is an error for 'Stotfold' (see p.38, n.10 above).

[5] Documents especially useful are *Feudal Aids*; *Rotuli Hundredorum*, 2 vols. (Record Commission, London, 1812–18); R.E. Glasscock (ed.), *The Lay Subsidy of 1334*, Brit. Acad. Records of Social and Economic Hist. ns 2 (London, 1975).

[6] An example of probability is on ff.145–145v, where Lathbury, Tyringham and Stoke Goldington lie between Little Linford, which is below a Bunsty hundred head, and Weston Underwood, which is below one elsewhere in the text (f.146v). Lathbury itself is said to be in Bunsty Hundred on f.145.

[7] For example, Addingrove lay in Ixhill Hundred in 1284–6, see *Feudal Aids*, i. 84. The Horton (in Ivinghoe) that is represented by three entries is ill-attested in later times but the natural boundary places it in Yardley Hundred.

[8] The map in Darby and Campbell (eds.), *Domesday Geography*, 139, shows the unnecessary complexity that arises when little attempt is made to restore hundred headings.

[9] A. Bryant, *The County of Buckinghamshire from an Actual Survey* (London, 1824).

[10] For example, in 'Seckley' Hundred the places which name the parishes of Stony Stratford, Willen, Fenny Stratford and Bletchley are not mentioned in DB. Even fewer parishes are named in the Chiltern hundreds.

[11] Shipton Lee, Quainton and Oving are not directly beneath hundred heads in the text, but lie with places that were certainly in Ashendon Hundred.

[12] For Oving, see n.2 above; for Hoggeston, see n.3 above.

[13] See Baring, *Domesday Tables*, 137. Alternatively, Haddenham could always have been in Stone Hundred, and Ixhill Hundred could have been continuous by incorporating a tract of land that was later in Oxfordshire.

boundary may well have integrated the two portions.[1] In later times Moreton (in Dinton parish) was a detached portion of Desborough Hundred, lying within Stone Hundred. Since it is then evidenced as a remote part of West Wycombe manor, held by the Bishop of Winchester in 1086 as later, it was probably also detached, though unnamed, in 1086.[2]

Caversfield with dependent land in Stratton Audley was isolated from 'Rowley' Hundred by the county boundary,[3] as perhaps was a part of Biddlesden parish, although, if the 1086 county boundary followed the tributary of the Great Ouse at this point, it would have lain within the county.[4] No vills were certainly divided by hundred boundaries,[5] but Ibstone and Edlesborough were shared with Oxfordshire and Bedfordshire respectively.[6]

A few detached parts of other counties lay within Buckinghamshire: Lillingstone Lovell and Boycott were clearly parts of Oxfordshire in 1086 as later, perhaps annexed to the royal manor of Kirtlington (Oxon.)[7]; while Ackhampstead, although not named in Domesday Book, was presumably an outlier of Abingdon Abbey's seventeen-hide Oxfordshire manor of Lewknor.[8] Two other detachments are found on the later map of Buckinghamshire—Coleshill or 'Stoke' manor, a detached part of Hertfordshire lying south of Amersham, and part of Aspley Heath (now in Wavendon parish), a detached portion of Bedfordshire. Their 1086 status is uncertain.[9]

Such complications suggest that although Domesday Book provides the first evidence for the hundredal pattern of Buckinghamshire, it does not record any original arrangement. At an earlier stage, for example, Saunderton may well have been part of Risborough Hundred, although in 1086, as a headland of Desborough, it nearly isolated Bledlow from the rest of Risborough Hundred. Moreover, since it is often members of the same group of three hundreds that intersect each other (perhaps because the division into separate hundreds was influenced by considerations of tenure), it is apparent that the original six greater hundredal units were more compact and distinct.

Domesday records all the names of the Buckinghamshire hundreds in recognizable form, except that some forms of Cottesloe show assimilation to a name such as Courteenhall (Northants)[10] and all but two of the forms of Moulsoe are evidently influenced by Mursley.[11]

Only two hundreds—Aylesbury and Risborough—are named from 1086 royal manors, but several—Ashendon, Burnham, Moulsoe, Mursley, Stoke,[12] Stone and Waddesdon—are called after Domesday estates held by others. Of the remaining hundred names Bunsty is now represented by Bunsty Farm in Gayhurst;[13] North and South Cottesloe are found in Wing parish;[14] Desborough is in West Wycombe;[15] and Ixhill and Yardley are now both the names of farms, the former lying in Oakley parish,[16] the latter in Pitstone.[17] The other hundreds are named from places that are now lost. 'Mow' Hundred was called after some mound or structure, perhaps in Park Meadow in Steeple Claydon, which was the traditional moot site.[18] 'Rowley' survived as a hill-name until the eighteenth century and may have lain just north of Stockingwood inside Gawcott parish.[19] 'Seckley' was the name of fields lying in Loughton and Bradwell parishes, while 'Stotfold' was a site in Lamport, in Stowe parish.[20]

Unlike those of the adjacent Berkshire, the hundreds of Buckinghamshire, although normally grouped in threes, stayed remarkably constant from the eleventh century to the nineteenth. 'Mow' Hundred was sometimes later called Buckingham, and lands belonging to the honour of Berkhamsted (Herts.) were sometimes treated as a hundred, but the only lasting changes were the transfer of a few vills to adjacent hundreds. Thus Eton moved from Burnham

[1] But most of this part of Tring Hundred is well represented in Hertfordshire DB.

[2] NGR SP 7909; see *VCH Buckinghamshire*, ii (1908), 278.

[3] *VCH Buckinghamshire*, iv (1927), 157–60; *VCH Oxfordshire*, vi (1959), 3.

[4] This detachment of Biddlesden was transferred to Syresham parish, Northants, in 1884, see F. A. Youngs, Jun., *Guide to the Local Administrative Units of England: 1 Southern England* (London, 1979), 31. In this corner of the county, the boundary especially near Luffield Abbey (NGR SP 6642) looks artificial.

[5] DB appears to place *Hamdenham*, now represented by Great and Little Hampden, in Aylesbury Hundred, but it is possible that Little Hampden, not separately surveyed, was in Stone Hundred in 1086 as later.

[6] For other parts of Ibstone, see f.160v; for Edlesborough, see f.215.

[7] See *VCH Buckinghamshire*, iv. 191, 235–6; *VCH Oxfordshire*, vi. 3.

[8] See *VCH Buckinghamshire*, iii (1925), 65, 68; *VCH Oxfordshire*, viii (1964), 1, 103.

[9] On Coleshill (NGR SU 9495), see Davies, 'Hundreds of Buckinghamshire and Oxfordshire', 248; *VCH Buckinghamshire*, iii. 150. For Aspley Heath (NGR SP 9234), see *VCH Bedfordshire*, iii (1912), 338.

[10] The forms *Coteslau*, *Coteslai* correctly represent the personal name *Cott* and OE *hlaw*, but *Coteshala* and *Coteshale* show the termination *halh* as in *Cortenhale*, *Cortenhalo*, for Courteenhall (Northants). The form *Corteshala* in the Farley text on f.150v is misprinted.

[11] The correct forms *Molesoueslau* and *Moleslou* alternate with *Moslai*, *Moslei*, *Mosleie*, *Moselai*, and *Moisselai*, influenced by Mursley (*Mursalai*, *Muselai*); see Davies, 'Ancient Hundreds of Buckinghamshire', 106; Mawer and Stenton, *Place-Names of Buckinghamshire* (abbr. *PNBU*), 29.

[12] Named from the manor of Stoke Poges.

[13] NGR SP 8347; see Mawer and Stenton, *PNBU*, 3, 5; O.S. Anderson, *The English Hundred-Names: The South-Eastern Counties* (abbr. *EHNSE*) (Lund, Leipzig, 1939), 15; *VCH Buckinghamshire*, iv. 268.

[14] NGR SP 8622; see Mawer and Stenton, *PNBU*, 75, 87; Anderson, *EHNSE*, 13; *VCH Buckinghamshire*, iii. 326.

[15] NGR SP 8493; see Mawer and Stenton, *PNBU*, 174, 207; Anderson, *EHNSE*, 9; *VCH Buckinghamshire*, iii. 33.

[16] NGR SP 6510; see Mawer and Stenton, *PNBU*, 114, 127; Anderson, *EHNSE*, 5; *VCH Buckinghamshire*, iv. 1.

[17] NGR SP 933163; see Mawer and Stenton, *PNBU*, 90, 100; Anderson, *EHNSE*, 13; *VCH Buckinghamshire*, iii. 326.

[18] Mawer and Stenton, *PNBU*, 51; Anderson, *EHNSE*, 3; *VCH Buckinghamshire*, iv. 135. The name is OE *muga*, 'mow', 'heap', 'mound', giving the Normanized DB form *Lammua* etc. by the addition of the French *la*. It is *Moue* in 1346, see *Feudal Aids*, i. 125.

[19] NGR SP *c*.6831; see Mawer and Stenton, *PNBU*, 58; Anderson, *EHNSE*, 2; *VCH Buckinghamshire*, iv. 135.

[20] See Mawer and Stenton, *PNBU*, 40; Anderson, *EHNSE*, 2; *VCH Buckinghamshire*, iv. 135.

to Stoke,[1] while Farnham Royal reversed the process. Great and Little Missenden were later in Aylesbury, Gawcott in 'Stotfold', Tickford in 'Seckley', Hogshaw in Ashendon, and Thornton in Buckingham (or 'Mow' Hundred). Much later still, Weston Turville and Halton formed a detachment of Stone Hundred, but in the fourteenth century, as in 1086, they lay in Aylesbury Hundred. Yet, despite these changes, the hundreds that survived into the nineteenth century were recognizably those of Domesday Book.

[1] If it really lay in Burnham in 1086; see p.39, n.2 above.

TABLE: The Hundreds of Buckinghamshire

| Modern Name | Form(s) found in Domesday Book | Number on map |
|---|---|---|
| Ashendon | *Esseden-e* | VIII |
| Aylesbury | *Elesberie* | XIV |
| Bunsty | *Bonestou* | I |
| Burnham | *Berneham, Burneham* | XVI |
| Cottesloe | *Coteshala, Coteshale, Coteslai, Coteslau* | X |
| Desborough | *Dusteberge, Dustenberg* | XVII |
| Ixhill | *Tichesela, Tichesele, Ticheshele, Tichessele* | XII |
| Moulsoe | *Moisselai, Moleslou, Molesoueslau, Moselai, Moslai, Moslei-e* | II |
| 'Mow' | *Lammua, Lammue, Lamua* | VI |
| Mursley | *Mursalai, Muselai* | VII |
| Risborough | *Risberg-e, Riseberg* | XV |
| 'Rowley' | *Rouelai* | V |
| 'Seckley' | *Sigelai* | IV |
| Stoke | *Stoches* | XVIII |
| Stone | *Stanes* | XIII |
| 'Stotfold' | *Stodfald, Stodfalt, Stofald* | III |
| Waddesdon | *Votesdon-e, Votesdune* | IX |
| Yardley | *Erlai* | XI |

# BIBLIOGRAPHY

# INDICES

## TO THE DOMESDAY FOLIOS

# BIBLIOGRAPHY

The following bibliography, arranged in date order, is derived by kind permission from D. Bates, *A Bibliography of Domesday Book*, published by Boydell and Brewer Ltd for the Royal Historical Society, 1986. Dr Bates has added certain entries to this county list in order to include appropriate references which are cited in the 'General Studies' section of his original work.

## BUCKINGHAMSHIRE


1. W. Bawden, *Dom.Boc. A Translation of the Record called Domesday, so far as Relates to the Counties of Middlesex, Hertford, Buckingham, Oxford and Gloucester* (Doncaster, 1812). Bawdwen produced a rather unsatisfactory translation of the whole of DB (British Library, Add. MS 27769), of which only sections were published.
2. G. Lipscomb, *The History and Antiquities of the County of Buckinghamshire*, 4 vols. (London, 1847). Translated and transcribed portions of the DB text in his descriptions of parishes.
3. H. James (director), *Domesday Book: or the Great Survey of England of William the Conqueror, A.D. MLXXXVI. Facsimile of the Part Relating to Buckinghamshire*. Photozincographed by Her Majesty's Command at the Ordnance Survey Office, Southampton (Southampton, 1862).
4. J. R. Boyle, 'Who was Eddeva?', *Trans. of the East Riding Ant. Soc.* 4 (1896), 11–22. For the DB holdings of Edith the Fair in Bucks. and six other counties.
5. F. H. Baring, 'The Conqueror's Footprints in Domesday', *EHR* 13 (1898), 17–25. Reprinted with 'some additions and alterations' in F. H. Baring, *Domesday Tables*, see 12 below, 207–16. An important article which used falls in manorial values to suggest the movement of William's army in 1066. Not all the detailed arguments have been accepted. See also 26, 27.
6. F. H. Baring, 'The Hidation of Some Southern Counties', *EHR* 14 (1899), 290–9.
7. F. H. Baring, Note on 'The Hidation of Buckinghamshire', *EHR* 15 (1900), 199. A correction to 6.
8. A. M. Davies, 'The Ancient Hundreds of Buckinghamshire', *The Home Counties Mag.* 6 (1904), 134–44. Reprinted with corrections in *Records of Buckinghamshire*, 9 (1909), 104–19. Davies' map was used by the *VCH*, see 9.
9. J. H Round, 'Introduction to the Buckinghamshire Domesday', *VCH Buckinghamshire*, ed. W. Page, i (London, 1905), 207–29.
10. F. W. Ragg, 'Text of the Buckinghamshire Domesday', ibid. 230–77.
11. L. Guilloreau, 'Les Possessions des Abbayes Mancelles et Angevines en Angleterre d'après le Domesday Book', *Revue Historique et Archéologique du Maine*, 60 (1906), 5–23.
12. F. H Baring, *Domesday Tables for the Counties of Surrey, Berkshire, Middlesex, Hertford, Buckingham and Bedford and the New Forest* (London, 1909).
13. A. M. Davies, 'Eleventh Century Buckinghamshire', *Records of Buckinghamshire*, 10 (1916), 69–74. A commentary on 12.
14. A. Mawer and F. M. Stenton, *The Place-Names of Buckinghamshire*, EPNS 2 (Cambridge, 1925).
15. W. Farrer, 'The Honour of Wallingford', *The Boarstall Cartulary*, ed. H. E. Salter (Oxford, 1930). For the holdings of Robert d'Oilly and Miles Crispin.
16. J. G. Jenkins, *A History of the Parish of Penn in the County of Buckingham* (London, 1935). At pp.5–6 corrects *VCH* and confirms EPNS on the identification of *Dilehurst*. See 10, 35.
17. B. W. Kissan, 'Lanfranc's Alleged Division of Lands between Archbishop and Community', *EHR* 54 (1939), 285–93. For the DB account of Canterbury's lands in nine counties.
18. A. M. Davies, 'Abefeld and Ackhamstead', *Records of Buckinghamshire*, 15 (1947–52), 166–71. Suggests identifications for unidentified estates.
19. A. M. Davies, 'The Hundreds of Buckinghamshire and Oxfordshire', ibid. 231–49. A reappraisal of 8 in the light of Assize Roll evidence. Compares the two counties.
20. M. W. Beresford, 'Glebe Terriers and Open-Field Buckinghamshire, with a Summary List of Deserted Villages of the County', *Records of Buckinghamshire*, 16 (1953–60), 5–28.
21. G. R. Elvey, 'Buckinghamshire in 1086', ibid. 342–62. A useful survey, with an important appendix devoted to anonymous estates and lost and doubtful names. There is an interesting reconstruction of DB Amersham with a map.
22. L. J. Ashford, *The History of the Borough of High Wycombe from its Origins to 1880* (London, 1960). Includes a map of the DB hundred of Desborough.
23. E. M. Elvey, 'The Abbot of Missenden's Estates in Chalfont St Peter', *Records of Buckinghamshire*, 17 (1961–5), 20–40. A piece of local DB geography.
24. H. C. Darby and E. M. J. Campbell (eds.), *The Domesday Geography of South-East England* (Cambridge, 1962).
25. A. C. Chibnall, *Sherington: Fiefs and Fields of a Buckinghamshire Village* (Cambridge, 1965).
26. D. Butler, *1066: the Story of a Year* (London, 1966). See for DB values and the route of the Conqueror's army. See 5, 27.
27. C. H. Lemmon, 'The Campaign of 1066', *The Norman Conquest: its Setting and Impact*, eds. D. Whitelock *et al.* (London, 1966), 77–122. For DB values and the campaign. See also 5, 26.
28. W. E. Wightman, *The Lacy Family in England and Normandy, 1066–1194* (Oxford, 1966).
29. G. K. Tull, 'Land Utilisation in the Newport Hundreds at the Time of the Domesday Survey', *Wolverton Archaeol. Soc. Jnl* 2 (1969), 32–48.
30. O. F. Brown, 'Cleyley in Domesday', ibid. 49–58.
31. D. and J. Hay, *Hilltop Villages of the Chilterns* (London, Chichester, 1971). See ch.8 for settlements not recorded in DB.
32. L. Bull, 'The Ancient Saltway from Droitwich to Princes Risborough', *Records of Buckinghamshire*, 20 (1975–8), 87–92.
33. M. Reed, 'Markets and Fairs in Medieval Buckinghamshire', ibid. 563–85. Discussion of the indirect evidence thereof in Bucks. DB.
34. B. Harvey, *Westminster Abbey and its Estates in the Middle Ages* (Oxford, 1977).
35. J. Morris (ed., from a draft translation by E. Teague and V. Sankaran), *Domesday Book: Buckinghamshire* (Chichester, 1978).
36. A. C. Chibnall, *Beyond Sherington: the Early History of the Region of Buckinghamshire Lying to the North-East of Newport Pagnell* (London, Chichester, 1979).
37. M. Reed, *The Buckinghamshire Landscape* (London, Sevenoaks, 1979).

# INDEX OF PLACES

## NOTES

In this edition, the place-names found in the translation, on the county map, and in the following Index of Places are all interrelated and have been established according to strict editorial policy. The central source for each of these three elements has been a specially compiled card-index containing a card for every mention of a place-name in Domesday Book: this index itself has been adjusted as research progressed. Thus the separate disciplines of identification, map-making, indexing, and rendering the Latin into readable English have all contributed to this compendium of Domesday place-names and to the manner of the presentation of each category. However, a word of caution is appropriate here, because the reader should be aware that the simple exchange of a Domesday name for even the most obvious modern equivalent does not necessarily mean that the original settlement lay precisely at that location, nor that it had a similar territorial form.

It is important to realise that the place-names of Domesday Book do not represent modern religious, social, administrative or agricultural units such as parishes, townships, villages, hamlets or farms, except by coincidence. They stand for estates or taxable units that may not in reality have been either independent or self-supporting. No bounds are given and these estates, depending on their size, may well have extended over more than one modern parish, be interlaced with other holdings, or possess a number of widely scattered members. Most Domesday estates will have contained several settlements, all of which had names in 1086, but which the survey leaves unnamed and whose statistics it engrosses with others. Frustratingly, Domesday says nothing that allows us to determine the centre, the extent, or the form of the estate.

Many Domesday estate-names will doubtless have been those actually current in the locality concerned; but others are 'book-names'—administrators' designations and often very general in scope—such as the name of a valley, hill, river or tract of land. These were probably known by more specific names on the ground, but Domesday Book does not record them. Especially where a vill is shown to have been in divided ownership in 1086, or where the Domesday unit is the fragment of some great multiple estate of pre-Conquest times, Domesday may well retain the 'charter' or 'book' name of its more extensive predecessor even though other evidence may indicate that a more precise appellation was almost certainly in use at the time.

The Domesday name may now be represented by a parish name, or by that of a township, hamlet or isolated farm. It may no longer survive as a settlement-name at all, but only as that of a river, wood, hill, road or bridge. The name may even have become lost before it appeared on any map; and finally it may have escaped identification altogether, either because the place designated scarcely survived the eleventh century or because the form in which Domesday transmits the place-name is corrupt and so far unintelligible.

A Domesday place can only be considered to be satisfactorily identified when the proposed name has passed a number of tests. Is the evolution of the 1086 name-form to the suggested modern equivalent philologically acceptable? Does it lie in the hundred indicated or implied by the text, or reconstructed from it? Do the details of land, equipment, resources and industry given by the entry in Domesday Book accord with what could have been practicable within the proposed area? Can the estate be identified among the possessions of the 1086 holder's heirs or successors in later centuries? In practice, by no means all published identifications satisfy these requirements and the accuracy and reliability of identifications varies considerably from county to county. Much depends on the quality of the work of the eighteenth and nineteenth century 'antiquarian' pioneers and of the sections on Domesday in the relevant volume of the *Victoria County Histories*. The standard of more recent work, the existence of a county volume among the publications of the English Place-Names Society, or of 'topographical' volumes from the *Victoria County History* make the identifications of some counties more secure than those of others. The evidence so gathered will have been reviewed for H.C. Darby's monumental series on Domesday Geography (1952–77) and for the Phillimore edition of Domesday Book (1975–86), but with varying thoroughness. For the present publication, it has been impractical to re-examine every item of this complex and widely scattered evidence afresh, but in cases where modern published identifications conflict or where there are other obvious reasons for doubt, the evidence has been rescrutinised.

In the following Index of Places, a system of square-bracketed editorial additions and of single or double inverted commas imply varying degrees of certainty in identification, and are set out in the key below. A further key precedes the translation in this volume and contains the related conventions employed there. Among the symbols on the county map, of which this index is also the gazetteer, will be found a system of circles, complete, broken, or interlinked, which serves the same function, besides a full treatment of the county- and hundred-boundaries in 1086.

By far the greater part of the evidence for the identification of place-names is derived from Great Domesday Book itself. However, occasionally a holding was entered without its eleventh-century name, or the name given has been replaced by a later one, and where possible these have been supplied from the testimony of certain other documents that are directly related to the making of Domesday Book or to its use. Such documents deemed admissable as evidence in this context are, for example, the Exon Book for the south-western counties, Evesham A for Worcestershire, and the Herefordshire Domesday. However, there is no source other than the Domesday folios accepted for identifications in this volume.

F. R. Thorn

### GENERAL

1. Scope of Index

The index refers to all place-names found in the text written at the time of the compilation of Great Domesday Book, 1086–87, including all contemporary corrections, notes and additions in the margins. Insertions added to the MS in medieval and later times are not indexed, but identifications are incorporated which have been assisted by the evidence of any secondary documents that might exist as indicated in the introduction to these notes above.

Only references to the folios and translation supplied with this volume are indexed. A section listing any named holdings in this county which are recorded in the folios of other shires will be found on the associated county map.

2. Use of suprascript numbers

Where a place-name occurs more than once on a folio, its incidence is indicated by a suprascript number.

Note that occasionally a named entry can be followed immediately by further reference(s) to the same vill, usually designated by terms such as *ibi*, 'there'; *ibidem*, 'in the same place'; *in eadem villa*, 'in the same vill'. Such entries are not indexed as the place-name itself is absent.

3. Use of "..."

Double inverted commas indicate a name found only in Domesday Book and for which there is no known later equivalent, or of which the form may be corrupt. The name so enclosed is printed in Roman type.

4. Use of '...'

Single inverted commas indicate the latest or most typical known form of a name which remained in use beyond the eleventh century, but which either has not survived into modern times at all, or which only appears on twentieth-century maps as the name of a feature such as a river, hill, wood etc., rather than as a place of habitation. This also applies to names without a continuous history and which have only recently been revived for antiquarian reasons.

## MODERN PLACE-NAMES (ROMAN TYPE)

5. Authority

The modern place-names are consistent with those marked on the particular 1:100,000 Ordnance Survey grey base-map employed as the background for each associated county map. Note that place-names can vary from edition to edition of OS maps and their absence from this particular map does not mean that they are necessarily lost.

6. Modern counties

Throughout this edition the county-boundaries are regarded as those that existed prior to the restructuring of the counties in 1974.

7. National Grid Reference

Four-figure National Grid References are given for modern place-names which represent settlements recorded in Domesday Book. Note that these NGRs do not necessarily pin-point the precise location of such settlements in 1086 for the reasons set out in the introduction to these notes above.

8. Common prefixes and suffixes: Great, Little, etc.

Modern places which are distinguished by common prefixes such as Old, Great and Little, Upper, Middle and Lower, Nether and Over, East and West, North and South have their main entry indexed under the relevant place-names, in the same way as those with distinguishing suffixes such as All Saints, St Andrew and Abbots.

9. Use of 'or', 'and'

Where a place is designated by two or more prefixes or suffixes and linked by 'or', e.g. Great or Little, All Saints or St Andrew, it is uncertain which of these two modern places represents the holding in question or whether both did so. Where the prefixes are linked by 'and', e.g. East and West, St Peter and St Martin, the inference is that both modern places lie within the territory of a single estate of 1086.

10. Use of 'in', 'near'

In the event of two or more places in one county having the same name, they are distinguished by the addition of the parish-names in square brackets, e.g. [in Compton]. The only exception is when the parish- and place-name are the same, or where the place-name forms part of the parish-name. In these cases one will be followed by the parish-name, [in Compton], while the other will be related to a prominent nearby town or feature, [near Wallingford].

11. Choice of representative names distinguished by affixes

In a given locality a single place-name in Domesday Book may now be represented by a number of variant names distinguished by different prefixes or suffixes. Where a major derivative name signifying a village or hamlet still exists, such as Great, Little, Higher, Lower, St Mary, St Peter, this is preferred to minor or dependent variant names, such as Park, Moor, Gate, Green, Manor. Similarly minor settlement-names, where only they survive, are preferred to non-settement names such as those of fields, hills, woods, streams, marshes.

Where the name in Domesday Book is represented on modern maps only by the name of a minor feature, the principal element alone is used in the index and in the translation, so that Weston Farm, Lodge, Hall, Bridge, Wood etc., appear only as Weston.

12. Places now 'lost'

A number of places named in Domesday Book either no longer exist as distinct settlements or have disappeared altogether due to urban development, inundation by reservoirs, coastal erosion, rural depopulation, and other causes. These 'lost' places are treated variously, both in the translation and in this index, according to the circumstances that have caused them to disappear.

*a.* Places which have been absorbed into an area of urban development, but have given their name to a distinct suburb or district. These are designated as 'in' the relevant town or city which is enclosed in square brackets, e.g. Knowle [in Bristol].

*b.* Places absorbed into urban development, as above, but of which the name has not survived as that of a distinct suburb or district. These are designated as 'in' the relevant town or city in square brackets, also as above, but the place-name is enclosed within single inverted commas, e.g. 'Tessall' [in Birmingham].

*c.* Places now lost under water have their names enclosed in single inverted commas and are followed by an indication of their former whereabouts in square brackets if known, e.g. 'Syndercombe' [in Clatworthy Reservoir].

*d.* Names of places lost in rural areas are enclosed in single or double inverted commas as set out in 3 and 4 above. However, they may also be designated as being 'in' the parish to which they belonged when this is known, e.g. "Sortelai" [in Quainton], 'Ashden' [in Compton].

*e.* Those lost places which can be reliably located have been plotted on the accompanying county map. Those which can only be approximately located are included in the Index and the translation but are not mapped.

13. Use of names other than Domesday derivatives

All modern names used in this edition are derived from those of 1086 with only the following exceptions:

*a.* Where the name of the Domesday Book estate has been entirely superseded by a more recent name that covers the same extent, e.g. Reigate (Surrey) for 'Churchfield'; Padstow (Corn.) for *Lanweneboc*.

*b.* Where the later name of the Domesday Book estate is derived from the TRE or TRW holder or his title, e.g. Dodington (Som.) for 'Stowey'; Bishopstone (Herefs.) for 'Mansell'.

*c.* Where it is now possible to identify places which were sited along the banks of a river and which bear only the river name in Domesday Book, as with many settlements on the Ottery (Devon) and the Piddle (Dorset).

*d.* Where the holding is un-named in Domesday Book, but its name can be reliably established from any other contemporary documents, such as those mentioned in the introduction to these notes above.

## PLACE-NAMES IN DOMESDAY BOOK *(ITALIC TYPE)*

14. Variant forms

All variant forms found in these county folios of Domesday Book are indexed.

15. Abbreviations

Place-names that are specifically shortened in the MS with abbreviation-marks are given in their extended form.

16. Use of *u*, *v*, *w*

Since *u* and *v* are used indiscriminately in this MS, as in others of the period, they are here transposed to be closest to the modern spelling of the place-names. Double-*u* (*uu*) is always transposed as *w*, except in names enclosed in double inverted commas (see 3 above) where the scribe's original orthography is maintained.

17. Use of hyphenated endings

Where the spelling of a name varies only by the addition of a final letter or letters, the shorter version is given followed by the variant ending after a hyphen. Thus *Evelai*, *Evelaia* appears as *Evelai-a*; *Heiford*, *Heiforde* as *Heiford-e*; *Winewic*, *Winewiche* as *Winewic-he*.

18. Page and folio references

References to the pages of editorial matter in this volume are printed in **bold**, and are followed by the references to the folio numbers of the facsimile and the translation, which are identical for both.

19. Recto and Verso

Folio numbers without suffix indicate the *recto* of the folio, while suffix 'v' indicates the *verso*.

20. Use of ‡

A double-dagger ‡ before a main entry refers to the errata section printed at the end of these indices, if such is required.

# BUCKINGHAMSHIRE

A



B



C

# INDEX OF PERSONS AND ECCLESIASTICAL BODIES

## NOTES

### 1. TRE, TRW

Most of the entries in Domesday Book record two distinct categories of landholder: those English or Anglo-Scandinavian owners who held land before the Conquest (TRE, *tempore regis Edwardi*, 'in the time of King Edward'), and those who dispossessed them after 1066 (TRW, *tempore regis Willelmi*, 'in the time of King William') – or more particularly twenty years later at the time of the Conqueror's survey. It is usual for the Church to maintain continuity of ownership throughout both periods, but it is rare for an individual to do so. Since Domesday Book is a description of the situation at the time of its compilation in 1086–87, the circumstances obtaining TRE are invariably entered in the past tense, TRW in the present.

### 2. Use of * †

Prefixed asterisks * indicate references to the names of English or Anglo-Scandinavian landholders or churches mentioned only in a TRE context. Daggers † signify those which are stated to have continued their tenancy from the TRE to the TRW period. Names found only TRW have no prefixed symbol.

### 3. The Kings

The references to King Edward and to King William are divided for convenience into categories which encompass various aspects of kingship. The references to King Edward implied by the abbreviation TRE are not indexed. Where the text shows that someone in the TRE period *tenuit de rege Edwardo*, 'held of King Edward', the references are indexed under the category of King Edward 'as lord'.

References to the equivalent TRW phrase *tenet de rege*, 'holds of the king', are not indexed as it was not used systematically and was anyway superfluous because in feudal theory current after the Conquest all land was technically held of the king.

### 4. Abbeys and Churches

The terms *Abbatia*, 'Abbey', and *Æcclesia*, 'Church' are sometimes used interchangeably in Domesday Book for large monastic institutions. In this index, irrespective of the text, 'Abbey' is always used for the Benedictine houses, both in England and on the continent, while 'Church' is reserved for secular houses, i.e. colleges of priests, non-monastic bishoprics, minsters, etc.

### 5. Personal Names TRE

All TRE names are standardized in accordance with O. von Feilitzen, *The Pre-Conquest Personal Names of Domesday Book* (Uppsala, 1937) with the following exceptions: Alfred, Edgar, Edith, Edmund, Edward, Edwin, Harold, Morcar, Siward, Stigand, Swein and Waltheof.

Old English forms are used in preference to Scandinavian variants. When no Old English form is attested, names are standardized first to their Anglo-Scandinavian, then to their Old Danish, Old Swedish, and finally Old Norse forms.

### 6. Personal Names TRW

There is no authority equivalent to von Feilitzen for TRW names, and their transposition into modern forms by individual historians has seldom been consistent. For this edition the editors have retained what they perceive to have become the 'accepted' forms of certain names despite inconsistencies. Thus, for example, *Albertus Lotharingensis* becomes Albert of Lorraine, not the Lotharingian, whilst *Walterius Flandrensis* remains Walter the Fleming, not of Flanders, in the style used for most non-Norman continentals. However, a policy of standardization has been established for the aspects of nomenclature which follow.

Modern anglicized forms of Christian names are preferred, e.g. Gilbert for *Giselbertus*, Geoffrey for *Goisfridus*, Hugh for *Hugo*, Ralph for *Radulfus*.

Continental and English toponymics appear in the modern form of the place-name e.g. Robert d'Oilly not *Robert de Oilgi*, Roger of Westerham not *Roger de Oisteram*. As in these examples, 'de' is used for continental places of origin, 'of' for English names.

Continental patronymics are expressed with the prefix 'fitz', e.g. Hugh fitzBaldric. The equivalent English or Anglo-Scandinavian names are expressed as 'son of', e.g. Swein son of Azur. This rule is also applied to patronymics in TRE names.

Ambiguous TRW personal names which are attested in both Anglo-Scandinavian and Continental sources are given their Continental forms unless the manuscript specifically identifies any person so named as English.

TRW names with obscure Latin forms or with no modern equivalent appear in the Index as they do in the manuscript, but without the *-us* ending, e.g. Otbert for *Otbertus*, Winemar for *Winemarus*.

### 7. Titles

Main entries are indexed under the toponymic, and the personal name(s), where known, are supplied in square brackets, e.g. Mortain, [Robert], Count of; Coutances, [Geoffrey de Mowbray], Bishop of. If these name(s) occur explicitly in the folios of this county, the square brackets are left off.

### 8. Occupational Names

Examples: Alwine the huntsman, Gilbert the cook, Regenbald the priest. Although Domesday Book describes many of these persons with other descriptive suffixes – for instance Regenbald occurs variously in different counties as 'the priest', 'the chaplain', 'the king's chaplain', and 'of Cirencester' – only that or those which occur in the folios of this particular county are listed here.

### 9. Cross-indexing

All patronymics, non-titular toponymics, rank-names, by-names and occupational names are cross-indexed with the main entry under the Christian name. Examples:

| Main Entry | Cross-reference |
|---|---|
| Eudo fitzHubert | Hubert, *see* Eudo fitzHubert |
| Alvred of Lincoln | Lincoln, *see* Alvred of Lincoln |
| Leofwine Cild | Cild, *see* Leofwine Cild |
| Alwine Cobbold | Cobbold, *see* Alwine Cobbold |
| Gilbert the cook | cook, *see* Gilbert the cook |

In the case of Abbeys, main entries will be found under the place-name with the dedication cross-indexed: Ramsey, Abbey of St Benedict (main entry); St Benedict, Ramsey, Abbey of.

Secular churches are indexed under Church with a cross-reference to the dedication, and also to the place-name: Church of Saint-Remy of Rheims (main entry); Saint-Remy of Rheims, Church of; Rheims, Church of Saint-Remy of.

### 10. Folio References

Only one reference to a name is indexed per folio. The frequent use of *idem*, 'the same man', is not indexed as the name itself is not present. References are linked by a hyphen when the consecutive entries for a holder's fief cover more than one folio.

Folio numbers without suffix indicate the *recto* of the folio, while suffix 'v' indicates the *verso*.

# BUCKINGHAMSHIRE

# TRANSLATION

# TRANSLATION

## NOTES TO THE TRANSLATION

### SOURCE AND STANDARDIZATION

THE translations in the County Edition of Domesday Book are based in the main upon those that appear in the *Victoria Histories of the Counties of England*, of which publication commenced in 1900 and is still in progress. The translator of the relevant county folios of Domesday Book in volume one of *VCH Buckinghamshire* (1905) was F. W. Ragg. Alecto Historical Editions are grateful to the publishers of *VCH* for permission to make use of this translation.

In order that the translations contained in each of the present county volumes can all be served by a common system of indices, the text of *VCH* has been standardized so that place- and personal names as well as technical terms and certain common phrases are consistent throughout. The opportunity has also been taken to correct such errors as may have become apparent as a result of subsequent research.

For a detailed statement of the policies governing the treatment of names, see the notes which precede the 'Index of Places' and the 'Index of Persons and Ecclesiastical Bodies' above.

### METHODS OF RELATING THE TRANSLATION TO THE FACSIMILE

Throughout the folios of Great Domesday Book there is considerable variation in the number of lines written per page, in the depth and width of the columns, and in the spaces that separate the numbered chapters. In order to assist the use of the facsimile and this translation together, the type-size and the lay-out of the pages of the translation have been designed to match the configuration of the MS text as closely as possible.

The MS was foliated in the seventeenth century on only the *recto* side of each page. In the translation the *verso* is also foliated with the number followed by v.

● to the left, within the column, signifies the presence of one of the larger rubricated initial letters that commonly begin each entry. This device is provided to enable the reader more easily to relate passages in the translation to those in the facsimile by counting the spots on the former against the more prominent initials in the latter.

#### TYPOGRAPHY

Roman type is reserved for the original text of Great Domesday, including all corrections and marginal additions made to the MS at the time of its compilation in the late eleventh century.

*Italic* type is used for all matter added subsequently during the Middle Ages and up to recent times.

The use of upper and lower case is the same as in the MS:

FULL CAPITALS represent the large rustic capitals used for county- and chapter-headings, which are all written in red.

LARGE AND SMALL CAPITALS represent matter written in black rustic capitals within the text and usually through-lined in red. Those not written in capitals, whether intentionally or in error, are here transposed in lower case.

### MARGINALIA

The translations of those passages entirely written in the margin are printed as close as is possible to the position they occupy in the MS, in smaller type where necessary. A complete key to the system of symbols employed here for the marginal notes and signs found in the MS, such as § for the transposition signs, M, B, S, etc. preceding ● in certain counties, and [1], [2], [3], □, ⬚, ☒, etc., is given in Appendix I, 'The Marginalia of Great Domesday Book', in the associated *Domesday Book Studies* volume, pp. 160–2.

### EDITORIAL CONVENTIONS

Square brackets are reserved for editorial insertions.

[*sic*] — indicates a scribal error in the MS, here reproduced in the translation. The only exception is the incorrect chapter numbering.

[. . .] — signifies a gap in the MS text, either left blank by the scribe for an insertion to be added later, or as a result of erasure. Three full points within the brackets are the standard length in the translations regardless of the actual extent of the gap in the MS.

† 7 hides † — Daggers enclose the tentative translation of a passage, phrase or numeral which is obscure in the MS, owing either to slips of the pen, to unclear alteration by the scribe, or to the worn condition of the parchment.

7 hides — Underlining indicated words or passages marked for deletion in the MS: the same convention is followed in the translation where no correction has been added suprascript. In the latter case, only the corrected text is given.

| it is worth 12*s.* | — Bars within the text enclose the full extent of a passage of which part is written in the margin, where a note will be found to that effect in square brackets.

[?] WESTON — The modern equivalent given for a Domesday place-name which is probable, but not certain.

[? Weston] — A place left un-named in Domesday Book, but which can be tentatively identified from internal evidence or from the evidence of other related documents.

WESTON [in Parishbrook] — Where a county contains two or more modern places with the same name, they are differentiated by indicating the parish 'in' which each of them lies.

WESTON [near Oldborough] — In the above instance, when one of the place-names is the same or partially the same as the name of the parish in which it lies, giving the awkward WESTON [in Weston], its situation is instead indicated as being 'near' a prominent town or feature.

[Great or Little] WESTON — The use of 'or' indicates that it is uncertain which of two or more modern places now represent the Domesday place-name, or whether all did so.

[Great and Little] WESTON — The use of 'and' indicates that two or more modern places lie within the territory of the same Domesday estate.

WESTON [Oxon.] — County abbreviations indicate that a locality recorded in the folios of this county lies within the boundaries of another in modern times. Throughout this edition the modern county boundaries are taken to be those that obtained prior to the restructuring of the counties in 1974.

## NOTES TO THE TRANSLATION

### Use of Inverted Commas

"CELVERDESCOTE" Double inverted commas indicate a place-name found only in Domesday Book and for which there is no known later equivalent, or of which the form may be corrupt.

Hundred- and wapentake-names are similarly treated, but a typical form is used if there are variants.

'SCULTHORP' Single inverted commas indicate the latest or most typical known form of a name which remained in use beyond the eleventh century, but which either has not survived into modern times at all, or which only appears on twentieth-century maps as the name of a feature such as a river, hill, wood etc., rather than as a place of habitation. This also applies to names without a continuous history and which have only recently been revived for antiquarian reasons.

Hundred- and wapentake-names which are antiquarian revivals are similarly treated. Single inverted commas also indicate such names derived from places which had disappeared before the compilation of the first OS 1-inch maps in the early nineteenth century, either because they never were the names of inhabited communities, or because they had fallen into disuse by that time. In such cases the name-form adopted is the latest, most typical or a regularized form.

## EDITOR'S NOTE

Almost from the beginning of the Buckinghamshire folios the numbering of the initial list of landholders on f.143 fails to correspond with the relevant chapter-headings in the text until the very end. Two stages of error are evident.

At the time when the red headings were being added, the scribe missed the fief of the Bishop of Lincoln (which should be number IIII according to the list), and designated the next chapter, that of the Bishop of Bayeaux, as IIII instead. As a result, the sequence of numbers in the text is one digit behind the list thereafter.

Then, as he worked through the text, he failed to notice that in the list he had inadvertently passed over the number XXXIX. This omission compounded the previous error and caused all further numbering in the text to be behind by two, right up to the last chapter LVII. Against this number the list gives the heading 'Thegns of the king and almsmen', while in the text on f.153 this block of entries is divided into three separate chapters: LV, Alric the cook; LVI, Alsige; and LVII, Leofwine of Nuneham Courtenay, so that the final number in the list and in the text does at last tally.

The faulty numbering is transposed in the translation as it is in the manuscript, but for the sake of simplicity the errors are noticed here only and are not signalled by [*sic*] where they occur.

• BUCKINGHAM with Bourton was assessed at 1 hide TRE, and is so now. There is land for 8 ploughs. In demesne are 2 [ploughs]; and the villans have $3\frac{1}{2}$ ploughs, and there could be $2\frac{1}{2}$ more. There are 26 burgesses and 11 bordars and 2 slaves. There is 1 mill rendering 14*s.*, meadow for 8 ploughs, [and] pasture for the livestock of the vill. In all it rendered TRE £10 by tale; now it renders £16 of blanch silver.

• Bishop Remigius holds the church of this borough, and land for 4 ploughs which belongs to it. There are 4 ploughs, and 3 villans and 3 bordars and 10 cottars, and 1 mill [rendering] 10*s.* [There is] meadow for 2 ploughs, [and] wood for fences. It is and was worth £6; TRE £7. This church Bishop Wulfwig held of King Edward.

• In this borough the Bishop of Coutances has 3 burgesses whom Wulfweard son of Eadgifu held. These pay 6*s.* 6*d.* yearly, and to the king they pay 11*d.*

Earl Hugh has 1 burgess who was a man of Burgheard of Shenley. This man pays 26*d.* yearly, and to the king 5*d.*

Robert d'Oilly has 1 burgess who was a man of Azur son of Toti. This man pays 16*d.*, and to the king 5*d.*

Roger d'Ivry has 4 burgesses who were men of the same Azur. These pay 7*s.* 6*d.*, and to the king 13*d.*

Hugh de Bolbec has 4 burgesses who were men of Ælfric. These pay 28*d.*, and to the king 12*d.*

Mainou the Breton has 4 burgesses who were men of Eadgifu wife of Sigeræd. These pay 29*d.* They owe nothing to the king.

Hascoit Musard has 1 burgess who was a man of Azur son of Toti. This man pays 16*d.*, and to the king 2*d.*

Ernulf de Hesdin has 1 burgess who was Wiglaf's [man]. This man pays 2*s.* yearly, and to the king 3*d.*

William de Castellion has of the Bishop of Bayeux's fief 2 burgesses who were men of Earl Leofwine. These pay 16*d.*, and to the king now nothing, but TRE they paid 3*d.*

1 burgess of Earl Aubrey's fief pays to the king 2*d.*

Leofwine of Nuneham Courtenay has 5 burgesses, and he had them TRE. These pay him 4*s.* yearly, and to the king 12*d.*

• I King WILLIAM
II The Archbishop of Canterbury
III The Bishop of Winchester
IIII The Bishop of Lincoln
V The Bishop of Bayeux
VI The Bishop of Coutances
VII The Bishop of Lisieux
VIII The Abbot of Westminster
IX The Abbot of St Albans
X The Abbess of Barking
XI The Canons of Oxford
XII Regenbald the priest
XIII The Count of Mortain
XIIII Earl Hugh of Chester
XV Walter Giffard
XVI William de Warenne
XVII William Peverel
XVIII William fitzAnsculf
XIX Robert de Tosny
XX Robert d'Oilly
XXI Robert Gernon
XXII Geoffrey de Mandeville
XXIII Gilbert de Ghent
XXIIII Miles Crispin
XXV Edward of Salisbury
XXVI Hugh de Beauchamp
XXVII Hugh de Bolbec
XXVIII Henry de Ferrers
XXIX Walter de Vernon
XXX Walter fitzOther
XXXI Walter the Fleming
XXXII William de Feugeres
XXXIII William the chamberlain
XXXIIII William fitzConstantine
XXXV William fitzManni [2]
XXXVI Turstin fitzRolf
XXXVII Turstin Mantel
XXXVIII Ralph de Feugeres
XL Bertram de Verdun
XLI Nigel d'Aubigny
XLII Nigel de Berville
XLIII Roger d'Ivry
XLIIII Richard Engaine
XLV Mainou the Breton
XLVI Joscelin the Breton
XLVII Urse de Bercheres
XLVIII Winemar [the Fleming]
XLIX Martin
L Hervey the legate
LI Hascoit Musard
LII Gunfrid de Chocques
LIII Giles brother of Ansculf
LIIII Queen Matilda
LV Countess Judith [2]
LVI Azelina wife of [Ralph] Taillebois
LVII Thegns of the king and almsmen

## THE LAND OF THE KING

• AYLESBURY, a demesne manor of the king, has always been assessed at 16 hides. There is land for 16 ploughs. In demesne are 2 [ploughs]. There 20 villans with 14 bordars have 10 ploughs, and there could be 4 more. There are 2 slaves, and 2 mills rendering 23*s.*, meadow for 8 ploughs, and from the remainder, 20*s.* In all it renders £56 assayed and weighed, and from the toll £10 by tale; TRE it rendered £25 by tale.

In this manor was and is 1 sokeman having 1 virgate of land, which he could give or sell to whom he wished, and yet he always does service to the king's sheriff. The church of this manor the Bishop of Lincoln holds.

M ● Wendover has always been assessed at 24 hides. There is land for 26 ploughs. In demesne are 3 ploughs. There 26 villans with 6 bordars have 17 ploughs, and there could be 6 more. There are 2 mills rendering 10*s.*, meadow for 3 ploughs, and from the remainder, 20*s.*, [and] woodland for 2,000 pigs. In all it renders yearly £38 assayed and weighed; TRE it rendered £25 by tale. In this manor are 2 sokemen holding $1\frac{1}{2}$ hides. They did not belong there TRE.

M ● Princes Risborough was Earl Harold's vill. It has always been assessed at 30 hides. There is land for 24 ploughs. In demesne [are] 20 hides, and there are 4 ploughs. There 30 villans with 12 bordars have 20 ploughs. There are 3 slaves, and 2 mills rendering 14*s.* 8*d.*, meadow for 7 ploughs, [and] woodland for 1,000 pigs. All together it renders yearly £47 of blanch silver, less 16*d.*; TRE it rendered £10 by tale. To this manor belongs and belonged a certain burgess of Oxford paying 2*s.* In addition a salt-worker of Droitwich [Worcs.] renders summae [*sic*] of salt, and in the same manor was and is a certain sokeman holding 3 virgates. He could indeed sell [his land], but yet he has done service to the sheriff.

M ● Swanbourne was Earl Harold's vill. It is assessed at $4\frac{1}{2}$ hides. There is land for 4 ploughs. In demesne [are] 3 hides and 3 virgates, and there is 1 plough and there could be another. There 3 villans have $1\frac{1}{2}$ ploughs, and there could be as many more. There is 1 slave, and meadow for 5 ploughs. All together it renders yearly 30*s.* of blanch silver; TRE 30*s.* by tale.

M ● Upton [in Slough] was Earl Harold's vill. It is assessed at 18 hides. There is land for 10 ploughs. In demesne [are]
[1] $2\frac{1}{2}$ hides, and there are 2 ploughs. There 19 villans with 5 bordars have 15 ploughs. There are 2 slaves, and 1 mill rendering 4*s.* From a fishery, 1,000 eels. [There is] meadow for 2 ploughs, [and] woodland for 200 pigs. All together it renders yearly £21 assayed and weighed; TRE it rendered £15 by tale.

M ● Brill was King Edward's manor. It has always been assessed at 20 hides. There is land for 25 ploughs. In demesne are 3 [ploughs]. There 19 villans with 13 bordars have 17 ploughs, and there could be 5 more. There are 2 slaves, and 1 mill rendering 10*s.*, meadow for 20 ploughs, [and] woodland for 200 pigs. All together it renders yearly £38 of blanch silver, and for the forest £12 assayed and weighed; TRE it rendered £18 by tale.

In 'Stotfold' Hundred

M ● King William holds Biddlesden. Earl Aubrey had it of him. There are 4 hides and 1 virgate. There is land for 8 ploughs. In demesne [are] 2 hides, and there is 1 plough, and there could be 2 more. There 4 villans and 5 bordars have 2 ploughs, and there could be 3 more. There are 4 slaves, and 2 mills rendering 28*d.*, meadow for 1 plough, [and] woodland for 200 pigs. It is worth 30*s.*; when received £4; TRE 40*s.* Azur son of Thorth, a thegn of King Edward, held this manor.

## II. THE LAND OF ARCHBISHOP LANFRANC

In Stone Hundred

M ● Archbishop Lanfranc holds Haddenham. It is assessed at 40 hides. There is land for 30 ploughs. In demesne [are] 18 hides, and there are 6 ploughs. There 40 villans with 16 bordars have 14 ploughs, and there could be 10 more. There are 15 slaves, and 2 mills rendering 20*s.*, meadow for 6 ploughs, pasture for the livestock, and for the farm of the archbishop 8 days' hay. In all it is worth £40; when received £20; TRE £40. Of this land Gilbert the priest holds of the archbishop 3 hides and 1 church with the tithes. There is land for 1 plough, and there is [1 plough] with 1 villan and 3 bordars. It is and always was worth 60*s.* This manor Earl Tosti held.

M ● The archbishop himself holds Halton. It is assessed at 5 hides. There is land for 7 ploughs. In demesne [are] $2\frac{1}{2}$ hides, and there are 2 ploughs. There 10 villans with 15 bordars have 5 ploughs. There is 1 mill rendering 15*s.*, meadow for 2 ploughs, woodland for 100 pigs and 2*s.* [besides]. In all it is and always was worth £8. This manor Earl Leofwine held.

In Risborough Hundred

M ● The archbishop himself holds Monks Risborough. It is assessed at 30 hides. There is land for 14 ploughs. In demesne [are] 16 hides, and there are 2 ploughs. There 32 villans with 8 bordars have 12 ploughs. There are 4 slaves, meadow for 6 ploughs, [and] woodland for 300 pigs. In all it is worth £16; when received 100*s.*; TRE £16. This manor Esger the staller held of Christ Church, Canterbury, but with the condition that it could not be separated from that church TRE.

## III. THE LAND OF THE BISHOP OF WINCHESTER

M ● Walkelin, Bishop of Winchester, holds West Wycombe. It is assessed at 19 hides. There is land for 23 ploughs. In demesne [are] 5 hides, and there are 3 ploughs. There 27 villans with 8 bordars have 19 ploughs. There are 7 slaves, and 3 mills rendering 20*s.*, and 1 fishery rendering 1,000 eels, meadow for 7 ploughs, [and] woodland for 1,000 pigs. In all it is worth £15; when received £10; TRE £12. This manor was and is for the sustenance of the monks of the Church of Winchester. Stigand held it TRE.

In Yardley Hundred

M ● The Bishop of Winchester himself holds Ivinghoe. It is assessed at 20 hides. There is land for 25 ploughs. In demesne [are] 5 hides, and there are 3 ploughs, and there could be a fourth. There 28 villans with 4 bordars have 20 ploughs, and there could be 1 more. There are 6 slaves, meadow for 5 ploughs, woodland for 600 pigs and 10*s.* [besides]. In all it is worth £18; when received £10; TRE £15. This manor belonged and belongs to the demesne of the Church of St Peter of Winchester.

## THE LAND OF BISHOP OF LINCOLN

In Aylesbury Hundred

M ● Remigius, Bishop of Lincoln, holds Stoke Mandeville. It is assessed at 8 hides. There is land for 21 ploughs. In demesne [are] 3 hides, and there are 6 ploughs. There 20 villans with 4 bordars have 15 ploughs. There are 3 slaves, and 1 mill rendering 10*s.*, woodland for 30 pigs, [and] meadow for 3 ploughs. This manor belongs to the Church of Aylesbury. There are 18 bordars who pay 20*s.* yearly. In all it is worth £20; when received £12; TRE £18. This manor with the church Bishop Wulfwig held TRE. From the 8 hundreds which lie round Aylesbury each sokeman who has 1 hide or more renders 1 summa of corn to this church. Besides this also 1 acre of corn or 4*d.* was paid by each sokeman to this church TRE, but after the coming of King William it was not paid.

M • Walter holds Buckland of Bishop Remigius. It is assessed at 10 hides. There is land for 8 ploughs. In demesne are 2 [ploughs]; and and [*sic*] 14 villans with 6 bordars have 6 ploughs. [There is] meadow for 2 ploughs, [and] woodland for 300 pigs. In all it is worth £8; when received £3; TRE £10. This manor Godric, brother of Bishop Wulfwig, held; he could not give or sell it without his leave.

In Burnham Hundred

• The same Walter holds of the same bishop half a hide. There is land for half a plough. It is and always was worth 5*s*. This land Leofric, a man of Earl Harold, held and could sell.

In Desborough Hundred

M • Walter himself holds of the same bishop Wooburn. It is assessed at 8½ hides. There is land for 9 ploughs. In demesne are 2 [ploughs]; and 12 villans with 13 bordars have 10 ploughs. There is 1 slave, and 8 mills rendering 104*s*., [and] meadow for 6 ploughs and for the horses. From a fishery, 300 eels. [There is] woodland for 200 pigs and 7*s*. 4*d*. [besides]. In all it is worth £15; when received 100*s*.; TRE £12. This manor Earl Harold held.

• In Lude Walter holds of the same bishop 1½ hides. There is land for 2 ploughs. There are 1½ [ploughs], and there could be half [a plough more]. There are 2 villans with 1 bordar. There is 1 slave, and 3 mills rendering 14*s*. It is and always was worth 30*s*. Leofric, a man of Earl Harold, held this manor and could sell it.

In 'Rowley' Hundred

• The bishop himself holds Gawcott, which belongs to the Church of Buckingham. There is 1 hide. There is land for 1½ ploughs, and there are [1½ ploughs] with 2 bordars and 1 slave. [There is] meadow for half a plough. It is and was worth 30*s*.; TRE 40*s*. This land Bishop Wulfwig held.

## IIII. THE LAND OF THE BISHOP OF BAYEUX

In Stone Hundred

M • The Bishop of Bayeux holds in Stone 7 hides. Helto holds of him. There is land for 7 ploughs. In demesne are 3 [ploughs]; and 1 villan with 15 bordars have 1 plough, and there could be 2 more. There are 7 slaves. [There is] meadow for plough [*sic*]. In all it is and was worth 100*s*.; TRE £6. This manor 2 brothers held: one a man of Ulf, and the other a man of Eadgifu. They could give or sell it to whom they wished.

M • The same Helto holds of the same bishop Dinton. It is assessed at 15 hides. There is land for 13 ploughs. In demesne are 3 [ploughs]; and 35 villans with 7 bordars have 10 ploughs. There are 8 slaves, meadow for 13 ploughs, and 1 mill rendering 4*s*. In all it is and always was worth £15. This manor Avelin, a thegn of King Edward, held.

• In Lower Hartwell Helto holds of the bishop 3 hides. There is land for 3 ploughs, and there are [3 ploughs] with 1 villan and 7 bordars, and 1 mill rendering 8*s*. In all it is and always was worth 50*s*. This land 3 sokemen held. One, a man of Archbishop Stigand, [held] half a hide; another, a man of Earl Leofwine, 2 hides; the third, a man of Avelin, half a hide; and they could sell and give [their land].

• In the same vill Robert holds of the bishop 1 hide. There is land for 2 ploughs. There is 1 [plough], and there could be another. There is 1 villan and 4 slaves. It is and was worth 20*s*.; TRE 40*s*. This land Avelin, a thegn of King Edward, held and could sell.

M • Roger holds Weston Turville of the bishop. It is assessed at 20 hides. There is land for 17 ploughs. In demesne are 3 [ploughs], and there could be a fourth. There 12 villans have 12 ploughs, and there could be 1 more. There are 12 slaves, and 4 mills rendering 33*s*. 4*d*., meadow for 10 ploughs and 6*s*. [besides], [and] woodland for 100 pigs. In all it is worth £15; when received £8; TRE £15.

Of the land of this manor Earl Leofwine held 9½ hides, and Godric the sheriff 3½ hides as 1 manor, and 2 men of the same Godric 3½ hides, and 1 man of Earl Tosti 2 hides, and 2 men of Earl Leofwine 1½ hides. All could sell [their land]. Of these hides, the Bishop of Lisieux has 1 of the Bishop of Bayeux. There is land for 1 plough, but the plough is not there. It is and always was worth 5*s*. Those men whom Roger holds in Weston Turville [. . .] did not belong to Earl Leofwine TRE.

M • Roger himself holds Bedgrove. It is assessed at 2 hides. There is land for 3 ploughs. In demesne is 1 [plough]; and 5 villans with 5 bordars have 2 ploughs. [There is] meadow for 1 plough. It is worth 30*s*.; when received 10*s*.; TRE 40*s*. This manor Swein, a man of Alwine Varus, held and could sell.

• In Bierton the same Roger holds of the bishop 1 hide and 3 virgates. There is land for 1½ ploughs, and there are [1½ ploughs] with 3 bordars. It is and was worth 20*s*.; TRE 50*s*. This land 2 sokemen held: one a man of Alwine Varus, and the other a man of Earl Leofwine, and they could sell.

In Risborough Hundred

• In Horsenden Roger holds of the bishop half a hide. There is land for half a plough, and there is [half a plough] with 1 bordar. It is and was worth 3*s*.; TRE 5*s*. This land a man of Earl Leofwine held and could sell.

• In the same vill Robert holds of the bishop half a hide. There is land for half a plough, but the plough is not there. It is and was worth 2*s*.; TRE 5*s*. This land Godwine, a man of Earl Leofwine, held and could sell.

In Burnham Hundred

M • In Chalfont St Peter Roger holds of the bishop 4 hides and 3 virgates. There is land for 15 ploughs. In demesne is 1 [plough]; and 14 villans with 4 bordars have 14 ploughs. There are 2 slaves, and 1 mill rendering 6*s*., meadow for 2 ploughs, woodland for 600 pigs, and a hawk's eyrie. In all it is worth 110*s*.; when received 60*s*.; TRE 110*s*. This manor Earl Leofwine held.

• In Amersham Roger holds of the bishop half a hide. There is land for 1 plough, and there is [1 plough] with 3 bordars, and 1 mill rendering 4*s*., [and] meadow for 1 plough. This land is and always was worth 20*s*. This land Alwine, a man of Queen Edith, held and could sell.

• In Chesham Roger holds half a hide. There is land for 2 ploughs. In demesne [is] 1 plough; and 1 villan with 2 bordars have 1 plough. [There is] woodland for 50 pigs. It is and always was worth 20*s*.

• In Chesham the Bishop of Bayeux himself holds 1½ hides. There is land for 3 ploughs. In demesne is 1 hide, and there is 1 plough; and 2 villans with 3 bordars have 2 ploughs. There are 2 slaves, and 2 mills rendering 3*s*., [and] meadow for 3 ploughs. It is and always was worth 60*s*. This manor 2 sokemen held: one a man of Earl Leofwine, the other a man of Earl Harold, and they could sell.

M • Gilbert, Bishop of Lisieux, holds of the Bishop of Bayeux 'Dilehurst' [in Taplow]. It is assessed at 10 hides. There is land for 10 ploughs. In demesne are 2 [ploughs], and there could be a third. There 14 villans with 1 bordar have 6 ploughs, and there could be a seventh. There is 1 slave, and 1 mill rendering 3*s*., meadow for 2 ploughs, [and] woodland for 300 pigs. In all it is worth £6; when received 40*s*.; TRE £6. This manor Earl Leofwine held in demesne.

M • Roger holds of the bishop Taplow. It is assessed at 8 hides and 1 virgate. There is land for 16 ploughs. In demesne is 1 [plough]; and 18 villans with 4 bordars have 15 ploughs. There are 2 slaves. From a fishery, 1,000 eels. [There is] meadow for 1 plough, [and] woodland for 700 pigs. In all it is worth £8; when received 60*s*.; TRE £9. This manor Asgot, a man of Earl Harold, held, and in the same place 1 man of Archbishop Stigand had 1 hide and could sell it.

IN DESBOROUGH HUNDRED

M ● WILLIAM fitzOgier holds of the bishop HUGHENDEN. It is assessed at 10 hides. There is land for 10 ploughs. In demesne are 2 [ploughs]; and 15 villans with 3 bordars have 8 ploughs. There are 5 slaves, meadow for 2 ploughs, [and] woodland for 600 pigs. In all it is worth £10; when received £6; TRE £7. This manor Queen Edith held.

● In West Wycombe Roger holds of the bishop half a hide. There is land for 1 plough, and there is [1 plough] with 1 bordar. It is and was worth 7*s*.; TRE 10*s*. This land a man of Archbishop Stigand held; he could not sell or give it away from West Wycombe, his manor, as the hundred testifies.

● In MARLOW [Marlow or Little Marlow] Tedald holds of the bishop 5 hides. There is land for 4 ploughs. In demesne [are] 1½ hides, and there are 1½ ploughs. There 6 villans with 4 bordars have 2½ ploughs. There is 1 slave, and 1 mill [rendering] 20*s*. From a fishery, 500 eels. [There is] meadow for 2 ploughs, [and] woodland for 50 pigs. In all it is worth £7; when received £4; TRE as much. This manor Queen Edith held.

● In Saunderton Roger holds of the bishop 5 hides. There is land for 5 ploughs. In demesne are 2 [ploughs]; and 13 villans with 3 bordars have 3 ploughs. There are 2 slaves, and 1 mill, meadow for 1 plough, [and] woodland for 50 pigs. It is and was worth 100*s*.; TRE £6. This manor a man of Earl Leofwine held and could sell.

● In "Hanechedene" Tedald held of the bishop 3 hides. Now it is of the king's farm. There is land for 7 ploughs. In demesne [is] half a hide, and there are 2 ploughs. There 6 villans, with 3 bordars, and 5 slaves have 5 ploughs. In all it is and was worth 100*s*.; TRE £4. Of this manor Fridebert, a man of Earl Leofwine, held 2½ hides, and Alric Gangemere and his sister held half a hide which TRE was unjustly taken from them.

IN IXHILL HUNDRED

● In Waldridge Helto holds of the bishop 2 hides and 1 virgate. There is land for 2 ploughs. In demesne is 1 [plough]; and 2 villans have 1 plough. There is 1 slave, and meadow for 2 ploughs. It is and was worth 20*s*.; TRE 40*s*. This land 2 sokemen held: one a man of Avelin, and the other a man of Ælfgifu, sister of Earl Harold; they could sell.

● In Ilmer Robert holds of the bishop 4 hides. There is land for 5 ploughs. In demesne are 2 [ploughs]; and 8 villans with 1 bordar have 3 ploughs. There are 4 slaves, and 1 mill rendering 10*s*., [and] meadow for 5 ploughs. It is worth £4; when received 100*s*.; and as much TRE. This manor Godwine, a man of Earl Leofwine, held and could sell.

● The same Robert holds of the bishop Aston Sandford as 2 hides. There is land for 5 ploughs. In demesne are 2 [ploughs]; and 7 villans have 3 ploughs. There are 4 slaves, [and] meadow for 5 ploughs. It is worth £4; when received 100*s*.; and as much TRE. This manor Avelin, a thegn of King Edward, held.

IN ASHENDON HUNDRED

● In Beachendon 2 Englishmen hold of the bishop 1 virgate. There is land [. . .]. It is and always was worth 5*s*. They themselves held it TRE: one a man of Beorhtric, and the other a man of Azur; they could sell.

IN WADDESDON HUNDRED

● In [?North] Marston Robert holds 1 hide of the bishop. There is land for 1 plough, and there is [1 plough], [and] meadow for 1 plough. It is and was always worth 20*s*. This land a man of Azur son of Toti held and could sell.

IN YARDLEY HUNDRED

● In Whaddon [in Slapton] Roger holds 3 virgates of the bishop. There is land for half a plough, and there is [half a plough] with 1 villan, [and] meadow for half a plough. It is and was worth 5*s*.; TRE 10*s*. This land a man held; he could sell it.

IN MURSLEY HUNDRED

M ● TURSTIN de Gironde holds of the bishop DUNTON. It is assessed at 10 hides. There is land for 8 ploughs. In demesne are 2 [ploughs], and there could be a third. There 6 bordars have 3 ploughs, and there could be 2 more. There are 4 slaves, [and] meadow for 8 ploughs. All together it is and was always worth 100*s*. This manor Earl Leofwine held.

● In Drayton Parslow Roger holds of the bishop 3 virgates. There is land for 3 ploughs, and there are [3 ploughs] with 2 villans and 3 bordars. [There is] meadow for plough [*sic*]. It is and was worth 25*s*.; TRE 30*s*. This land 2 brothers, men of Alweard Cild, held, and they could sell it.

IN 'STOTFOLD' HUNDRED

● In Westbury [near Brackley] Roger holds of the bishop 2½ hides as 1 manor. There is land for 7 ploughs. In demesne are 2 [ploughs]; and 8 villans with 3 bordars have 5 ploughs. There is 1 slave, meadow for 5 ploughs, [and] woodland for 250 pigs. It is worth £3; when received 50*s*.; TRE 60*s*. This manor Æthelnoth Cild, a thegn of King Edward, held.

● The bishop himself holds SHALSTONE, 5 hides, as 1 manor. There is land for 5 ploughs. In demesne are 2 [ploughs]; and 4 villans with 1 bordar have 2 ploughs, and there could be a third. There are 3 slaves, [and] woodland for 50 pigs. It is worth 30*s*.; when received 20*s*.; TRE £4. This manor 2 thegns held as 2 manors, Godric 3 hides and Wiglaf 2 hides, and they could sell to whom they wished.

● Robert d'Oilly and Roger d'Ivry hold of the bishop STOWE. It is assessed at 5 hides. There is land for 5 ploughs. In demesne is 1 [plough], and there could be 2 more. There 3 bordars have half a plough, and there could be 1½ [ploughs more]. [There is] meadow for 6 ploughs, [and] woodland for 50 pigs. It is worth 40*s*.; [it was] waste when received; TRE [it was worth] 60*s*. This manor Thorgisl, a man of Baldwin son of Herluin, held and could sell.

● Turstin holds of the bishop Foscote. It is assessed at 6 hides. There is land for 4 ploughs. In demesne are 2 [ploughs]; and 1 villan with 2 bordars have 2 ploughs. There is 1 slave, and meadow for 4 ploughs, [and] woodland for 30 pigs. It is and always was worth £3. This manor Leithr, a thegn of King Edward, held and could sell.

● Gilbert Maminot holds of the bishop LECKHAMPSTEAD. It is assessed at 18 [hides]. There is land for 12 ploughs. In demesne are 3 [ploughs], and there could be a fourth. There 18 villans with 6 bordars have 4 ploughs, and there could be another 4. There are 2 slaves, meadow for 12 ploughs, [and] woodland for 400 pigs. In all it is and was worth £6; TRE £8. This manor Earl Leofwine held.

IN 'ROWLEY' HUNDRED

● Ernulf de Hesdin holds of the bishop in Lenborough 7 hides as 1 manor. There is land for 5 ploughs. In demesne are 2 [ploughs]; and 1 villan with 6 bordars have 1 plough, and there could be 2 more. There are 3 slaves, [and] meadow for 5 ploughs. From woodland, 4*s*. yearly. It is and was worth 60*s*.; TRE £4. This manor Wiglaf, a man of Earl Leofwine, held and could sell.

● Ansgot de Rots holds of the bishop Preston Bissett. It is assessed at 15 hides. There is land for 8 ploughs. In demesne are 3 [ploughs]; and 11 villans with 7 bordars have 5 ploughs. There are 6 slaves, and 1 mill rendering 32*d*., meadow for 8 ploughs, [and] woodland for 200 pigs. It is worth 100*s*.; when received £4; TRE as much. This manor Wiglaf, a man of Earl Leofwine, held and could sell.

• Robert of Thame holds of the bishop CHETWODE. It is assessed at 10 hides. There is land for 5 ploughs. In demesne are 2 [ploughs]; and 7 villans with 2 bordars have 2½ ploughs, and there could be half [a plough more]. There are 6 slaves, and 1 mill rendering 30*d.*, meadow for 5 ploughs, [and] woodland for 100 pigs. It is worth 60*s.*; when received 40*s.*; TRE 60*s.* This manor Æthelnoth the Kentishman, a thegn of King Edward, held and could sell.

• Ernulf de Hesdin holds of the bishop Barton Hartshorn. It is assessed at 10 hides. There is land for 5 ploughs. In demesne [are] 2 ploughs. There 3 bordars have 1 plough, and there could be 2 ploughs [more]. There are 4 slaves, [and] meadow for 3 ploughs. From pasture, 30*s.* [There is] woodland for 100 pigs. In all it is worth £14; when received 40*s.*; TRE 60*s.* This manor Wiglaf, a thegn of Earl Leofwine, held and could sell.

• Ilbert de Lacy holds of the bishop TINGEWICK. It is assessed at 10 hides. There is land for 8 ploughs. In demesne are 3 [ploughs]; and 3 villans with 2 bordars have 4 ploughs, and there could be a fifth. There are 10 slaves, and 1 mill rendering 4*s.*, and from other renders of the vill, 20*s.* [There is] meadow for 8 ploughs, [and] woodland for 800 pigs. All together it is worth £10; when received £6; TRE £10. This manor Æthelnoth, a thegn of King Edward, held and could sell.

IN 'MOW' HUNDRED

• The Bishop of Bayeux himself holds 3 hides and 3 virgates. There is land for 3 ploughs. In demesne [are] 2 hides, and there is half a plough, and there could be 1½ ploughs [more]. There 2 villans with 1 bordar have half a plough. There are 2 slaves, [and] meadow for 2 ploughs. It is worth 20*s.*; when received 13*s.* 4*d.*; TRE 40*s.*

• Robert of Romney holds of the bishop in Addington 6 hides. There is land for 6 ploughs. In demesne are 2 [ploughs]; and 8 villans with 2 bordars have 3 ploughs, and there could be a fourth. There are 4 slaves, [and] meadow for 6 ploughs. It is and was worth 60*s.*; TRE 100*s.* This manor Godwine, a man of Earl Leofwine, held and could sell.

IN BUNSTY HUNDRED

• In Lathbury the Bishop of Lisieux holds of the Bishop of Bayeux 1 hide, less 5 feet. There is land for 1 plough, and there is [1 plough] with 3 villans, [and] meadow for 1 plough. It is and was worth 10*s.*; TRE 20*s.* This land Sigeric, a man of Earl Leofwine, held and could sell.

• GAYHURST the Bishop of Lisieux holds of the Bishop of Bayeux, and Robert de Noyers [holds] of him. It is assessed at 5 hides. There is land for 4 ploughs. In demesne are 2 ploughs; and 10 villans have 2 ploughs. There are 2 slaves, and 1 mill rendering 13*s.* 4*d.*, meadow for 4 ploughs, [and] woodland for 80 pigs. All together it is and was worth 100*s.*; TRE £8. This manor Sigeric, a man of Earl Leofwine, held and could sell.

• In [Great or Little] Brickhill Turstin holds of the bishop 1 hide. There is land for 1 plough, but there is no plough, only 3 villans with 2 bordars. It is and was worth 14*s.*; TRE 20*s.* This manor Alwine, a man of Æstan, held. He could not give nor sell it away from [Great or Little] Brickhill, Æstan's manor.

## V. THE LAND OF THE BISHOP OF COUTANCES

IN IXHILL HUNDRED

• The Bishop of Coutances holds WORMINGHALL, and Robert holds of him. It has always been assessed at 5 hides. There is land for 5 ploughs. In demesne are 2 [ploughs]; and 16 villans with 6 bordars have 3 ploughs. There are 4 slaves, meadow for 2 ploughs, [and] woodland for 200 pigs. It is and was worth £6; TRE £7. This manor Eadgifu, wife of Wulfweard, held under Queen Edith and could sell.

IN ASHENDON HUNDRED

• The bishop himself holds LUDGERSHALL. It is assessed at 9 hides. There is land for 8 ploughs. In demesne [are] 4 hides, and there are 2 ploughs, and there could be a third. There 13 villans with 4 bordars have 5 ploughs. There are 5 slaves, meadow for 8 ploughs, [and] woodland for 40 pigs. In all it is and was worth 100*s.*; TRE £6. This manor Eadgifu held of Queen Edith and could sell.

• Two knights hold OVING of the bishop. It is assessed at 10 hides. There is land for 9 ploughs. In demesne are 4 [ploughs], and there could be a fifth. There 18 villans have 3 ploughs, and there could be a fourth. There are 8 bordars, meadow for 4 ploughs, [and] woodland for 200 pigs. In all it is worth £10; when received 100*s.*; TRE £7. This manor Edwin, a thegn of King Edward, held and could sell.

IN WADDESDON HUNDRED

• In [? North] Marston Ranulph holds under the bishop 1 virgate. There is land for half a plough, and there are 2 oxen. It is and always was worth 40*d.* This land Leofric, a man of Edwin, held and could sell.

IN MURSLEY HUNDRED

• In Stewkley William holds 3½ hides as 1 manor. There is land for 9 ploughs. In demesne are 2 ploughs. There 10 villans with 10 bordars have 6½ ploughs, and there could be half [a plough] more. There are 5 slaves, [and] meadow for 8 ploughs. It is and was always worth £4. This manor Wulfweard Cild, a thegn of King Edward, held.

IN 'SECKLEY' HUNDRED

• The bishop himself holds SIMPSON as 8 hides and 3 virgates, as 1 manor, of William Bonvalet in pledge. There is land for 8 ploughs. In demesne are 3 hides, and there are 3 ploughs. There 13 villans with 2 bordars have 5 ploughs. There are 6 slaves, and 1 mill rendering 10*s.*, [and] meadow for 8 ploughs. In all it is worth £6; when received 20*s.*; TRE £8. This manor Queen Edith held and could sell.

• The bishop himself holds EATON LEYS. It is assessed at 10 hides. There is land for 18 ploughs. In demesne [are] 4 ploughs. There 35 villans with 6 bordars have 14 ploughs. There are 12 slaves, and 1 mill rendering 20*s.*, [and] meadow for 12 ploughs. In all it is worth £12; when received £8; TRE £10. Eadgifu held this manor and could sell it to whom she wished.

IN BUNSTY HUNDRED

• LITTLE LINFORD Eadgifu holds of the bishop. It is assessed at 4 hides. There is land for 4 ploughs. In demesne are 2 [ploughs]; and 6 villans have 2 ploughs, and [there is] 1 mill rendering 8*s.* 8*d.*, meadow for 4 ploughs, [and] woodland for 40 pigs. It is and was worth 40*s.*; TRE 60*s.* This manor the same Eadgifu held TRE.

• In Lathbury William holds of the bishop 5 hides as 1 manor. There is land for 4 ploughs. In demesne are 2 [ploughs]; and 6 villans with 6 bordars have 2 ploughs. There are 3 slaves, and meadow for 4 ploughs, [and] woodland for 100 pigs. It is worth £4; when received 40*s.*; TRE 60*s.* This manor Edwin son of Burgræd, a thegn of King Edward, held.

• In Tyringham Ansketil holds of the bishop 2½ hides and 3 parts of 1 virgate as 1 manor. There is land for 4 ploughs. In demesne are 3 [ploughs]; and 3 villans with 6 bordars have 1 plough. There are 4 slaves.

All together it is worth 50*s*.; when received 20*s*.; TRE 60*s*. This land is in exchange for [?]Bleadon [Som.]. This manor 2 thegns held. One, a man of Earl Waltheof, had 2 hides and half a virgate as 1 manor, and the other held 3 parts of 1 virgate, and they could sell.

● In Stoke Goldington a certain Englishman holds of the bishop 1 hide and 1 virgate. There is land for 1 plough, and there is [1 plough] with 4 bordars. [There is] meadow for 1 plough, [and] woodland for 50 pigs. It is worth 20*s*.; when received 10*s*.; TRE 20*s*. This land 2 thegns held as 2 manors. Each held 2½ virgates and they could sell.

M ● In WESTON UNDERWOOD the bishop holds 7½ hides. There is land for 7 ploughs. In demesne is 1 hide, and 1 plough; and 4 villans with 3 bordars have 6 ploughs, and with them are 7 sokemen and a certain Frenchman. There are 3 slaves, meadow for 7 ploughs, [and] woodland for 200 pigs. It is and was worth 100*s*.; TRE £6. This manor 10 thegns, men of Burgræd, held and could sell, and in the same place was 1 man of Alric [who] had 3 virgates and could sell them.

M ● The bishop himself holds OLNEY. It is assessed at 10 hides. There is land for 10 ploughs. In demesne [are] 3 hides, and there are 3 ploughs. There 24 villans with 5 bordars have 7 ploughs. There are 5 slaves, and 1 mill rendering 40*s*. and 200 eels, meadow for 10 ploughs, [and] woodland for 400 pigs. All together it is worth £12; when received £7; TRE £12. This manor Burgræd held, and there 1 sokeman, his man, had 1½ virgates and could sell them.

M ● In Lavendon the bishop holds 2 hides as 1 manor. There is land for 4 ploughs. In demesne [is] 1 hide, and there are 2 ploughs; and 4 villans with 3 bordars have 2 ploughs. There are 3 slaves, meadow for 1 plough, [and] woodland for 100 pigs. It is worth 40*s*.; when received 20*s*.; TRE 60*s*. This manor a man of Burgræd held and could sell.

● In the same vill William holds of the bishop 4 hides and 2 parts of 1 virgate as 1 manor. There is land for 4 ploughs. In demesne [are] 2 ploughs; and 7 villans with 6 bordars have 2 ploughs. There are 3 slaves, and 1½ mills rendering 27*s*. and 250 eels, meadow for 4 ploughs, [and] woodland for 60 pigs. It is worth 60*s*.; when received 20*s*.; TRE £4. This manor 8 thegns held, and 1 of these, Alli, a man of King Edward, was lord of the others. All could sell their land.

● In the same vill Ansketil holds 1½ hides and 2 parts of 1 virgate of the bishop. There is land for 1½ ploughs, and there are [1½ ploughs]. [There is] meadow for the like number, [and] woodland for 12 pigs. It is worth 20*s*.; when received 5*s*.; TRE 20*s*. This land Burgræd and Wulfric, his man, held and could sell.

● In the same vill 3 sokemen hold 1 hide of the bishop, and 1 virgate. There is land for 1 plough. There is half [a plough], and there could be half [a plough more]. There is 1 villan with 2 bordars, meadow for 4 oxen, [and] woodland for 8 pigs. It is and was worth 10*s*.; TRE 20*s*. This land 2 thegns, Burgræd and Wulfric God's man held and could sell.

IN MOULSOE HUNDRED

● In Clifton Reynes Morcar holds 1½ hides of the bishop. There is land for 2 ploughs, and there are [2 ploughs], with 6 villans and 4 bordars. There is 1 slave, meadow for 2 ploughs, and 1 mill. All together it is and was worth 20*s*.; TRE 40*s*. This manor Alli, a thegn of King Edward, held and could sell. This land is in exchange for [?]Bleadon [Som.], as the bishop's men say.

● In the same vill Thorbert holds of the bishop 1 hide. There is land for 1 plough, and there is [1 plough], with 1 villan and 3 bordars. There is 1 slave, meadow for 1 plough, [and] woodland for 20 pigs. It is and was worth 10*s*.; TRE 20*s*. This land Wulfwine God's man held and could sell.

M ● The bishop himself holds SHERINGTON. It is assessed at 10 hides. There is land for 11 ploughs. In demesne [are] 3 hides, and there are 4 ploughs. There 22 villans with 6 bordars have 6 ploughs, and there could be a seventh. There are 8 slaves, and 1 mill rendering 26*s*., meadow for 4 ploughs, [and] woodland for 100 pigs. All together it is worth £10; when received £7; TRE £10. Of this manor Edwin son of Burgræd held 6 hides as 1 manor, and Alwine, his man, 1 hide as 1 manor, and Oswulf, a man of King Edward, had 3 hides as 1 manor. These 2 could give and sell their land.

● In Emberton 2 thegns hold of the bishop 3 hides. There is land for 2 ploughs, and there are [2 ploughs]. [There is] meadow for 2 ploughs, [and] woodland for 50 pigs. There are 2 villans and 2 bordars. It is and was worth 40*s*.; TRE £4. These men held it who now hold it. One of them, Godric, had 1 hide, and the other, Wulfric, 2 hides as 1 manor; and they could sell.

## VI. THE LAND OF THE BISHOP OF LISIEUX

IN COTTESLOE HUNDRED

● The Bishop of Lisieux holds in Crafton 2½ hides. Robert de Noyers holds them of him as 1 manor. There is land for 5 ploughs. In demesne are 2 [ploughs], and there could be a third; and 4 villans with 4 bordars have 2 ploughs. It is and was worth 60*s*.; TRE £4. This manor Blæcmann, a man of Earl Tosti, held. He could not sell without his leave.

IN MOULSOE HUNDRED

● In BOW BRICKHILL Robert holds of the bishop 5 hides. [. . .] There is land for 4 ploughs. In demesne is 1 [plough]; and 7 villans with 3 bordars have 3 ploughs. There is 1 slave, meadow for 4 ploughs, [and] woodland for 150 pigs. It is and was always worth £4. This manor Blæcmann, a man of Earl Tosti, held and could sell.

## VII. THE LAND OF ST PETER OF WESTMINSTER

IN STOKE HUNDRED

M ● THE ABBOT OF ST PETER of Westminster holds DENHAM. It is assessed at 10 hides. There is land for 12 ploughs. In demesne [are] 3 hides, and there are 2 ploughs. There 15 villans with 3 bordars have 7 ploughs, and there could be 3 more. [There is] meadow for 12 ploughs, and 2 mills rendering 7*s*., and 3 fisheries render 3*s*. yearly. [There is] woodland for 300 pigs. In all it is and was worth £7; TRE £10. This manor Wulfstan the thegn gave to ST PETER of Westminster and there it belonged in demesne on the day on which King Edward was alive and dead.

IN BURNHAM HUNDRED

M ● The abbot himself holds in EAST BURNHAM 8 hides. There is land for 6 ploughs. In demesne [are] 4 hides, and there is 1 plough; and 6 villans with 1 bordar have 5 ploughs. [There is] meadow for 6 ploughs, [and] woodland for 100 pigs. In all it is worth 100*s*. and 28*d*.; when received the same; TRE £6. This manor 3 thegns held TRE and could sell, and yet these 3 paid yearly 5 orae as a customary due to the minster of Staines. One of these, Wulfric, had 3 hides and 3 virgates, and another, a man of Eadric of Marlow, had 3 hides and 1 virgate, and the third had 1 hide: he was a man of Sæwulf.

## VIII. THE LAND OF ST ALBAN

IN WADDESDON HUNDRED

● THE ABBOT OF ST ALBAN'S holds GRANBOROUGH. It is assessed at 5 hides. There is land for 9 ploughs. In demesne [are] 2 hides, and there are 2 ploughs; and 7 villans with 4 bordars have 7 ploughs. There is 1 slave, [and] meadow for 2 ploughs. All together it is worth it is worth [*sic*] 100*s*.; when received £4; TRE 100*s*. This manor belonged and belongs to the demesne of the Church of St Alban.

IN COTTESLOE HUNDRED

M ● The abbot himself holds ASTON ABBOTS. It is assessed at 10 hides. There is land for 12 ploughs. In demesne [are] 6 hides, and there are 3 ploughs, and there could be 2 more. There 7 villans with 12 bordars have 6 ploughs. There is 1 slave, [and] meadow for 3 ploughs. It is worth £10; when received £6; TRE £10. This manor belonged and belongs to the demesne of the Church of St Alban.

IN MURSLEY HUNDRED

M • The abbot himself holds WINSLOW. It is assessed at 15 hides. There is land for 19 ploughs. In demesne [are] 5 hides, and there are 3 ploughs, and there could be a fourth. There 17 villans with 5 bordars have 15 ploughs. There are 3 slaves, [and] meadow for 19 ploughs. From woodland, 10*s.* yearly. In all it is and always was worth £11. 13*s.* 4*d.* This manor belonged and belongs to the demesne of the Church of St Alban.

## IX. THE LAND OF THE CHURCH OF BARKING

IN YARDLEY HUNDRED

• THE ABBESS of Barking holds SLAPTON. It is assessed at 6 hides. There is land for 6 ploughs. In demesne [is] 1 hide, and there are 2 ploughs; and 18 villans with 4 bordars have 4 ploughs. There are 4 slaves, [and] meadow for 6 ploughs. In all it is and always was worth £6. This manor belonged and belongs to the Church of Barking.

## X. THE LAND OF THE CANONS OF OXFORD

IN ASHENDON HUNDRED

• THE CANONS of Oxford hold of the king UPPER WINCHENDON. It is assessed at 10 hides. There is land for 9 ploughs. In demesne [are] 1½ hides, and there are 2 ploughs; and 18 villans with 1 bordar have 7 ploughs. There is 1 slave, [and] meadow for 2 ploughs. In all it is and was worth £6; TRE £8. This manor belonged and belongs to the demesne of the Church of the canons of Oxford.

## XI. THE LAND OF REGENBALD THE PRIEST

IN BURNHAM HUNDRED

• REGENBALD the priest holds of the king 1 hide in Boveney which belongs to the Church of Cookham. There is land for 1 plough, and there is [1 plough] with 1 villan. [There is] meadow for 1 plough. It is and always was worth 10*s.* This man held it in alms of King Edward.

## XII. THE LAND OF THE COUNT OF MORTAIN

IN STONE HUNDRED

• THE COUNT OF MORTAIN holds in Little Missenden 1 hide, and Vigot holds of him. There is land for 1½ ploughs. There is 1 plough, and there could be half [a plough more]. There are 4 bordars, meadow for 1 plough, [and] woodland for 100 pigs. It is and was worth 100*s.*; TRE 40*s.* This land Alwine, a man of Sigeræd son of Sibbi, held and could sell.

IN RISBOROUGH HUNDRED

• In Horsenden Ralph holds of the count 6 hides and 3 virgates. There is land for 4 ploughs. In demesne is 1 [plough]; and 7 villans with 1 bordar have 3 ploughs. There are 2 slaves, and 1 mill rendering nothing, [and] meadow for 1 plough. It is and was worth 50*s.*; TRE 100*s.* This manor 3 sokemen held; 2 of these, men of Earl Harold, had 2 hides, and the third, a man of Ingeld, had 4 hides and 3 virgates. All, however, could sell.

M • The count HIMSELF holds BLEDLOW. It is assessed at 30 hides. There is land for 18 ploughs. In demesne [are] 16 hides, and there are 4 ploughs; and 32 villans with 3 bordars have 14 ploughs. There are 8 slaves, and 1 mill rendering 24 summae of malt, woodland for 1,000 pigs and from the rents of the woodland enough iron for the ploughs, [and] meadow for 18 ploughs. In all it is worth £22; when received £12; TRE £20. This manor Eadmær Atule, a thegn of King Edward, held and could sell.

IN BURNHAM HUNDRED

• In Amersham Almær holds of the count half a hide. There is land for 2 ploughs, and there are [2 ploughs] with 1 villan and 1 bordar. [There is] meadow for 2 ploughs, [and] woodland for 20 pigs. It is and always was worth 20*s.* This land Siward, a man of Ealdgifu, held and could sell.

IN DESBOROUGH HUNDRED

• In West Wycombe William holds of the count half a hide. There is land for half a plough, and there is [half a plough] with 1 bordar. It is and always was worth 10*s.* This land 1 sokeman, a man of Archbishop Stigand, held. He could not give nor sell it away from the manor of West Wycombe on the day on which King Edward was alive and dead, as the hundred testifies.

IN IXHILL HUNDRED

• In Ickford the monks of Grestain hold 6 hides of the count. There is land for 6 ploughs. In demesne [are] 3 hides, and there are 2 ploughs, and there could be 2 others. There 3 villans with 10 bordars have 2 ploughs. [There is] meadow for 6 ploughs. It is and was worth £6; TRE £7. This manor Ulf, a man of Earl Harold, held and could sell.

IN COTTESLOE HUNDRED

M • The count himself holds WING. It is assessed at 5 hides. There is land for 40 ploughs. In demesne is 1 hide, and there are 4 ploughs. There 51 villans with 20 bordars have 21 ploughs, and there could be 15 more ploughs. [There is] meadow for 25 ploughs. From the pasture, iron for 5 ploughs. In all it is worth £31; when received the same; TRE £32. This manor Edward Cild, a man of Earl Harold, held and could sell.

• In Crafton the monks of Saint-Nicolas hold 2½ hides of the count. There is land for 5 ploughs. In demesne are 3 [ploughs]; and 8 villans have 2 ploughs. [There is] meadow for 5 ploughs. It is and was worth £4; TRE £6. This manor Edward Cild held and could sell.

• In Wingrave Alan holds 1½ hides of the count. There is land for 1 plough. There is 1 [plough], and there could be half [a plough more]. There is 1 villan and 1 bordar, [and] meadow for 1 plough. It is and always was worth 20*s.* This land Ordmær, a man of Beorhtric, held and could sell.

• In Helsthorpe Ranulph holds of the count 3 virgates. There is land for 1 plough, and there is [1 plough] with 2 bordars. There is 1 slave, and meadow for 1 plough. It is and always was worth 20*s.* This land Leofwine, a man of Godric, held and could sell.

• In Hardwick Almær holds of the count 2 hides. There is land for 2 ploughs, and there are [2 ploughs], with 2 villans and 1 bordar. There is 1 slave, [and] meadow for 2 ploughs. It is and always was worth 40*s.* This land Sæweard, a man of Earl Harold, held and could sell.

• In [Lower or Upper] Burston Alan holds of the count 2 hides. There is land for 2 ploughs. In demesne is 1 [plough]; and 3 villans with 1 bordar have 1 plough. [There is] meadow for 2 ploughs. It is worth 30*s.*; when received 10*s.*; TRE 40*s.* This land 3 thegns held. V [*sic*] Of these one [was] a man of Earl Leofwine, another a man of Godwine Cild, Abbot of Westminster, the third a man of Alfred of Wing; and all could sell their land. ☒

• In the same vill Almær holds 1 virgate of the count, and there are 2 villans. It is and was worth 5*s.* This land Siward, a man of Earl Harold, held and could sell.

IN YARDLEY HUNDRED

• In Drayton Beauchamp William fitzNigel holds 1½ hides. There is land for 1 plough. [There is] meadow for 1 plough, [and] woodland for 25 pigs. It is and always was worth 20*s.* This land a widow held of Beorhtric and could sell.

• In the same vill Leofsige holds of the count 1½ hides and 2 parts of 1 virgate. There is land for 1 plough. There are 2 villans and 2 slaves, meadow for 1 plough, [and] woodland for 25 pigs. It is and always was worth 20*s.* This land Wicga, a man of King Edward, held and could sell.

• In Pitstone Ralph holds of the count 3 hides and 1 virgate as 1 manor. There is land for 1 plough, and there is [1 plough] with 1 bordar. [There is] woodland for 30 pigs. It is worth 20*s.*; when received 5*s.*; TRE 25*s.* This land Ælfgeat of Aylesbury held and could sell.

• In the same vill Bernard holds of the count 3 hides and 1 virgate as 1 manor. There is land for 1 plough. There is half [a plough], and there could be half [a plough more]. There are 2 bordars, [and] woodland for 30 pigs. It is and always was worth 20*s.* This land 2 men of the Abbot of St Alban's held and could sell.

• In the same vill Fulcold holds of the count 1 hide and 1 virgate. There is land for 4 oxen, and there are [4 oxen]. [There is] woodland for 10 pigs. It is and always was worth 10*s.* This land Glædwine, a man of the Abbot of St Alban's, held and could sell.

From the manor of Pitstone, Turgis the count's man, took away 6 hides which the count himself holds unjustly in his demesne.

• In Ivinghoe Aston Ralph holds of the count 3 virgates. There is land for half a plough, and there is [half a plough] with 1 villan. It is and was worth 5*s.*; TRE 10*s.* This land Godwine, a priest of Archbishop Stigand, held and could sell.

• In Cheddington Ralph holds of the count 1 hide and 1 virgate. There is land for 1 plough, and there is [1 plough] with 1 bordar. It is and always was worth 10*s.* This land 3 men of Archbishop Stigand held and could sell.

• In the same vill Ranulph holds of the count half a hide. There is land for half a plough, and there is [half a plough] with 1 villan. It is and always was worth 10*s.* This land Lyfing, a man of the Abbot of St Alban's, held and could sell.

• In Horton [in Ivinghoe] Ælfstan holds of the count 1 virgate. There is land for 2 oxen. It is and was worth 2*s.*; TRE 3*s.* This land Brunmann, a man of Archbishop Stigand, held and could sell.

In Mursley Hundred

• In Swanbourne Ralph and Almær hold 5 hides. There is land for 5 ploughs. There is 1 [plough], and there could be 4 [more]. There are 2 villans, [and] meadow for 5 ploughs. This land is worth 40*s.*; when received £6; TRE 100*s.* Of this manor Beorhtwine, a thegn of King Edward, held $4\frac{1}{2}$ hides, and Almær, a man of Earl Harold, $1\frac{1}{2}$ hides, and they could sell.

• In Salden Ralph holds of the count 3 hides and half a virgate as 1 manor. There is land for 3 ploughs, and there are [3 ploughs], with 3 villans and 2 bordars. [There is] meadow for 3 ploughs. It is and was worth 30*s.*; TRE 40*s.* This manor 4 thegns held. Of these one [was] a man of Alwine, and another a man of Alwine of Newham, and the third a man of Alweard, and the fourth a man of Azur. All these could sell.

• In Mursley Alvred holds of the count 1 hide. There is land for half a plough. It is and was worth 7*s.*; TRE 10*s.* This land Edwin, a man of Azur, held and could sell.

In 'Stotfold' Hundred

• In Biddlesden the same count holds 3 virgates. There is land for 1 plough, but it has been laid waste. This land Alric, a man of Alwine son of Goding, held and could sell.

In 'Rowley' Hundred

• In Hillesden Ranulph holds of the count 1 hide. There is land for 1 plough, and there is [1 plough] with 3 bordars. [There is] meadow for 1 plough, [and] woodland for 10 pigs. It is worth 30*s.*; when received 12*s.*; TRE 30*s.* This land Leofwine, a man of Ælfric son of Goding, held and could sell.

In 'Mow' Hundred

• In Marsh Gibbon the monks of Grestain hold 11 hides of the count. There is land for 13 ploughs. In demesne [are] 4 hides, and there are 3 ploughs. There 17 villans with 3 bordars have 10 ploughs. There are 8 slaves. All together it is and always was worth £8. This manor Ulf son of Burgræd held and could sell, and a man of Bondi the staller had there half a hide and could sell it.

In 'Seckley' Hundred

• In Caldecote Alvred holds 4 hides and 1 virgate of the count as 1 manor. There is land for 4 ploughs. In demesne are $1\frac{1}{2}$ [ploughs], and there could be half [a plough] more. There are 2 vavasours paying 32*s.* 6*d.*, and 1 villan and 5 bordars with 2 ploughs. There is 1 slave, and a mill rendering 5 orae and 4*d.*, meadow for 2 ploughs, [and] woodland for 24 pigs and 28*d.* as a customary due. In all it is and always was worth £4. This manor 4 thegns held TRE and they could sell and give it to whom they wished.

• In Woughton on the Green Ralph holds of the count 4 hides as 1 manor. There is land for 4 ploughs. In demesne is 1 [plough], and there could be another. There 3 villans with 6 bordars have 1 plough, and there could be another. There are 2 slaves, [and] meadow for 4 ploughs. All together it is worth £3; when received £4; TRE £3. This manor 8 thegns held. Of these, 4, the men of Ælfric Varus, had half a hide, and 1, a man of Ælfric son of Goding, 1 hide and half a virgate, and 1, a man of Wulfweard son of Eadgifu, 1 hide and 1 virgate, and 1, a man of Leofwine son of Æstan, half a hide, and 1, a man of Baldwin, half a hide, and 1, a man of Morcar, half a hide, and 1, a man of Sæweald, had 1 virgate. All these could sell.

• In Loughton Walter holds of the count half a hide. There is land for half a plough, and there is [half a plough] with 1 villan. This land is worth 20*s.*; when received 5*s.*; TRE 20*s.* This land Almær, a man of Ælfric son of Goding, held and could sell.

• In Great Linford Ranulph holds of the count 2 hides. There is land for 2 ploughs, and there are [2 ploughs], with 4 villans and 3 bordars and 1 slave. [There is] meadow for 2 ploughs. It is and was always worth 40*s.* This land 2 men of Ælfric son of Goding held and could sell.

In Bunsty Hundred

• In Weston Underwood Ivo holds of the count 1 hide and 2 parts of 1 virgate. There is land for 1 plough. There are 2 oxen with 2 bordars, meadow for 1 plough, [and] woodland for 20 pigs. It is and always was worth 20*s.* This land 3 thegns held. Of these, 2, men of Burgræd, had 3 virgates and 2 parts of 1 virgate, the third, a man of Ælfric son of Goding, 1 virgate, and they could sell.

• In Lavendon Humphrey holds of the count $2\frac{1}{2}$ hides as 1 manor. There is land for $2\frac{1}{2}$ ploughs. In demesne [are] $1\frac{1}{2}$ hides, and there is 1 plough; and 3 villans with 5 bordars have $1\frac{1}{2}$ ploughs. There are 2 slaves, and 1 mill rendering 10*s.* and 50 eels, meadow for 2 ploughs, [and] woodland for 40 pigs. It is worth 40*s.*; when received 20*s.*; TRE £4. This manor a man of Ælfric son of Goding held and could sell.

In Moulsoe Hundred

• In Wavendon Ralph holds of the count 2 hides as 1 manor. There is land for $2\frac{1}{2}$ ploughs. In demesne is 1 [plough]; and 2 villans with 3 bordars have 1 plough, and there could be half [a plough more]. There is 1 slave, and meadow for 2 ploughs, [and] woodland for 15 pigs. It is worth 20*s.*; when received 10*s.*; TRE 40*s.* This manor Goldnir, a housecarl of King Edward, held and could sell.

• In the same [vill], Walter holds of the count 2 hides as 1 manor. There is land for $2\frac{1}{2}$ ploughs. In demesne is 1 [plough]; and 2 villans with 3 bordars have 1 plough, and there could be half [a plough] more. There are 2 slaves, meadow for 2 ploughs, [and] woodland for 15 pigs. It is worth 20*s.*; when received 10*s.*; TRE 40*s.* This manor Beorhtwine, a man of Earl Harold, held and could sell.

• In the same vill Humphrey holds of the count 3 virgates. There is land for 1 plough. There is 1 bordar, [and] meadow for 1 plough. It is and was worth 5*s.*; TRE 10*s.* This land Centisc, a man of Leofnoth son of Osmund, held and could sell.

## XIII. THE LAND OF EARL HUGH

In Cottesloe Hundred

M • Earl Hugh holds Mentmore. Robert holds it of him. It is assessed at 18 hides. There is land for 10 ploughs. In demesne [are] 4 ploughs; and 18 villans have 6 ploughs. There are 3 slaves, [and] meadow for 4 ploughs. In all it is worth £12; when received £10; TRE £14. This manor Eadgifu the Fair held.

In 'Seckley' Hundred

• Hugh holds of the earl Shenley Church End. It is assessed at 2 hides. There is land for 10 ploughs. In demesne are 3 ploughs; and 5 villans with 6 slaves have 5 ploughs, and there could be 2 more. [There is] meadow for 5 ploughs, [and] woodland for 50 pigs. It is and was worth 100*s.*; TRE £6. This manor Burgheard, a housecarl of King Edward, held and could sell.

☒

• In Shenley Church End Hugh holds of Earl Hugh 5 hides as 1 manor. There is land for 5 ploughs, and there are 4 ploughs, and there could be a fifth. There are 8 villans, meadow for 5 ploughs, [and] woodland for 50 pigs. In all it is and was worth £3; TRE £4. This manor Burgheard, a thegn of King Edward, held.

IN MOULSOE HUNDRED

• William holds [Great or Little] BRICKHILL. It is assessed at 9 hides. There is land for 9 ploughs. In demesne [are] 4 ploughs; and 16 villans with 6 bordars have 6 s[*sic*] ploughs. There are 6 slaves, and 2 mills rendering 30*s*., meadow for 10 ploughs, [and] woodland for 100 pigs. All together it is worth £9; when received £7; TRE £10. This manor Earl Tosti held.

## XIIII. THE LAND OF WALTER GIFFARD

IN STONE HUNDRED

• WALTER Giffard holds in Lower Hartwell 2 hides, and Hugh de Bolbec [holds] of him. There is land for 2 ploughs, and there are [2 ploughs], with 4 villans and 3 bordars. There are 4 slaves. It is and always was worth 30*s*. This land 2 men of Sigeræd held and could sell, and they now hold it.

M • Hugh himself holds of Walter GREAT KIMBLE. It is assessed at 20 hides. There is land for 11½ ploughs. In demesne are 2 [ploughs], and there could be a third. There 22 villans with 8 bordars have 8½ ploughs. There are 6 slaves, meadow for 11 ploughs, [and] wood for fences. In all it is and always was worth £10. This manor Sigeræd, a thegn of King Edward, held and could sell.

M • Turstin fitzRolf holds of Walter GREAT MISSENDEN. It is assessed at 10 hides. There is land for 8 ploughs. In demesne are 2 [ploughs]; and 9 villans with 1 bordar have 6 ploughs. There are 2 slaves, meadow for 2 ploughs, woodland for 500 pigs, and from the rents of the woodland, 4 orae yearly. In all it is and was worth £4; TRE £7. This manor Sigeræd son of Ælfgifu, a thegn of King Edward, held and could sell.

IN DESBOROUGH HUNDRED

M • Herbrand holds of Walter FAWLEY. It is assessed at 10 hides. There is land for 14 ploughs. In demesne are 2 ploughs; and 13 villans with 1 bordar have 12 ploughs. There are 5 slaves, meadow for 2 ploughs, [and] woodland for 100 pigs. All together it is worth £6; when received 100*s*.; TRE £6. This manor Earl Tosti held.

IN IXHILL HUNDRED

M • Walter himself holds LONG CRENDON. It is assessed at 20 hides. There is land for 25 ploughs. In demesne [are] 10 hides, and there are 5 ploughs; and 52 villans with 10 bordars have 20 ploughs. There are 10 slaves, and 1 mill rendering 18*s*., meadow for 10 ploughs, woodland for 100 pigs, and there is a park for wild beasts. In all it is worth £20; when received and TRE £15. This manor Særic son of Ælfgifu held.

M • Hugh holds of Walter ADDINGROVE. It is assessed at 3½ hides. There is land for 4 ploughs. In demesne are 2 [ploughs]; and 2 villans with 7 bordars have 3 ploughs. There is 1 slave, [and] meadow for 1 plough. All together it is worth 60*s*.; when received 40*s*.; TRE £4. This manor Wulfweard, a man of Queen Edith, held and could sell.

M • Walter himself holds CHILTON. It is assessed at 10 hides. There is land for 10 ploughs. In demesne [are] 4 hides, and there are 4 ploughs; and 10 villans with 4 bordars have 6 ploughs. There are 3 slaves, meadow for 3 ploughs, [and] woodland for 100 pigs. All together it is worth £7; when received £8; and as much TRE. This manor, Ælfric son of Goding, a thegn of King Edward, held.

M • Roger holds of Walter EASINGTON. It is assessed at 5 hides. There is land for 4 ploughs. In demesne are 2 [ploughs]; and 5 villans have 2 [ploughs]. There are 2 slaves, and meadow for 2 ploughs. It is and always was worth 60*s*. This manor Ælfric son of Goding held and could sell.

M • Walter himself holds DORTON. It is assessed at 5 hides. There is land for 7 ploughs. In demesne [are] 2½ hides, and there are 3 ploughs. There 12 villans with 6 bordars have 4 ploughs. There are 3 slaves, meadow for 3 ploughs, [and] woodland for 100 pigs. In all it is and always was worth 100*s*. This manor Ælfric, a thegn of King Edward, held and could sell.

IN ASHENDON HUNDRED

M • Walter himself holds [Lower or Upper] POLLICOTT. It is assessed at 10 hides. There is land for 8 ploughs. 2 knights hold it of Walter. In demesne [are] 4 ploughs; and 13 villans with 1 bordar have 4 ploughs. There are 4 slaves, [and] meadow for 8 ploughs. In all it is and was worth £6; TRE £7. Ælfric son of Goding held 5 hides of this manor, and 3 brothers held 5 hides, and they could sell to whom they wished.

M • In ASHENDON Richard holds of Walter 8 hides. There is land for 6 ploughs. In demesne are 2 [ploughs]; and 4 villans with 4 bordars have 4 ploughs. There are 2 slaves, and meadow for 6 ploughs. In all it is worth £3; when received £4; TRE 100*s*. This manor 3 brothers held and could sell to whom they wished.

M • In CHEARSLEY Earnwulf and Geoffrey hold of Walter 8½ hides. There is land for 6 ploughs. In demesne [are] 4 ploughs; and 6 villans with 2 bordars have 2 ploughs. There are 4 slaves, [and] meadow for 6 ploughs. It is and was worth £6; TRE £7. This manor 6 thegns held and could sell to whom they wished.

M • Walter himself holds LOWER WINCHENDON. It is assessed at 10 hides. There is land for 11 ploughs. In demesne [are] 3 hides, and there are 3 ploughs; and 23 villans with 8 bordars have 8 ploughs. There is 1 slave, and meadow for 7 ploughs, and 1 mill rendering 20*s*. and 80 eels. In all it is and always was worth £12. This manor Edith held of Queen Edith.

M • Ralph holds of Walter WOTTON UNDERWOOD. It is assessed at 10 hides. There is land for 10 ploughs. In demesne are 3 [ploughs]; and 10 villans with 13 bordars have 7 ploughs. There are 5 slaves, and meadow for 5 ploughs, [and] woodland for 200 pigs. All together it is and was worth £7; TRE £8. This manor Eadgifu, wife of Wulfweard, held and could sell.

IN COTTESLOE HUNDRED

• Two Englishmen hold of Walter in this hundred 1 virgate. There is land for half a plough, [and] meadow for half a plough. It is and always was worth 3½*s*. These men who hold it held it TRE and could sell.

M • Hugh de Bolbec holds of Walter WHITCHURCH. It is assessed at 8 hides. There is land for 12 ploughs. In demesne [are] 3 ploughs, and there could be 2 [more]. There 14 villans with 2 bordars have 7 ploughs. There are 8 slaves, [and] meadow for 6 ploughs. All together it is and was worth £8; TRE £10. This manor 2 brothers, thegns of King Edward, held as 2 manors and could sell. ☒

• In Littlecote Robert holds of Walter 2½ hides as 1 manor. There is land for 3 ploughs. In demesne [are] 2 ploughs; and 2 villans with 3 bordars have 1 plough. There are 3 slaves, and meadow for 1 plough. This land is and was worth 40*s*.; TRE 60*s*. This manor Wicga, a thegn of King Edward, held and could sell.

• In [Lower or Upper] Burston Turstin holds of Walter 1 hide. There is land for 1 plough, and there is [1 plough], with 2 bordars and 1 slave. [There is] meadow for 1 plough. It is worth 20*s*.; when received 10*s*.; TRE 20*s*. This land Alwynn, a certain woman, held under Siward, and she could sell it.

IN YARDLEY HUNDRED

• Ralph holds of Walter in Pitstone 5½ hides as 1 manor. There is land for 2 ploughs, and there are [2 ploughs], with 3 villans and 3 bordars and 1 slave. [There is] woodland for 40 pigs. It is worth 40*s*.; when received 20*s*.; TRE 40*s*. This manor Thorulf, a man of Earl Leofwine, held and could sell.

IN MURSLEY HUNDRED

• William holds of Walter in SWANBOURNE 7 hides and 3 virgates as 1 manor. There is land for 7 ploughs. In demesne are 2 [ploughs]; and 7 villans with 5 bordars have 4 ploughs. There are 2 slaves, [and] meadow for 6 ploughs. All together it is and was worth £4; TRE 100*s*.

This manor 2 thegns held—Alweard 5 hides all but 1 virgate, and Alwig his man, 2 hides and 3 virgates. They had them as 2 manors and could sell them.

M ● Walter himself holds [Great and Little] HORWOOD. It is assessed at 10 hides. There is land for 9 ploughs. In demesne [are] 5 hides, and there are 4 ploughs; and 8 villans with 10 bordars have 5 ploughs. There are 2 slaves, and meadow for 9 ploughs, [and] woodland for 100 pigs. In all it is and always was worth £7. This manor Alweard Cild, a thegn of King Edward, held.

● Walter de Bec holds of Walter Singleborough. It is assessed at 6 hides. There is land for 6 ploughs. In demesne are 3 ploughs; and 4 villans with 4 bordars have 3 ploughs. There are 4 slaves, and meadow for 3 ploughs, [and] woodland for 40 pigs. In all it is and always was worth £4. This manor Edward Cild, a thegn of King Edward, held.

M ● Walter himself holds WHADDON [near Bletchley]. It is assessed at 10 hides. There is land for 10 ploughs. In demesne [are] 5 hides, and there are 5 ploughs; and 14 villans with 9 bordars have 5 ploughs. There are 10 slaves, meadow for 10 ploughs, [and] woodland for 100 pigs. In all it is and always was worth £8. This manor Edward Cild, a thegn of King Edward, held.

M ● In MURSLEY William holds of Walter 5 hides as 1 manor. There is land for 4 ploughs. In demesne are 2 [ploughs]; and 2 villans with 5 bordars have 2 ploughs. There are 2 slaves, [and] meadow for 2 ploughs. It is and always was worth £3.

● In LAMPORT Berner holds of Walter 3½ hides as 1 manor. There is land for 4 ploughs. In demesne is 1 [plough], and there could be another. There 2 villans with 2 bordars have 2 ploughs. There are 2 slaves, meadow for 2 ploughs, [and] woodland for 50 pigs. It is and always was worth 40*s*. This manor Swein Swart, a man of Earl Edwin, held and could sell.

● Robert holds of Walter AKELEY. It is assessed at 3 hides. There is land for 4 ploughs. In demesne are 4 oxen, and there could be 2 ploughs [more]. There 2 villans with 4 bordars have 2½ ploughs. There are 2 slaves, meadow for 1 plough, [and] woodland for 806 pigs. In all it is and was worth 40*s*.; TRE 60*s*. This manor Ælfric son of Goding held and could sell.

M ● Hugh holds of Walter LILLINGSTONE DAYRELL. It is assessed at 5 hides. There is land for 5 ploughs. In demesne are 1½ [ploughs], and there could be half [a plough more]. There 6 villans with 5 bordars have 2 ploughs, and there could be a third. [There is] meadow for 5 ploughs, [and] woodland for 1,200 pigs. It is worth 60*s*.; when received 40*s*.;TRE 50*s*. This manor Sigeric, a man of Queen Edith, held and could sell.

● In MAIDS MORETON Turstin holds of Walter 2 hides. There is land for 2 ploughs, and there are 1½ [ploughs], and there could be half [a plough more]. There are 2 villans and 4 bordars, [and] meadow for 2 ploughs. It is worth 30*s*.; when received 10*s*.; TRE 20*s*. This manor Wulfric, a man of Ælfric son of Goding, held and could sell.

● In the same vill the same Turstin holds of Walter 4 hides as 1 manor. There is land for 4 ploughs. In demesne are 2 [ploughs], and there could be another 2. There is 1 villan with 3 bordars, [and] meadow for 4 ploughs. It is worth £4; when received 20*s*.; TRE 60*s*. Of this manor Ælfric son of Goding held 2 hides as 1 manor, and Eadric, a man of Esger the staller, 1½ hides as 1 manor, and Sæweard, a man of Azur son of Toti, held half a hide, and they could give and sell [their land].

● In Leckhampstead Hugh holds of Walter 2 hides. There is land for 1 plough, and there is [1 plough], with 1 villan and 2 bordars and 1 slave. There is 1 mill rendering 20*d*., meadow for 1 plough, [and] woodland for 50 pigs. In all it is worth 30*s*.; when received 20*s*.; TRE 30*s*. This manor Swærting, a man of Esger the staller, held. He could neither sell nor give it but by his leave.

### IN 'ROWLEY' HUNDRED

● In Beachampton Hugh holds of Walter 5 hides as 1 manor. There is land for 5 ploughs. In demesne are 2 [ploughs]; and 5 villans with 9 bordars have 3 ploughs. There is 1 slave, and 1 mill rendering 10*s*., [and] meadow for 2 ploughs. In all it is worth £4; when received 30*s*.; TRE £4. 10*s*. This manor Ælfric, a man and thegn of King Edward, held and could sell.

● The same Hugh holds Bourton of Walter. It is assessed at 1 hide. There is land for 2 ploughs. In demesne is 1 [plough]; and 2 villans with 2 bordars have 1 plough. [There is] meadow for 2 ploughs. It is and was worth 30*s*.; TRE 20*s*. This manor Ælfric, a thegn of King Edward, held and could sell.

● In Lenborough Ralph holds of Walter 3 hides as 1 manor. There is land for 2 ploughs. There is 1 [plough], and there could be another. There are 2 bordars, and meadow for 2 ploughs. It is worth 30*s*.; when received 60*s*.; TRE 40*s*. This manor Tovi, a man of Ælfric son of Goding, held and could sell.

● In Hillesden Hugh holds of Walter 18 hides as 1 manor. There is land for 14 ploughs. In demesne are 4 [ploughs]; and 17 villans with 9 bordars have 10 ploughs. There are 7 slaves, and 1 mill rendering 4*s*., meadow for 14 ploughs, [and] woodland for 100 pigs. In all it is worth £6; when received £8; and as much TRE. This manor Ælfric, a thegn of King Edward, held and could sell.

● Ralph holds of Walter EDGCOTT. It is assessed at 5 hides. There is land for 8 ploughs. In demesne are 2 [ploughs]; and 10 villans with 9 bordars have 6 ploughs. There are 2 slaves, meadow for 2 ploughs, [and] woodland for 100 pigs. In all it is and was always worth 100*s*. This manor 4 thegns held. One of these, Alwine, had 2½ hides as 1 manor, and another, Edwin, 1 hide and 1 virgate as 1 manor, and Almær half a hide, and Thorir, a housecarl of King Edward, 3 virgates. All could sell [their land].

● In Woolstone Ralph [. . .] holds of Walter 3½ hides as 1 manor. There is land for 3 ploughs. In demesne are 2 [ploughs]; and 4 villans have 1 plough. [There is] meadow for 2 ploughs, and 1 mill rendering 10*s*. It is worth 40*s*.; when received 20*s*.; TRE 60*s*. This manor Edward, a thegn of King Edward, held and could sell.

● In Woolstone the monks of Saint-Pierre-de-la-Couture hold of Walter 5 hides as 1 manor. There is land for 5 ploughs. In demesne are 2 [ploughs]; and 8 villans with 1 bordar have 3 ploughs. There is 1 mill rendering 6*s*. 4*d*., meadow for 4 ploughs, [and] woodland for 100 pigs. It is and was worth £3; TRE £4. This manor Ælfric son of Goding held and could sell.

M ● Walter himself holds NEWTON LONGVILLE. It is assessed at 10 hides. There is land for 12 ploughs. In demesne [are] 4 hides, and there are 4 ploughs; and 20 villans with 8 bordars have 8 ploughs. There are 11 slaves, and meadow for 6 ploughs. In all it is worth £12; when received £10; and as much TRE. This manor Edward Cild held.

● In Loughton Ivo holds of Walter 4½ hides. There is land for 4½ ploughs. In demesne are 2 [ploughs]; and 5 villans with 2 bordars have 1 plough, and there could be another 1½ [ploughs]. [There is] meadow for 4 ploughs. It is worth 60*s*.; when received 30*s*.; TRE £4. This manor 5 thegns held and could sell.

● In Bradwell Walter Hackett holds of Walter Giffard 1½ hides. There is land for 2 ploughs. In demesne is 1 [plough], and there could be another. There is 1 bordar and 1 slave, [and] meadow for 1 plough. It is worth 20*s.*; when received 10*s.*; TRE 30*s.* This land Ælfgeat, a man of Queen Edith, held and could sell.

M ● In Great Linford Hugh holds of Walter 2 hides and 1½ virgates as 1 manor. There is land for 5 ploughs. In demesne is 1 [plough]; and 16 villans with 2 bordars have 4 ploughs. There are 4 slaves, and meadow for 4 ploughs. It is worth £3; when received 40*s.*; TRE £4. This manor Ælfric son of Goding held and could sell.

In Bunsty Hundred

M ● The same Hugh holds of Walter Ravenstone. It is assessed at 5 hides. There is land for 6 ploughs. In demesne are 2 [ploughs]; and 10 villans with 6 bordars have 4 ploughs. There are 4 slaves, and 1 mill rendering 25*s.*, meadow for 6 ploughs, [and] woodland for 300 pigs. It is and was worth 100*s.*; TRE £6. This manor Leofwine, a thegn of King Edward, held and could sell.

● In Lavendon Ralph holds of Walter 2 hides and 1 virgate and the fourth part of 1 virgate. There is land for 2 ploughs. In demesne is 1 [plough]; and 5 villans with 8 bordars have 1 plough. [There is] meadow for 1 plough, [and] woodland for 30 pigs. It is worth 25*s.*; when received 10*s.*; TRE 40*s.* This land a man of Bishop Wulfwig held and could sell.

In Moulsoe Hundred

M ● In Hardmead Hugh holds of Walter 2½ hides as 1 manor. There is land for 2½ ploughs, and there are [2½ ploughs], with 4 villans and 2 bordars. [There is] meadow for 1 plough, [and] woodland for 50 pigs. It is and always was worth 40*s.* This manor a man of Ælfric son of Goding held and could sell.

M ● Richard holds of Walter Moulsoe. It is assessed at 10 hides. There is land for 7 ploughs. In demesne is 1 [plough]; and 7 villans with 9 bordars have 6 ploughs. There is 1 slave, and meadow for 5 ploughs, [and] woodland for 100 pigs. All together it is worth £6; when received 100*s.*; TRE £8. This manor 8 thegns held and could sell. One of these, Alwine, held 2 hides as 1 manor; and another, Ulf, a man of Esger the staller, 2 hides as 1 manor; and Algar, a man of Edward Cild, 1½ hides as 1 manor; Alsige 1 hide; Thorkil 1 hide; Lodi 1 hide; Oswulf 1 hide; Alric half a hide.

M ● In Broughton [near Moulsoe] Hugh holds of Walter 4 hides as 1 manor. There is land for 5 ploughs. In demesne [is] 1 plough; and 8 villans with 5 bordars have 4 ploughs. There are 2 slaves, and 1 mill in demesne, [and] meadow for 3 ploughs. It is and was worth 60*s.*; TRE £4. This manor Oswig, a man of Ælfric son of Goding, held and could sell.

● In Milton Keynes Hugh holds of Walter half a hide. There is land for 1 plough, but no [plough] is there. [There is] meadow for 1 plough. It is worth 4*s.*; TRE 10*s.* This land Oswig, a man of Ælfric, held and could sell.

M ● In Bow Brickhill Ralph holds of Walter 5 hides as 1 manor. There is land for 5 ploughs. In demesne are 2 [ploughs]; and 8 villans with 2 bordars have 3 ploughs. There are 2 slaves, [and] meadow for 5 ploughs. It is worth 60*s.*; when received 40*s.*; TRE 100*s.* Of this land Godwine, a man of Bishop Wulfwig, held 2 hides as 1 manor; Godbald 1 hide; Ælfric 1 hide; Ordric 1 hide; and they all could sell their land.

M ● In the same vill Robert holds of Walter 4 hides as 1 manor. There is land for 5 ploughs. In demesne are 3 [ploughs]; and 9 villans with 5 bordars have 2 ploughs. There are 3 slaves, and 1 mill rendering 10*s.*, meadow for 5 ploughs, [and] woodland for 100 pigs. It is and always was worth 100*s.* Of this land Godwine, a man of Bishop Wulfwig, held 2 hides as 1 manor, and 5 other thegns held the other land, that is, 2 hides, and they could sell.

## XV. THE LAND OF WILLIAM DE WARENNE

In Aylesbury Hundred

● William de Warenne holds Broughton [in Aylesbury]. It is assessed at 10 hides. There is land for 8 ploughs. In demesne [are] 2 hides, and there are 2 ploughs; and 13 villans with 5 bordars have 6 ploughs. There are 4 slaves, and 1 mill rendering 10*s.*, meadow for 5 ploughs, [and] woodland for 100 pigs. In all it is and was worth £8; TRE £10. This manor Edward, a thegn of King Edward, held and could sell.

In 'Rowley' Hundred

M ● Brian holds of William Caversfield [Oxon.]. It is assessed at 5 hides. There is land for 8 ploughs. In demesne are 3 [ploughs]; and 12 villans with 9 bordars have 5 ploughs. There is a fishpond. In all it is and always was worth 100*s.* This manor Edward, a man of Earl Tosti, held and could sell.

## XVI. THE LAND OF WILLIAM PEVEREL

In Stone Hundred

M ● William Peverel holds Lower Hartwell, 6 hides and 3 virgates. Tehel holds of him. There is land for 8 ploughs. In demesne are 3 [ploughs]; and 16 villans with 4 bordars have 5 ploughs. There are 4 slaves, and meadow for 8 ploughs. In all it is and was worth 100*s.*; TRE £7. This manor Alwine, a thegn of King Edward, held and could sell.

● In Upton [in Dinton] Robert holds of William 3½ hides. There is land for 5 ploughs. In demesne are 2 [ploughs]; and 8 villans with 3 bordars have 3 ploughs. There are 3 slaves, and meadow for 5 ploughs. It is and always was worth 60*s.* This manor Alwine, a man of Queen Edith, held and could sell.

In Ashendon Hundred

M ● Payne holds of William Tetchwick as 2 hides. There is land for 2 ploughs. In demesne is 1 [plough]; and 3 villans have 2 ploughs. There is 1 slave, meadow for 2 ploughs, [and] woodland for 50 pigs. This land is worth 30*s.*; when received 20*s.*; TRE 30*s.* This manor Alwine, a thegn of King Edward, held and could sell.

● In Shipton Lee William holds 1 hide. There is land for half a plough, and there is [half a plough] with 1 villan. It is and was worth 5*s.* This land Alwine, a thegn of King Edward, held.

In Waddesdon Hundred

M ● William himself holds Middle Claydon. It is assessed at 10 hides. There is land for 10 ploughs. In demesne [are] 3 hides, and there are 3 ploughs; and 16 villans with 2 bordars have 5 ploughs, and there could be 2 more. There are 3 slaves, meadow for 4 ploughs, [and] woodland for 150 pigs. In all it is worth £10; when received £12; TRE £10. This manor Alwine, a thegn of King Edward, held.

M ● William himself holds Hogshaw. It is assessed at 5 hides. There is land for 3½ ploughs. In demesne [are] 3 hides, and there are 2 ploughs; and 6 villans with 2 bordars have 1½ ploughs. [There is] meadow for 3 ploughs, [and] woodland for 40 pigs. It is and always was worth 60*s.* This manor Alwine, a thegn of King Edward, held.

M ● Ralph holds in [Botolph or East] Claydon of William 3 hides and 1 virgate as 1 manor. There is land for 3 ploughs. In demesne is 1 [plough]; and 4 villans have another, and there could be a third. [There is] meadow for 1 plough, [and] wood for fences. It is and always was worth 40*s.* This manor Alwine, a thegn of King Edward, held and could sell. Of this land a certain man of his held 1 virgate and could sell it without his leave.

M ● Ambrose holds of William Adstock. It is assessed at 10 hides. There is land for 7 ploughs. In demesne are 3 [ploughs]; and 5 villans with 2 bordars have 3 ploughs, and there could be a fourth. [There is] meadow for 7 ploughs. In all it is and was worth 100*s.*; TRE £8. This manor Gytha, wife of Earl Ralph, held and could sell.

M ● William himself holds Haversham. It is assessed at 10 hides. In Bunsty Hundred
There is land for 10 ploughs. In demesne are hides [*sic*], and there are 1½ ploughs, and there could be another 1½. There 16 villans with 8 bordars have 7 ploughs. There are 5 slaves, and 1 mill rendering 8*s.* and 75 eels, meadow for 9 ploughs, [and] woodland for 300 pigs. It is and was worth £6; TRE £7. This manor Countess Gytha held.

M ● Drogo holds of William Stoke Goldington, 3 hides and 3 virgates, as 1 manor. There is land for 4 ploughs. In demesne are 2 [ploughs]; and 5 villans with 4 bordars have 2 ploughs. There are 2 slaves, meadow for 4 ploughs, [and] woodland for 200 pigs. It is and always was worth £4. This manor Countess Gytha held.

## XVII. THE LAND OF WILLIAM FITZANSCULF

IN STONE HUNDRED

• WILLIAM fitzAnsculf holds in this hundred half a hide, and a certain Englishman [holds] of him. There is land for half a plough, and there is [half a plough], with 1 bordar. It is and always was worth 10*s*. This land Leofwine brother of Alsige held and could sell.

IN AYLESBURY HUNDRED

M • Ralph holds of William in ELLESBOROUGH 13½ hides. There is land for 11 ploughs. In demesne are 2 [ploughs]; and 17 villans with 3 bordars have 9 ploughs. There are 2 slaves, and meadow for 2 ploughs, [and] woodland for 105 pigs. In all it is and was worth £8; TRE £9. This manor Earl Harold held, and this same manor Ansculf de Picquigny exchanged for half of Princes Risborough with Ralph Taillebois, by order of King William.

• In the same vill Otbert holds of William 1½ hides. There is land for 2 ploughs, and there are 2 oxen with 1 villan. It is and was worth 5*s*.; TRE 20*s*. This land Baldwin, a man of Archbishop Stigand, held and could sell.

M • The same Otbert holds of William [Great and Little] HAMPDEN. It is assessed at 3 hides. There is land for 5 ploughs. In demesne are 2 [ploughs]; and 4 villans have 3 ploughs. There are 2 slaves, woodland for 500 pigs, and from the rents of the woodland, iron for 2 ploughs. It is and was worth £4; TRE 100*s*. This manor Baldwin, a man of Archbishop Stigand, held and could sell.

IN STOKE HUNDRED

• Walter holds of William DITTON. It is assessed at 5 hides. There is land for 3 ploughs. In demesne is 1 [plough]; and 4 villans have 2 ploughs. There is 1 slave, and meadow for 3 ploughs, [and] woodland for 16 pigs. It is and was worth 30*s*.; TRE 40*s*. This manor Sigeræd, a man of Earl Harold, held and could sell.

M • The same Walter holds of William STOKE POGES. It is assessed at 10 hides. There is land for 10 ploughs. In demesne are 2 [ploughs]; and 10 villans with 3 bordars have 6 ploughs, and there could be 2 more. There are 4 slaves, and 1 mill rendering 4*s*., [and] woodland for 500 pigs. In all it is worth £5; when received £3; TRE £6. This manor Sigeræd, a man of Earl Harold, held and could sell, and 1 hide of this land a certain sokeman, a man of Tubbi, held and could sell.

IN WADDESDON HUNDRED

M • In NORTH MARSTON Ranulph holds of William 6½ hides as 1 manor. There is land for 6 ploughs. In demesne are 2 [ploughs]; and 8 villans with 3 bordars have 3 ploughs, and there could be a fourth. [There is] meadow for 2 ploughs. All together it is worth 100*s*.; when received 60*s*.; TRE £4. Of this manor Leofric, a man of Earl Edwin, held 5 hides as 1 manor; and another man had 1 hide and 1 virgate of King Edward's soke; and Beorhtwine, a man of Earl Tosti, had 1 virgate. All these could sell.

• In the same vill Bernard holds of William 1 hide. There is land for 1 plough, and there is [1 plough], with 1 bordar. It is and was worth 10*s*.; TRE 20*s*. This land Alwig, a man of Beorhtric, held, and it was of the king's soke, and he could sell it.

• In Hoggeston Payne holds of William 8 hides and 2½ virgates. There is land for 10 ploughs. In demesne are 2 [ploughs]; and 12 villans with 7 bordars have 8 ploughs. There are 5 slaves, [and] meadow for 10 ploughs. All together it is and was worth £7; TRE 100*s*. Of this manor Almær, a man of Bondi the staller, held 7 hides as 1 manor; and a man of the Abbess of Barking 1 hide, and a man of Eadgifu the Fair held 2½ virgates; and all these could sell [their land].

IN COTTESLOE HUNDRED

• In Soulbury Payne holds of William 5½ hides and the third part of 1 virgate. There is land for 17 ploughs. In demesne are 3 [ploughs]; and 14 villans with 5 bordars have 9 ploughs, and there could be 5 ploughs more. There are 3 slaves, and 1 mill rendering 16*s*., [and] meadow for 3 ploughs. All together it is and was worth £7; TRE £8. This manor 11 sokemen held and could sell.

• In Hollingdon Payne holds of William 3½ virgates. There is land for 1 plough, and there is [1 plough] with 3 villans. It is and always was worth 10*s*. This land 4 sokemen held: of these, 3 men of Beorhtric had 2½ virgates, and the fourth, a man of Wicga, had 1 virgate; and all these could sell their land.

• In Littlecote Payne holds of William 1½ hides. There is land for 1½ ploughs. There is 1 [plough] with 1 bordar, and there could be half [a plough more]. [There is] meadow for 1 plough. It is worth 20*s*.; when received 40*s*.; TRE 30*s*. This land 2 men of Beorhtric held and could sell.

IN YARDLEY HUNDRED

• In CHEDDINGTON Swærting holds of William half a hide. There is land for 2 oxen. It is and was worth 5*s*.; TRE 10*s*. This land Lyfing, a man of King Edward, held and could sell.

IN MURSLEY HUNDRED

• In Swanbourne Payne holds of William 1 virgate. There is land for 2 oxen. It is and always was worth 2*s*. This land Oswig, a man of Beorhtric, held and could sell.

IN 'MOW' HUNDRED

• Baldwin holds of William at farm 2 hides. There is land for 1½ ploughs, and there are [1½ ploughs], with 1 villan and 1 bordar. [There is] meadow for 1 plough. All together it is and was worth 26*s*. This man held it TRE and could sell it.

• In MARSH GIBBON Æthelric holds of William 4 hides as 1 manor. There is land for 5 ploughs. In demesne [are] 2 [ploughs]; and 5 villans with 3 bordars have 3 ploughs. There are 3 slaves, meadow for 5 ploughs, [and] woodland for 30 pigs. It is and always was worth 70*s*.This man held it TRE, but he now holds it at farm of William in heaviness and misery.

IN 'SECKLEY' HUNDRED

M • William himself holds NEWPORT PAGNELL. It is assessed at 5 hides. There is land for 9 ploughs. In demesne [are] 4 carucates of land, and there are 4 ploughs; and 5 villans have 5 ploughs. The burgesses have 6½ ploughs, and †[the ploughs] of other men working outside the 5 hides†. There are 9 slaves, and 2 mills rendering 40*s*., meadow for all the ploughs and 10*s*. [besides], woodland for 300 pigs and 2*s*. [besides], and, in addition, 4*s*. from men who dwell in the woodland; and in all other rents it renders yearly 100*s*. and 16*s*. 4*d*. In all it is and was worth £20; TRE £24.This manor Ulf, a thegn of King Edward, held.

• In Caldecote William holds 3 hides and 1 virgate. There is land for 2 ploughs. In demesne is 1 [plough], and there could be another. There is 1 villan, and 1 mill rendering 8*s*.; and a certain knight has there half a hide with half a plough. [There is] meadow for 1 plough, [and] woodland for 100 pigs. It is and always was worth 40*s*. This manor 2 men of Ulf held and could sell.

• In Woolstone William holds 1½ hides. There is land for 1½ ploughs. In demesne is 1 [plough]; and 1 villan has half a plough. There are 2 slaves. It is and was worth 20*s*.; TRE 30*s*. This land Ulf, a thegn of King Edward, held and could sell.

• In Bradwell William holds 3 virgates. There is land for 1 plough, and there is [1 plough], with 1 villan and 2 bordars and 1 slave. [There is] meadow for 1 plough. It is and always was worth 10*s*. This land Alweard, a man of Goding, held and could sell. Of this land Ansculf, when he was sheriff, dispossessed William of Cholsey, unjustly, as the men of the hundred say, and without the livery officer of the king or of anyone.

• In Great Linford Robert holds of William 1 virgate. There is land for 2 oxen, and there is 1 villan. It is and always was worth 2*s*. This land Grimbold, a man of Bisi, held and could sell.

• In TYRINGHAM Acard holds of William 7 hides and 1 virgate and the fourth part of 1 virgate as 1 manor. There is land for 8 ploughs. In demesne are 3 [ ploughs]; and 9 villans with 6 bordars have 5 ploughs. There are 6 slaves, meadow for 8 ploughs, [and] woodland for 200 pigs and 26*d*. from minor customary dues. All together it is worth £6;

when received £8; and as much TRE. This manor 5 thegns held: one of them, Harold, had 3 hides as 1 manor, and Godwine the priest half a hide, Æstan 2 hides as 1 manor, Godric, a man of Harold, 1 virgate, and Ælfgifu, wife of Harold, 1½ hides as 1 manor. All these could sell to whom they wished.

In Moulsoe Hundred

• Wibert holds of William 4 hides as 1 manor. There is land for 4 ploughs. In demesne is 1 [plough]; and 7 villans with 6 bordars have 3 ploughs. There is 1 slave, and 1 mill rendering 20*s*., meadow for 3 ploughs, [and] woodland for 150 pigs and 16*d*. [besides]. It is and was worth 40*s*.; TRE £4. This manor 2 thegns, Harold and Alwig, held and could sell.

• In Chicheley Baldwin holds of William 3 hides as 1 manor. There is land for 3 ploughs. In demesne is 1 [plough]; and 5 villans with 4 bordars have 2 ploughs. [There is] meadow for 1 plough, [and] woodland for 100 pigs. It is and always was worth 40*s*. This man held it TRE and could sell it.

• In the same [vill], Andrew holds of William 3 hides as 1 manor. There is land for 3 ploughs. In demesne is 1 [plough]; and 7 villans with 4 bordars have 2 ploughs. There are 2 slaves, meadow for 2 ploughs, [and] woodland for 100 pigs. It is and always was worth 40*s*. This manor Eadstan, a man of Æthelnoth the Kentishman, held and could sell.

• In the same [vill], Payne holds of William 3 hides and 3 virgates as 1 manor. There is land for 4 ploughs. In demesne is 1 [plough]; and 5 villans with 6 bordars have 3 ploughs. [There is] meadow for the ploughs. It is worth 60*s*.; when received 100*s*.; TRE £4. This manor 9 thegns held and could sell without leave of their lords.

M • William himself holds Tickford End. It is assessed at 5 hides. There is land for 8 ploughs. Besides the 5 hides, [there are] in demesne 2 carucates of land, and there are 2 ploughs. There 6 villans with 4 slaves have 6 ploughs. [There is] meadow for 5 ploughs, [and] woodland for 50 pigs. There 5 sokemen pay 27*s*. It is worth 100*s*.; when received £6; and as much TRE. This manor Ulf, a thegn of King Edward, held, and there were 5 thegns who held 3½ virgates of this land and could sell to whom they wished.

• In Hardmead Hervey holds 1 hide all but half a virgate, as 1 manor, of William. There is land for 1 plough, and there is [1 plough], with 2 villans and 2 bordars and 1 slave. [There is] woodland for 24 pigs. It is and was worth 12*s*.; TRE 20*s*. This land Godwine, a man of Ulf, held and could sell.

• In the same [vill], Payne holds of William half a virgate. There is land for 2 oxen, and there are [2 oxen]. [There is] meadow for 2 oxen, [and] woodland for 5 pigs. It is and was worth 2*s*.; TRE †£†2 [. . .]. This land Godric, a man of Oswig, held and could sell.

• In the same [vill], Baldwin holds 1 hide of William as 1 manor. There is land for 1 plough, and there is [1 plough] with 3 villans. It is and always was worth 1 mark of silver. This manor 3 brothers held. One of them [was] a man of Toki, and 2 were men of Baldwin, and they could sell. Of this land half a virgate belongs to the minster of St Firmin of [North] Crawley and it belonged to it TRE.

• In Milton Keynes Otbert holds of William 1 hide. There is land for 1 plough. There is 1 villan and 5 bordars and 1 slave, [and] meadow for 1 plough. It is worth 5*s*.; when received 20*s*.; and as much TRE. This land Sæweald, a man of Wulfweard Cild, held and could sell.

## XVIII. THE LAND OF ROBERT DE TOSNY

In Stone Hundred

• Robert de Tosny holds 7 hides in Stone, and Gilbert [holds] of him. There is land for 6 ploughs. In demesne are 2 [ ploughs]; and 7 villans with 11 bordars have 4 ploughs. There are 4 slaves; and 1 sokeman pays 15*s*. yearly. In all it is and always was worth 100*s*. This manor Ulf, a housecarl of King Edward, held.

In Yardley Hundred

M • In Cheddington Gilbert holds of Robert 5½ hides as 1 manor. There is land for 3½ ploughs. In demesne is 1 [plough], and there could be another. There 6 villans have 1½ ploughs. There are 4 slaves, [and] meadow for 2 ploughs. It is and was worth 60*s*.; TRE 100*s*. This manor Oswulf son of Frani, a thegn of King Edward, held and could sell.

In Moulsoe Hundred

M • In Clifton Reynes William de Boisrohard and his brother hold of Robert 4 hides as 1 manor. There is land for 4 ploughs. In demesne are 2 [ploughs]; and 6 villans with 7 bordars have 2 ploughs. There are 3 slaves, meadow for 4 ploughs, [and] woodland for 400 pigs. All together it is and was worth 100*s*.; TRE £6. This manor Oswulf, a thegn of King Edward, held and could sell. In this vill of Clifton Reynes, Sigefrith and Thorbert held 3 virgates which William and Roger have taken possession of and concealed, to the king's hurt, as the men of the hundred say. Of the 4 above-mentioned hides Alric, a man of Oswulf, held 1 virgate and could sell to whom he wished.

## XX. THE LAND OF ROBERT D'OILLY

In Stoke Hundred

M • Robert d'Oilly holds Iver. It is assessed at 17 hides. There is land for 30 ploughs. In demesne [are] 2 hides, and there are 4 ploughs; and 32 villans have 26 ploughs. Of these villans, 5 have 6 hides. There are 6 bordars and 4 slaves, and 3 mills rendering 44*s*., [and] meadow for 30 ploughs. From 4 fisheries, 1,500 eels and fish on Fridays for the use of the reeve of the vill. [There is] woodland for 800 pigs, and 2 arpents of vineyard. In all it is worth £22; when received 100*s*.; TRE £12. This manor Toki, a thegn of King Edward, held, and there were 3 sokemen. Of these, one, a man of Toki, held 3 virgates, but he could not sell except by his leave, and another, a man of Queen Edith, [held] 2½ hides, and the third, a man of Sæwulf, had 2½ hides: these 2 could give or sell [their land] to whom they wished, and they did not belong to this manor. This manor Robert exchanged with Clarenbold de Le Marais for Padbury, and it is [part] of his wife's fief.

In Desborough Hundred

M • Robert himself holds High Wycombe from his wife's fief. It is assessed at 10 hides. There is land for 30 ploughs. In demesne [are] 4 hides, and there are 3 ploughs. There 40 villans with 8 bordars have 27 ploughs. There are 8 slaves and 4 boors, and 6 mills rendering 75*s*. yearly, meadow for 3 ploughs and for the horses of the court and the villans' ploughs, [and] woodland for 500 pigs. In all it is worth £26; TRE £12.
when received £10. This manor Beorhtric held of Queen Edith.

In Ixhill Hundred

• Robert fitzWalter holds of Robert Oakley. It is assessed at 5 hides and 3 virgates. There is land for 7 ploughs. In demesne are 3 [ploughs]; and 9 villans with 7 bordars have 4 ploughs. There are 3 slaves. There is woodland for 200 pigs, if it were not for the king's park in which it lies. In all it is and was worth £6; TRE £7. These 5 hides and 3 virgates are 8 hides. Of these, Ælfgyth the maid held 2 hides which she could give or sell to whom she wished, and of the demesne farm of King Edward she herself had half a hide which Godric the sheriff granted her as long as he was sheriff, on condition of her teaching his daughter gold embroidery work. This land Robert fitzWalter holds now, as the hundred testifies.

In Yardley Hundred

● Ralph Basset holds of Robert Marsworth. It is assessed at 20 hides. There is land for 9 ploughs. In demesne are 4 [ploughs]; and 22 villans have 5 ploughs. There are 8 slaves, and 3 mills rendering 15*s.*, meadow for 6 ploughs, [and] woodland for 800 pigs. In all it is and always was worth £20. This manor Beorhtric, a thegn of King Edward, held and could sell.

● In Cheddington Ralph holds of Robert 1½ hides. There is land for 1 plough, and there is [1 plough] with 2 bordars. [There is] meadow for 1 plough. It is and always was worth 20*s.* This land Fin the Dane held and could sell.

In 'Stotfold' Hundred

● In Shalstone Robert holds of Robert 4 hides as 1 manor. There is land for 5 ploughs. In demesne [are] 2 ploughs; and 4 villans with 3 bordars have 3 ploughs. There are 4 slaves, [and] woodland for 50 pigs. This land is worth 40*s.*; when received 30*s.*; TRE 60*s.* This manor Azur son of Toti held and could sell.

M ● Turstin holds of Robert Water Stratford. It is assessed at 8 hides. There is land for 8 ploughs. In demesne are 3 [ploughs]; and 10 villans with 5 bordars have 5 ploughs. There are 3 slaves, and 1 mill rendering 8*s.*, [and] meadow for 6 ploughs. It is worth £7; when received 100*s.*; TRE £7. This manor Azur son of Toti held and could sell.

## XX. THE LAND OF ROBERT GERNON

In Stoke Hundred

M ● Robert Gernon holds Wraysbury. It is assessed at 20 hides. There is land for 25 ploughs. In demesne [are] 5 hides, and there are 2 ploughs; and 32 villans with 18 bordars have 15 ploughs, and there could be 8 ploughs more. There are 7 slaves, and 2 mills rendering 40 yearly [*sic*], meadow for 5 ploughs and hay for the beasts of the court, woodland for 500 pigs, and 4 fisheries in the Thames rendering 27*s.*, less 4*d.* In all it is and was worth £20; TRE £22. This manor Edmund, a thegn of King Edward, held.

## XXI. THE LAND OF GEOFFREY DE MANDEVILLE

In Burnham Hundred

M ● Geoffrey de Mandeville holds Amersham. It is assessed at 7½ hides. There is land for 16 ploughs. In demesne [are] 2 hides, and there are 3 ploughs; and 14 villans with 4 bordars have 9 ploughs. There could be 4 more. There are 7 slaves, meadow for 16 ploughs, [and] woodland for 400 pigs. In all it is and was worth £9; TRE £16. This manor Queen Edith held.

In Ixhill Hundred

● In Waldridge Swærting holds of Geoffrey half a hide. There is land for 1 plough, and there is [1 plough, and] meadow for 1 plough. It is and was worth 10*s.*; TRE 15*s.* This land Doding, a man of Esger the staller, held and could sell.

In Waddesdon Hundred

M ● In [Botolph or East] Claydon Geoffrey holds 7 hides as 1 manor. There is land for 5 ploughs. In demesne [are] 3 hides, and there are 2 ploughs; and 4 villans with 3 bordars have 3 ploughs. [There is] meadow for 2 ploughs, [and] woodland for 40 pigs. All together it is worth £4; when received £3; TRE £5. This manor Swein, a man of Esger the staller, held. He could not give nor sell it without his leave.

M ● Geoffrey himself holds Quarrendon. It is assessed at 10 hides. There is land for 10 ploughs. In demesne [are] 4 hides, and there are 4 ploughs; and 20 villans with 8 bordars have 8 ploughs. [There is] meadow for 10 ploughs, [and] woodland for 300 pigs. In all it is worth £8; when received 100*s.*; TRE £6. This manor Swein, a man of Esger the staller, held. He could not sell it without his leave.

In Yardley Hundred

M ● In Ivinghoe Aston Germund holds of Geoffrey 4 hides and 1 virgate as 1 manor. There is land for 3½ ploughs. In demesne are 2 ploughs; and 1 villan with 4 slaves has 1½ ploughs. [There is] meadow for 3 ploughs. It is and was worth 50*s.*; TRE 60*s.* This manor Esger the staller held in demesne.

In Mursley Hundred

● Geoffrey himself holds in Swanbourne 2 hides. There is land for 2 ploughs. In demesne [is] 1 hide, and there is 1 plough; and 3 villans with 2 bordars have 1 plough. [There is] meadow for 2 ploughs. It is and always was worth 30*s.* This manor Swein, a man of Esger the staller, held. He could not sell it without his leave.

In 'Stotfold' Hundred

M ● In Leckhampstead Osbert holds of Geoffrey 3 hides. There is land for 3 ploughs. In demesne is 1 [plough]; and [. . .] villans have 1½ ploughs, and there could be half [a plough] more. [There is] woodland for 150 pigs. It is worth 30*s.*; when received 20*s.*; TRE 30*s.* This manor Swærting, a man of Esger, held. He could not sell it.

In 'Mow' Hundred

● William de Keynes holds of Geoffrey 3½ hides as 1 manor. There is land for 3½ ploughs. In demesne is 1 [plough]; and 3 villans with 1 bordar have 2 ploughs, and there could be half [a plough more]. There is 1 slave, [and] meadow for 3 ploughs. In all it is and always was worth 40*s.* This manor Ulf, a man of Esger the staller, held and could sell, and of the same land Alwig held half a hide; he was a man of Alwine Varus and could sell it.

## XXII. THE LAND OF GILBERT DE GHENT

In Yardley Hundred

M ● Gilbert de Ghent holds Edlesborough. It is assessed at 20 hides. There is land for 14 ploughs. In demesne [are] 10 hides, and there are 4 ploughs; and 26 villans with 4 bordars have 10 ploughs. There are 10 slaves, and 2 mills rendering 15*s.* 4*d.*, meadow for 4 ploughs, [and] woodland for 400 pigs. In all it is and was worth £13; TRE £14. This manor Ulf, a thegn of King Edward, held and could sell.

● In Horton [in Ivinghoe] Swærting holds of Gilbert 3 virgates. There is land for half a plough, and there is a plough. This land is and always was worth 6*s.* 8*d.* This land a certain man of Ulf held. He could not give nor sell it without his leave.

## XXIII. THE LAND OF MILES CRISPIN

In Stone Hundred

● Miles Crispin holds in Upton [in Dinton] 1½ hides, and Alric holds of him. There is land for 1 plough, and there is [1 plough], with 1 villan and 2 bordars. There are 2 slaves. It is and always was worth 20*s.* This thegn held it TRE.

In Burnham Hundred

M ● Ralph holds of Miles Dorney. It is assessed at 3 hides. There is land for 3 ploughs. In demesne is 1 [plough]; and 5 villans with 4 bordars have 2 ploughs. There are 2 slaves, meadow for 3 ploughs and for the horses, and 1 fishery rendering 500 eels, [and] woodland for 150 pigs. It is worth 30*s.*; when received 10*s.*; TRE 60*s.* This manor Ealdræd, a man of Earl Morcar, held and could sell.

● Ralph and Roger hold of Miles Hitcham. It is assessed at 6 hides. There is land for 6 ploughs. In demesne are 2 [ploughs]; and 8 villans have 4 ploughs. There are 3 slaves, meadow for the ploughs, [and] woodland for 100 pigs.

From a fishery, 500 eels. In all it is worth £4; when received 20*s.*; TRE 100*s.* This manor Hemming, a thegn of King Edward, held and could sell.

In Desborough Hundred

• In Marlow [Marlow or Little Marlow] Ralph and Roger hold of Miles $8\frac{1}{2}$ hides and half a virgate. There is land for 6 ploughs. In demesne are 2 [ploughs]; and 14 villans with 6 bordars have 4 ploughs. There are 2 slaves, meadow for 6 ploughs, [and] woodland for 200 pigs and 12*d.* [besides]. It is and was worth 60*s.*; TRE £4. This land Hemming, a thegn of King Edward, held and could sell.

• In Saunderton Osbert holds of Miles 5 hides. There is land for 5 ploughs. In demesne are 2 [ploughs]; and 13 villans with 5 bordars have 3 ploughs. There are 2 slaves, and 2 mills rendering 8*s.*, meadow for 1 plough, [and] woodland for 50 pigs. It is and was worth 100*s.*; TRE £6. This manor Alric, a man of Earl Harold, held and could sell.

• In Aston Sandford 2 men hold of Miles half a hide. There is land for half a plough, and there is [half a plough] with 2 villans. [There is] meadow for half a plough. It is and was worth 10*s.*; TRE 15*s.* This land Wulfric and Coleman, men of Beorhtric, held and could sell.

In Ixhill Hundred

M • Miles himself holds Shabbington. It is assessed at 10 hides. There is land for 10 ploughs. In demesne are 3 hides, and there are 3 ploughs; and 12 villans with 7 bordars have 7 ploughs. There are 6 slaves, and 1 mill rendering 10*s.*, [and] meadow for 6 ploughs. From a fishery, 100 eels. [There is] woodland for 100 pigs. This manor is and always was worth £10. Vigot of Wallingford held it.

• In Ickford Richard holds of Miles 4 hides. There is land for 4 ploughs. In demesne is 1 [plough]; and 6 villans have 3 ploughs. There are 2 slaves, [and] meadow for 4 ploughs. In all it is worth £3; when received £4; TRE as much.

In Ashendon Hundred

• In Ashendon Viking holds of Miles 2 hides. There is land for 2 ploughs, and there are [2 ploughs] with 3 bordars. [There is] meadow for 2 ploughs. It is and always was worth 30*s.* This man held it TRE and could sell.

• In Chearsley Richard holds of Miles $1\frac{1}{2}$ hides. There is land for 1 plough, and there is [1 plough], with 1 villan and 1 bordar. There are 2 slaves, [and] meadow for 1 plough. It is and always was worth 22*s.* This land Healfdene, a man of Earl Harold, held and could sell.

• In 'Shortley' [in Quainton] 2 men hold of Miles 1 hide. There is land for 1 plough, and there is [1 plough], with 1 villan and 1 bordar. [There is] meadow for 1 plough, [and] woodland for 30 pigs. It is and always was worth 10*s.* This land 2 thegns, men of Beorhtric, held and could sell.

M • In Quainton Miles holds $7\frac{1}{2}$ hides. There is land for 9 ploughs. In demesne [are] 3 hides, and there are 3 ploughs; and 21 villans with 6 bordars have 6 ploughs. There are 6 slaves, meadow for 2 ploughs, [and] woodland for 100 pigs, meadow for 2 ploughs, [and] woodland for 100 pigs [*sic*]. In all it is and was worth £7; TRE £8. This manor Vigot of Wallingford held.

• Two men hold of Miles Beachendon as 2 hides. There is land for 3 ploughs, and there are [3 ploughs], with 2 villans and 3 bordars. [There is] meadow for 2 ploughs. It is and always was worth 25*s.* These men held it TRE—one a man of Beorhtric, and the other a man of Azur—and could sell it.

In Waddesdon Hundred

M • Miles himself holds Waddesdon. It is assessed at 27 hides. There is land for 28 ploughs. In demesne [are] 10 hides, and there are 8 ploughs; and 50 villans with 10 bordars have 20 ploughs. There are 17 slaves, and 1 mill rendering 12*s.*, meadow for 28 ploughs, [and] woodland for 150 pigs. In all it is worth £30; when received £16; TRE £30. This manor Beorhtric, a man of Queen Edith, held.

• In [Botolph or East] Claydon 2 Englishmen hold of Miles 2 hides. There is land for 1 plough, and there is [1 plough] with 3 bordars. [There is] meadow for 1 plough. It is and always was worth 20*s.* These men held it TRE. They were men of Hemming, and they could sell.

• In [Botolph or East] Claydon Geoffrey holds of Miles 7 hides and 3 virgates as 1 manor. There is land for 5 ploughs. In demesne are 2 [ploughs]; and 4 villans with 3 bordars have 3 ploughs. There are 3 slaves, meadow for 2 ploughs, [and] woodland for 100 pigs. All together it is worth £4; when received 20*s.*; TRE £4.

• In [?North] Marston Særic holds of Miles 1 hide. There is land for 1 plough, and there is [1 plough] with 1 bordar. [There is] meadow for 1 plough. It is and always was worth 20*s.* This man held it TRE; he was a man of Beorhtric and could sell it.

In Cottesloe Hundred

• In Soulbury Roger holds of Miles 1 hide and $1\frac{1}{2}$ virgates. There is land for 3 ploughs. In demesne is 1 [plough]; and 2 villans have another, and there could be a third. [There is] meadow for 2 ploughs. It is and always was worth 20*s.* This land Almær, a man of Beorhtric, held. He could not sell it without his leave.

• In Hollingdon Nigel holds of Miles 1 virgate. There is land for half a plough, and there is [half a plough] with 1 villan. It is and was worth 3*s.*; TRE 4*s.* He who held this land could not give nor sell it TRE.

• In Wingrave Nigel holds of Miles 5 hides as 1 manor. There is land for 5 ploughs. There 7 villans with 2 bordars have $2\frac{1}{2}$ ploughs and there could be as many [more]. There is 1 slave, [and] meadow for 5 ploughs. It is worth 40*s.*; when received 100*s.*; and as much TRE. This manor Beorhtric, a man of Queen Edith, held and could sell.

• In the same vill Turstin the priest holds of Miles half a hide. There is land for half a plough. There is 1 villan, [and] meadow for half a plough. It is and always was worth 10*s.* This land Leofmær, a man of Beorhtric, held and could sell.

• In the same vill Almær holds of Miles 2 hides as 1 manor. There is land for 3 ploughs. In demesne is 1 [plough]; and 7 villans have 2 ploughs. [There is] meadow for 3 ploughs. It is and always was worth 40*s.* This manor Almær, a man of Beorhtric, held and could sell.

• In Littlecote Robert holds of Miles 1 hide. There is land for 1 plough, and there is [1 plough] with 1 villan, [and] meadow for 1 plough. It is worth 15*s.*; when received 5*s.*; TRE 25*s.* This land Herch, a man of Beorhtric, held and could sell.

• In Hardwick William holds of Miles 1 hide. There is land for 1 plough, and there is [1 plough] with 2 bordars. [There is] meadow for 1 plough. It is worth 20*s.*; when received 10*s.*; TRE 20*s.* This land Oswulf held and could sell.

• In [Lower or Upper] Burston William holds of Miles 3 virgates. There is land for 1 plough. There are 3 villans, [and] meadow for 1 plough. It is and was worth 15*s.*; TRE 20*s.* This land Oswulf, a man of Beorhtric, held and could sell.

In Yardley Hundred

M • In Pitstone Roger holds of Miles 5 hides as 1 manor. There is land for 2 ploughs. In demesne is 1 [plough]; and 3 villans with 1 bordar have half a plough, and there could be half [a plough more. There is] woodland for 40 pigs. It is worth 30*s.*; when received 20*s.*; TRE 40*s.* This manor Leofsige, a man of Beorhtric, held and could sell.

• In the same vill Swærting holds of Miles 2 hides. There is land for 1 plough, and there is [1 plough], with 1 bordar and 2 slaves. [There is] woodland for 25 pigs. It is and was worth 10*s.*; TRE 20*s.* This land Leofsige, a man of Beorhtric, held and could sell.

• In Horton [in Ivinghoe] Swærting holds of Miles 1 hide. There is land for half a plough.

There is a plough, with 1 villan and 2 slaves, [and] meadow for half a plough. It is and always was worth 13*s.* 4*d.* Leofsige, a man of Beorhtric, held and could sell it.

IN MURSLEY HUNDRED

● In Stewkley Nigel holds of Miles 3½ hides as 1 manor. There is land for 9 ploughs. In demesne is 1 [plough], and there could be 2 [more]. There 9 villans with 2 bordars have 3½ ploughs, and there could be 2½ [ploughs] more. [There is] meadow for 9 ploughs. It is and was worth £4. This manor Beorhtric, a thegn of King Edward, held and could sell.

IN 'MOW' HUNDRED

● In Addington Eadwulf holds half a hide. There is land for half a plough, and there is [half a plough]. It is worth 10*s.*; when received 5*s.*; TRE 10*s.* This land Leofwig, a man of Eadwig, held and could sell.

IN 'SECKLEY' HUNDRED

● In Bradwell William holds of Miles 2 hides and 3 virgates. There is land for 3 ploughs. In demesne [are] 2 ploughs; and 5 villans there could have 1 plough. There are 2 slaves, [and] meadow for 2 ploughs. It is worth 40*s.*; when received 20*s.*; TRE 60*s.* This manor 2 thegns, Sibbi and Godwine, men of Ælfric son of Goding, held and could sell.

M ● Ralph holds Stanton Bury of Miles. It is assessed at 5 hides. There is land for 5½ ploughs. In demesne are 2 [ploughs]; and 7 villans with 3 bordars have 3 ploughs, and there could be half [a plough] more. There are 4 slaves, and 1 mill rendering 10*s.* 8*d.* and 50 eels, [and] meadow for 4 ploughs. In all it is worth £6; when received 100*s.*; TRE £6. This manor Bisi, a thegn of King Edward, held and could sell.

IN MOULSOE HUNDRED

● Almær of Wotton holds 1 hide of Miles. There is land for 1 plough, and there is [1 plough], with 3 villans and 2 bordars. [There is] meadow for 1 plough. It is and always was worth 10*s.* This land Ordwig, a man of Vigot of Wallingford, held and could sell.

## XXIIII. THE LAND OF EDWARD OF SALISBURY

IN AYLESBURY HUNDRED

M ● EDWARD of Salisbury holds ASTON CLINTON. It is assessed at 20 hides. There is land for 17 ploughs. In demesne [are] 9 hides and 1 virgate, and there are 6 ploughs; and 28 villans with 4 bordars have 11 ploughs, and there could be a twelfth besides. There are 13 slaves, and 1 mill rendering 5 orae of silver, meadow for 17 ploughs, [and] woodland for 300 pigs and iron for the demesne ploughs. In all it is worth £18; when received £10; TRE £20. This manor Wulfwynn, a man of King Edward, held and could sell.

IN WADDESDON HUNDRED

● Ranulph holds of Edward 1 hide and 1½ virgates. There is land for 1 plough, and there is [1 plough], with 1 villan and 1 bordar and 4 slaves. [There is] meadow for 1 plough. It is and was worth 10*s.*; TRE 20*s.* This land Almær held of Wulfwynn of Creslow and could sell.

● The same Ranulph holds CRESLOW. It is assessed at 5 hides. There is land for 6 ploughs. In demesne are 4 [ploughs]; and 6 villans with 1 bordar have 2 ploughs. There are 5 slaves, [and] meadow for 5 ploughs. In all it is worth 100*s.*; when received £4; TRE £6. This manor Wulfwynn, a certain woman, held TRE and could sell.

## XXV. THE LAND OF HUGH DE BEAUCHAMP

IN COTTESLOE HUNDRED

M ● HUGH de Beauchamp holds LINSLADE [Beds.]. It is assessed at 15 hides. There is land for 16 ploughs. In demesne [are] 5 hides, and there are 2 ploughs, and there could be 3 more. There 22 villans with 6 bordars have 11 ploughs. There are 5 slaves, and 1 mill rendering 20*s.*, [and] meadow for 2 ploughs. All together it is worth £10; when received 100*s.*; TRE £10. This manor Alwine, a man of Queen Edith, held and could sell.

● In Soulbury Hugh holds 2 parts of 1 virgate. There is land for 4 oxen. It is and was worth 3*s.*; TRE 4*s.* This land Dot God's man held; he could sell to whom he wished.

IN BUNSTY HUNDRED

● In Lathbury William d'Orange holds 4 hides of Hugh as 1 manor. There is land for 3 ploughs. In demesne are 2 [ploughs]; and 4 villans with 4 bordars have 1 plough. There are 3 slaves, meadow for 3 ploughs, [and] woodland for 100 pigs. It is worth £4; when received 20*s.*; TRE 60*s.* This manor 2 thegns, Leofric and Wulfgeat, held as 2 manors and could sell.

## XXVI. THE LAND OF HUGH DE BOLBEC

IN STONE HUNDRED

● HUGH de Bolbec holds in Little Missenden half a hide, and Wulfgeat [holds] of him. There is land for 1 plough, and there is [1 plough] with 1 bordar. [There is] meadow for 1 plough, [and] woodland for 30 pigs. It is and always was worth 10*s.* This man held it TRE. He was a man of Bishop Wulfwig and could sell.

IN BURNHAM HUNDRED

● In Amersham Wulfgeat holds of Hugh half a hide. There is land for 2 ploughs, and there are [2 ploughs], with 2 villans and 3 bordars. There is 1 mill rendering 5*s.*, [and] woodland for 20 pigs. It is and always was worth 20*s.* This man held it TRE and could sell.

● Hugh himself holds in CHESHAM 8½ hides. There is land for 16 ploughs. In demesne [are] 1½ hides, and there are 2 ploughs; and 16 villans with 6 bordars have 12 ploughs, and there could be 2 more. There are 6 slaves, and 1 mill rendering 10*s.*, meadow for 16 ploughs, [and] woodland for 800 pigs and iron for the ploughs. In all it is worth £10, less 3*s.*; TRE £12. This manor Beorhtric, a man of Queen Edith, held, and there 2 sokemen held 4 hides: they were men of Beorhtric and they could sell.

IN DESBOROUGH HUNDRED

M ● Hugh himself holds MEDMENHAM. It is assessed at 10 hides. There is land for 10 ploughs. In demesne [are] 4 hides, and there are 2 ploughs; and 10 villans with 8 bordars have 8 ploughs. There are 4 slaves. From a fishery, 1,000 eels. [There is] meadow for all the ploughs, [and] woodland for 50 pigs. All together it is and was worth 100*s.*; TRE £8. This manor Wulfstan, a thegn of King Edward, held and could sell to whom he wished.

● Hugh himself holds "BROCH" [? in Medmenham] as 1 hide. There is land for 1 plough, and there is [1 plough], with 1 villan and 2 bordars. It is and always was worth 10*s.* This land Oda held; he was a man of Beorhtric and could sell it.

IN YARDLEY HUNDRED

● In Cheddington Hugh holds half a hide, but it has been laid waste. This land Wulfwine of Whaddon held and could sell.

● In Whaddon [in Slapton] Hugh holds holds [*sic*] 1 hide. There is land for 1 plough, and there is [1 plough] with 1 villan. [There is] meadow for 1 plough. It is and was worth 10*s.*; TRE 20*s.* This land 2 men of Beorhtric held and could sell.

IN 'SECKLEY' HUNDRED

M ● Hugh himself holds CALVERTON. It is assessed at 10 hides. There is land for 10 ploughs. In demesne [are] 3 hides, and there are 3 ploughs; and 18 villans with 8 bordars have 7 ploughs and there could be a ninth [*sic*]. There are 9 slaves, and 1 mill rendering 13*s.* 4*d.*, [and] meadow for 5 ploughs. In all it is and was worth £10; TRE £12. This manor Bisi, a thegn of King Edward, held; and there 1 man of Queen Edith had 2 hides as 1 manor and could sell them.

M ● In Great Linford Hugh holds 2 hides and 1½ virgates as 1 manor. There is land for 2 ploughs. In demesne is 1 [plough]; and 5 villans with 2 bordars have 1 plough. There is meadow for 1 plough. It is and was worth 20*s.*; TRE 40*s.* This manor 3 thegns held and could give and sell.

● In Hardmead Hugh holds half a virgate. There is land for 2 oxen, meadow for 2 oxen, [and] woodland for 5 pigs. It is and was worth 2*s.* This land Wulfgrim, a man of Earl Leofwine, held and could sell.

● In Wavendon Ansel holds of Hugh 3 hides, less 1 virgate, as 1 manor. There is land for 3 ploughs. There are 4 oxen, with 2 villans and 3 bordars, [and] meadow for 3 ploughs. It is and was worth 40*s*.; TRE 60*s*. This land Swein, a man of Earl Harold, held and could sell.

## XXVII. THE LAND OF HENRY DE FERRERS

IN ASHENDON HUNDRED

M • HENRY de Ferrers holds Grendon Underwood. It is assessed at 2 hides. There is land for 8 ploughs. In demesne [is] 1 hide, and there are 3 ploughs; and 12 villans with 2 bordars have 5 ploughs. There are †4† slaves, meadow for 2 ploughs, [and] woodland for 500 pigs. In all it is and was worth £6; TRE £7. This manor Bondi the staller held TRE and could sell.

M • In Shipton Lee Henry holds 7 hides. There is land for 7 ploughs. In demesne [are] 3 hides, and there are 2 ploughs, and there could be 2 others. There 4 villans with 1 bordar have 2 ploughs, and there could be a third. There is 1 slave, [and] meadow for 1 plough. It is and was worth 60*s*.; TRE 100*s*. This manor Bondi the staller held TRE.

## XXVIII. THE LAND OF WALTER DE VERNON

IN STONE HUNDRED

• WALTER de Vernon holds in in [*sic*] Lower Hartwell half a hide. There is land for half a plough, but there is no plough. It is and always was worth 10*s*. This land Thorgot, a thegn of King Edward, held and could sell.

• In Marlow [Marlow or Little Marlow] Walter holds 6 hides and 1½ virgates. There is land for 6 ploughs. In demesne [are] 3½ hides, and there are 2 ploughs; and 8 villans with 6 bordars have 2½ ploughs, and there could be 1½ ploughs more. There is 1 slave, and meadow for 2 ploughs. It is and was worth 100*s*.; TRE £4. This land Godric, a man of Esger the staller, held and could sell.

IN WADDESDON HUNDRED

M • Walter himself holds [? Fleet] MARSTON. It is assessed at 3 hides. There is land for 6 ploughs. In demesne is 1 hide, and there is 1 plough, and there could be another. There 6 villans with 5 bordars have 3 ploughs, and there could be a fourth. There is 1 slave, [and] meadow for 2 ploughs. It is worth 40*s*.; when received 100*s*.; and as much TRE. This manor Thorgot, a man of Earl Leofwine, held and could sell.

## XX. THE LAND OF WALTER FITZOTHER

IN STOKE HUNDRED

M • WALTER fitzOther holds HORTON [near Slough]. It is assessed at 10 hides. There is land for 9 ploughs. In demesne [are] 2 hides, and there are 2 ploughs; and 15 villans with 5 bordars have 6 ploughs, and there could be a seventh. There are 4 slaves, and 1 mill rendering 20*s*., [and] meadow for 3 ploughs. In all it is worth £6; when received 50*s*.; TRE £6. This manor Ealdræd, a man of Archbishop Stigand, held and could sell.

IN BURNHAM HUNDRED

M • Walter himself holds ETON. It is assessed at 12 hides. There is land for 8 ploughs. In demesne [are] 3 hides, and there are 2 ploughs; and 15 villans with 4 bordars have 6 ploughs. There are 4 slaves, and 2 mills rendering 20*s*., meadow for 2 ploughs, [and] woodland for 200 pigs. From a fishery, 1,000 eels. In all it is worth £6; when received 100*s*.; TRE £6. This manor Queen Edith held.

M • Walter himself holds BURNHAM. It is assessed at 18 hides. There is land for 15 ploughs. In demesne [are] 3 hides, and there are 3 ploughs; and 28 villans with 7 bordars have 12 ploughs. There are 2 slaves, meadow for 3 ploughs, [and] woodland for 600 pigs and iron for the ploughs. In all it is worth £10; when received £6; TRE £10. This manor Almær, a thegn of King Edward, held.

IN MOULSOE HUNDRED

• Ralph holds of Walter 4 hides as 1 manor. There is land for 6 ploughs. In demesne are 2 [ploughs]; and 9 villans with 7 bordars have 4 ploughs. There are 2 slaves, meadow for 2 ploughs, [and] woodland for 100 pigs. All together it is worth 60*s*.; when received 100*s*.; TRE £4. This manor Oswig, a man of Alric, held and could sell.

## XXX. THE LAND OF WALTER THE FLEMING

IN MOULSOE HUNDRED

• WALTER the Fleming holds 1 hide and 1 virgate as 1 manor, and Fulkwin [holds] of him. There is land for 1 plough. There is 1 villan, [and] meadow for 1 plough. It is worth 10*s*.; when received 20*s*.; and as much TRE. This land Swening, a man of Earl Harold, held and could sell.

## XXXI. THE LAND OF WILLIAM DE FEUGERES

IN 'STOTFOLD' HUNDRED

• WILLIAM de Feugeres holds TURWESTON. It is assessed at 5 hides. There is land for 8 ploughs. Besides these 5 hides there are 3 carucates of land in demesne, and there is 1 plough, and there could be 2 more; and 6 villans with 4 bordars have 5 ploughs. There are 4 slaves, and 1 mill rendering 7*s*. 6*d*., [and] meadow for 8 ploughs. In all it is and was worth £4; TRE 100*s*. This manor Wynsige, the chamberlain of King Edward, held and could sell.

## XXXII. THE LAND OF WILLIAM THE CHAMBERLAIN

IN STONE HUNDRED

• WILLIAM the chamberlain holds 2 hides in Lower Hartwell, and Robert [holds] of him. There is land for 2 ploughs. In demesne is 1 [plough]; and 2 villans with 4 bordars have 1 plough. It is and always was worth 30*s*. This land Wulfmær, a priest of King Edward, held and could sell.

## XXXIII. THE LAND OF WILLIAM FITZCONSTANTINE

IN STONE HUNDRED

• WILLIAM fitzConstantine holds in 'Southcote' [in Stone] 1 virgate of land and 6 acres, and Sweeting [holds] of him. There is land for half a plough. It is and always was worth 6*s*. This land Wulfric, a man of Archbishop Stigand, held and could sell.

## XXXIIII. THE LAND OF WILLIAM FITZMANNI

IN ASHENDON HUNDRED

• WILLIAM fitzManni holds in Ludgershall 2 hides. There is land for 2 ploughs. In demesne [are] 1 hide and 1 virgate, and there is 1 plough; and 3 villans have 1 plough. [There is] meadow for 1 plough. It is and always was worth 20*s*. This manor Ælfric, the chamberlain of King Edward, held and could sell.

## XXXV. THE LAND OF TURSTIN FITZROLF

IN STONE HUNDRED

• TURSTIN fitzRolf holds Little KIMBLE, and Albert [holds] of him. It is assessed at 10 hides. There is land for 10 ploughs. In demesne are 2 [ploughs], and there could be another 2. There 10 villans with 1 bordar have 3 ploughs, and there could be 3 others. There are 2 slaves, and 1 mill rendering 16*s*., [and] meadow for 10 ploughs. In all it is and was worth 100*s*.; TRE £6. This manor Beorhtric, a thegn of King Edward, held.

IN COTTESLOE HUNDRED

M • In HARDWICK Turstin holds 19 hides. There is land for 19 ploughs. In demesne [are] 9½ hides, and there are 3 ploughs, and there could be a fourth. There 24 villans with 4 bordars have 14½ ploughs, and there could be half [a plough] more. There are 8 slaves, [and] meadow for 10 ploughs. In all it is worth £15; when received £10; TRE £16. This manor Saxi, a thegn of King Edward, held.

• In [Lower or Upper] Burston Reginald holds 1 hide of Turstin. There is land for 1 plough, and there is [1 plough], with 2 bordars and 1 slave. [There is] meadow for 1 plough. It is worth 20*s*.; when received 10*s*.; TRE 20*s*. Alwynn, a certain woman of Siward, held this land, and she could give it to whom she wished. §

## XXXVI. THE LAND OF TURSTIN MANTEL

IN STONE HUNDRED

• TURSTIN Mantel holds half a hide in Little Missenden. There is land for 2 ploughs. In demesne is 1 [plough]; and 2 villans with 1 bordar have 1 plough. [There is] meadow for 2 ploughs, [and] woodland for 30 pigs. It is and was worth 20*s*.; TRE 30*s*. This land Særic, a man of Sigeræd, held and could sell.

IN BURNHAM HUNDRED

• In Amersham Turstin holds half a hide. There is land for 2 ploughs. There is 1 [plough], and there could be another. There are 2 villans with 1 bordar, meadow for 2 ploughs, [and] woodland for 30 pigs. It is and was worth 13*s*. 4*d*.; TRE 20*s*. This land Thorkil, a man of King Edward, held and could sell.

• In Chesham Turstin holds half a hide. There is land for 1 plough, but it has been laid waste. It is and always was worth 5*s*. This land Øpi, a man of Beorhtric, held and could sell.

## XXXVII. THE LAND OF RALPH DE FEUGERES

IN 'MOW' HUNDRED

M • RALPH de Feugeres holds TWYFORD. It is assessed at 17 hides. There is land for 18 ploughs. In demesne [are] 6 hides, and there are 3 ploughs, and there could be 2 more. There 15 villans with 10 bordars have 11 ploughs, and there could be 2 more. There are 9 slaves, meadow for 3 ploughs, [and] woodland for 100 pigs. In all it is worth £10; when received £8; TRE £12. This manor Countess Goda held, and there a certain man of Earl Harold had 3 hides as 1 manor and could sell it.

M • Ralph himself holds CHARNDON. It is assessed at 10 hides. There is land for 10 ploughs. In demesne [are] 2 hides, and there are 2 ploughs; and 18 villans with 11 bordars have 8 ploughs. There are 4 slaves, [and] meadow for 2 ploughs. All together it is and was worth £8; TRE £9. This manor Einger, a man of Earl Harold, held and could sell.

## XXXVIII. THE LAND OF BERTRAM DE VERDUN

IN STOKE HUNDRED

M • BERTRAM de Verdun holds FARNHAM ROYAL. It is assessed at 10 hides. There is land for 8 ploughs. In demesne [are] 5 hides, and there are 2 ploughs; and 5 villans with 3 bordars have 4 ploughs, and there could be 2 more. There are 2 slaves, meadow for 2 ploughs, [and] woodland for 600 pigs. All together it is worth 100*s*.; when received £4; and as much TRE. This manor Countess Goda held. Of this manor, Geoffrey de Mandeville holds in Amersham half a hide, of which he dispossessed the aforesaid Bertram whilst he was overseas in the service of the king; the HUNDRED testifies to this; and Ralph Taillebois set up on Bertram's land a mill which was not there TRE, as the hundred testifies.

## XXXIX. THE LAND OF NIGEL D'AUBIGNY

IN DESBOROUGH HUNDRED

M • NIGEL d'Aubigny holds TURVILLE, and Roger [holds] of him. It is assessed at 5 hides. There is land for 11 ploughs. In demesne are 3 [ploughs]; and 13 villans with 1 bordar have 7 ploughs, and there could be an eighth. [There is] woodland for 20 pigs. All together it is worth £7; when received 100*s*.; TRE £7. This manor Thorbert, a man of Earl Ælfgar, held and could sell.

IN IXHILL HUNDRED

M • In TOWERSEY [Oxon.] Nigel de Le Vast holds of Nigel 9 hides and 1 virgate. There is land for 7 ploughs. In demesne are 3 [ploughs]; and 10 villans have 4 ploughs. There are 4 slaves, [and] meadow for 7 ploughs. In all it is worth £7; when received 100*s*.; TRE £8. This manor 7 thegns, men of King Edward, held and could sell.

## XL. THE LAND OF NIGEL DE BERVILLE

IN MURSLEY HUNDRED

• NIGEL de Berville holds in Drayton Parslow 2 hides and 1 virgate as 1 manor. There is land for 8 ploughs. In demesne is 1 [plough], and there could be 2 more. There 8 villans with 2 bordars have 4½ ploughs, and there could be half [a plough] more. There are 3 slaves, [and] meadow for 8 ploughs. It is worth 40*s*.; when received 100*s*.; and as much TRR [*sic*]. This manor Leofwine of Nuneham Courtenay held of the king, and afterwards, TRW, Ralph Passaquam held it of the same Leofwine, and found 2 men with hauberks for the guard of Windsor [Berks.]. The Bishop of Coutances dispossessed this Ralph and delivered [the manor] to the aforesaid Nigel.

## XLI. THE LAND OF ROGER D'IVRY

IN IXHILL HUNDRED

• ROGER d'Ivry holds NASHWAY, and Picot [holds] of him. It is assessed at 2 hides. There is land for 4 ploughs. In demesne are 2 [ploughs]; and 4 villans with 2 bordars have 2 ploughs. There are 2 slaves, meadow for 1 plough, [and] woodland for 200 pigs. In all it is worth 40*s*.; when received 30*s*.; TRE 50*s*. This manor Azur son of Toti, a man of Queen Edith, held and could sell.

IN MURSLEY HUNDRED

• In Westbury [in Shenley] Payne holds of Roger 2½ hides as 1 manor. There is land for 7 ploughs. In demesne are 2½ ploughs; and 8 villans with 2 bordars have 4½ ploughs. There is 1 slave, and 2 mills rendering 18*s*., meadow for 5 ploughs, [and] woodland for 250 pigs. In all it is worth 60*s*.; when received 50*s*.; TRE 60*s*. This manor Alwine, brother of Bishop Wulfwig, held and could sell.

• In Dadford Haimard holds of Roger 2 hides as 1 manor. There is land for 4 ploughs. There is 1 [plough], and there could be 3 more. There are 4 bordars and 1 slave, meadow for 4 ploughs, [and] woodland for 200 pigs. All together it is and was worth 20*s*.; TRE 30*s*. This manor Leofwine, a man of Burgræd, held and could give and sell.

M • Fulk holds of Roger RADCLIVE. It is assessed at 5 hides. There is land for 8 ploughs. In demesne are 3 [ploughs]; and 6 villans with 4 bordars have 3 ploughs, and there could be 2 more. There are 3 slaves, and 1 mill rendering 5*s*., [and] meadow for 8 ploughs. All together it is worth 100*s*.; when received £4; TRE £6. This manor Azur son of Toti held and could sell.

IN 'ROWLEY' HUNDRED

• In Beachampton Leofwine holds of Roger 1 hide. There is land for 1 plough, and there is [1 plough] with 2 villans. [There is] meadow for 1 plough. It is and always was worth 10*s*. This land Leofric, a man of Azur, held and could sell.

M • Godfrey holds of Roger THORNTON. It is assessed at 8 hides. There is land for 10 ploughs. In demesne are 3 [ploughs], and there could be a fourth. There 12 villans with 5 bordars have 5 ploughs, and there could be a sixth. There are 3 slaves, and 1 mill rendering 10 orae, [and] meadow for 6 ploughs. In all it is and was worth £6; TRE £8. This manor Azur son of Toti held and could sell.

• Fulk holds of Roger 'Haseley' [in Thornton] as 1 hide. There is land for 1½ ploughs. There is 1 plough, and there could be half [a plough more]. There is 1 bordar and 1 slave, [and] meadow for 1½ ploughs. It is and was worth 30*s*.; TRE 40*s*. This manor Thorir, a man of King Edward, held and could sell.

## XLII. THE LAND OF RICHARD ENGAINE

IN MURSLEY HUNDRED

• RICHARD Engaine holds in SHENLEY BROOK END 2½ hides as 1 manor. There is land for 2 ploughs, and there are [2 ploughs] with 8 villans and 2 slaves. [There is ] meadow for 2 ploughs, [and] woodland for 50 pigs. It is and always was worth 40*s*. This manor Wulfweard, a thegn of King Edward, held.

## XLIII. THE LAND OF MAINOU THE BRETON

IN AYLESBURY HUNDRED

M • MAINOU the Breton holds in ELLESBOROUGH 14½ hides. There is land for 11 ploughs. In demesne [are] 5 hides, and there are 3 ploughs; and 8 villans with 10 bordars have 8 ploughs. There are 4 slaves, meadow for 3 ploughs, [and] woodland for 100 pigs. In all it is worth £6; when received £4; TRE £10. This manor Leofnoth, a man of King Edward, held.

IN BURNHAM HUNDRED

• In Chalfont St Giles Mainou holds 4 hides and 3 virgates. There is land for 15 ploughs.

In demesne [is] 1 hide, and there are 3 ploughs; and 13 villans and 8 bordars have 12 ploughs. There are 4 slaves, and 3 mills: 1 renders 5 orae and the other 2 render nothing. [There is] meadow for 1 plough, woodland for 600 pigs, and in the same woodland a hawk's eyrie. In all it is worth £6. 10*s*.; when received 100*s*.; TRE £6. 10*s*. This manor Tovi, a thegn of King Edward, held, and there Alweard, his man, had half a hide and could sell it.

• In Aston Sandford Odo holds of Mainou 4½ hides. There is land for 4½ ploughs. In demesne are 3 [ploughs]; and 3 villans with 4 bordars have 1½ ploughs. There are 6 slaves, [and] meadow for 2 ploughs. All together it is worth 100*s*.; when received £4; TRE 100*s*. This manor Soting, a man of Earl Tosti, held and could sell.

IN COTTESLOE HUNDRED

• In Helsthorpe Helgot holds of Mainou 4 hides and 1 virgate as 1 manor. There is land for 3 ploughs. In demesne [are] 2 ploughs; and 2 villans with 1 plough. There are 2 slaves, [and] meadow for 3 ploughs. It is worth 40*s*.; when received 20*s*.; TRE £4. This manor 4 thegns held, one a man of Earl Leofwine, another a man of Wulfwynn, and the third a man of Leofwine of Mentmore, and the fourth a man of Beorhtric. All could sell.

IN YARDLEY HUNDRED

• In Drayton Beauchamp Helgot holds of Mainou 6 hides and 3 virgates as 1 manor, and 3 acres. There is land for 4 ploughs. In demesne is 1 [plough]; and 13 villans have 3 ploughs. There are 2 slaves, meadow for 3 ploughs, [and] woodland for 200 pigs. All together it is and was worth £4; TRE 100*s*. This manor Ælfric, a thegn of King Edward, held and could sell.

IN 'STOTFOLD' HUNDRED

• In Lamport Gerard holds of Mainou 2½ hides. There is land for 3 ploughs. In demesne is 1 [plough]; and 1 villan with 3 bordars have 1 plough, and there could be another. There is 1 slave, meadow for 1 plough, [and] woodland for 40 pigs. All together it is worth 30*s*.; when received 16*s*.; TRE 30*s*. This land Rawn, a man of Bishop Wulfwig, held and could sell.

IN 'MOW' HUNDRED

• In Thornborough Berner holds of Mainou 14 hides and 1 virgate as 1 manor. There is land for 11 ploughs. In demesne are 3 [ploughs]; and 14 villans with 8 bordars have 8 ploughs. There are 3 slaves, and 1 mill rendering 20*s*., [and] meadow for 4 ploughs. In all it is worth £8; when received £6; TRE £8. This manor Thorir, a thegn of King Edward, held.

M • Mainou himself holds PADBURY. It is assessed at 20 hides. There is land for 14 ploughs. In demesne are 3 [ploughs], and there could be a fourth. There 15 villans with 6 bordars have 8 ploughs, and there could be 3 more. There are 8 slaves, and 1 mill rendering 15*s*., [and] woodland for 30 pigs. In all it is worth £12; when received £7; TRE £12.

IN 'SECKLEY' HUNDRED

M • Mainou himself holds STOKE HAMMOND. It is assessed at 10 hides. There is land for 10 ploughs. In demesne [are] 3 hides, and there are 3 ploughs; and 12 villans with 4 bordars have 6 ploughs, and there could be a seventh. There are 6 slaves, and 1 mill rendering 8*s*., [and] meadow for 6 ploughs. In all it is and always was worth £10. This manor 8 thegns held. 1 of them held 6 hides, less half a virgate, as 1 manor, and he and all the other 7 could sell their land to whom they wished.

• In Loughton 2 knights hold of Mainou 5 hides as 1 manor. There is land for 5 ploughs. In demesne are 2 [ploughs]; and 6 villans with 2 bordars have 1½ ploughs, and there could be half [a plough more]. There is 1 slave, [and] meadow for 5 ploughs. In all it is and was worth £3; TRE £4. This manor Ælfric, a thegn of King Edward, held and could sell.

M • Mainou himself holds Wolverton. It is assessed at 20 hides. There is land for 20 ploughs. In demesne [are] 9 hides, and there are 5 ploughs; and 32 villans with 8 bordars have 10 ploughs, and there could be 5 more. There are 10 slaves, and 2 mills rendering 32*s*. 8*d*., [and] meadow for 9 ploughs. In all it is worth £20; when received £15; TRE £20. This manor 3 thegns held. One of these, Godwine, a man of Earl Harold, had 10 hides, and another, Thorir, a housecarl of King Edward, had 7½ hides, and the third, Ælfric, a man of Queen Edith, had 2½ hides. All these could sell to whom they wished.

## XLIIII. THE LAND OF JOSCELIN THE BRETON

IN BURNHAM HUNDRED

M • JOSCELIN the Breton holds in Amersham half a hide. There is land for 1 plough, and there is [1 plough] with 5 bordars, and 1 mill rendering 4*s*. [There is] meadow for 1 plough. It is and always was worth 20*s*. This land Ælfric, a man of Godric the sheriff, held and could sell.

IN COTTESLOE HUNDRED

• In Soulbury Joscelin holds 1½ hides and the third part of a virgate as 1 manor. There is land for 4 ploughs. In demesne [is] half a hide, and there is 1 plough; and 4 villans with 2 bordars have 3 ploughs. There are 3 slaves, and 1 mill rendering 16*s*., [and] meadow for 1 plough. It is and always was worth 40*s*. This manor Alwine, a man of Eadgifu the Fair, held and could sell.

M • Joscelin himself holds CUBLINGTON. It is assessed at 10 hides. There is land for 9 ploughs. In demesne [are] 6 hides, and there are 4 ploughs; and 8 villans with 8 bordars have 5 ploughs. There are 5 slaves, [and] meadow for 4 ploughs. All together it is worth £6; when received £3; TRE £6. This manor 2 men of King Edward held as 2 manors—Godwine 2 hides and Thorkil 8 hides—and they could sell.

• In Grove Robert holds of Joscelin 2½ hides. There is land for 2 ploughs. In demesne is 1 [plough]; and 2 villans have another plough. It is and was worth 20*s*.; TRE 27*s*. This manor 2 brothers held and could sell.

IN YARDLEY HUNDRED

• Ralph holds of Joscelin 1½ hides. There is land for 1 plough, and there is [1 plough] with 1 villan and 2 bordars, [and] meadow for 1 plough. It is and was worth 15*s*.; TRE 20*s*. This land Alwine, a man of Eadgifu the Fair, held and could sell.

## XLV. THE LAND OF URSE DE BERCHERES

IN MURSLEY HUNDRED

• URSE de Bercheres holds in SHENLEY BROOK END 2½ hides as 1 manor. There is land for 2 ploughs. In demesne [are] 1½ hides, and there is 1 plough; and the villans have 1 plough. [There is] woodland for 50 pigs. It is and was worth 30*s*.; TRE 40*s*. This manor Morcar, a man of Earl Harold, held and could sell.

## XLVI. THE LAND OF WINEMAR THE FLEMING

IN BUNSTY HUNDRED

M • WINEMAR holds HANSLOPE. It is assessed at 10 hides. There is land for 26 ploughs. In demesne are 5 hides, and, besides these, 5 carucates of land, and there are 2 ploughs, and there could be 4 more. There 36 villans with 11 bordars have 18 ploughs, and there could be 2 more ploughs. There are 8 slaves, and 1 mill rendering 12*s*., meadow for 11 ploughs, [and] woodland for 1,000 pigs. In all it is worth £24; when received £20; TRE £24. This manor Healfdene, a housecarl of King Edward, held and could sell.

## XLVII. THE LAND OF MARTIN

IN 'SECKLEY' HUNDRED

• MARTIN holds in Woughton on the Green 5½ hides as 1 manor. There is land for 5 ploughs. In demesne are 1½ [ploughs], and there could be half [a plough more]. There 6 villans with 3 bordars have 3 ploughs. [There is] meadow for 2 ploughs. There are 4 slaves. All together it is and was worth 100*s*.; TRE £6. This manor Azur son of Toti, a thegn of King Edward, held, and another thegn, his man, held 1 hide and could sell it.

## XLVIII. THE LAND OF HERVEY

IN DESBOROUGH HUNDRED

● HERVEY the legate holds in Ibstone [Ibstone and Ibstone Common] 2 hides of the king. There is land for 5 ploughs. In demesne [is] half a hide, and there are 2 ploughs; and 7 villans have 2 ploughs, and there could be a third. There is 1 smith, and 4 slaves, [and] woodland for 100 pigs. In all it is and was worth £4; TRE 100*s*. This manor Tovi, a thegn of King Edward, held and could sell.

## XLIX. THE LAND OF HASCOIT MUSARD

● HASCOIT Musard holds in Quainton 2½ hides as 1 manor, and Eudo [holds] of him. There is land for 4 ploughs. In demesne [are] 2 ploughs; and 4 villans with 3 bordars have 1 plough, and there could be another. There are 2 slaves, meadow for 2 ploughs, [and] woodland for 100 pigs. All together it is and always was worth 50*s*. This manor Azur son of Toti, a housecarl of King Edward, held and could sell.

## L. THE LAND OF GUNFRID DE CHOCQUES

IN COTTESLOE HUNDRED

● GUNFRID de Chocques holds in Wingrave 6 hides as 1 manor, and Wibald [holds] of him. There is land for 5 ploughs. In demesne are 3 [ploughs]; and 8 villans with 3 bordars have 2 ploughs. There is 1 slave, [and] meadow for 5 ploughs. In all it is and was worth 100*s*.; TRE £6. This manor Swein, a thegn of King Edward, held and could sell.

## LI. THE LAND OF GILES BROTHER OF ANSCULF

IN STOKE HUNDRED

● GILES brother of Ansculf holds DATCHET as 13½ hides. There is land for 12 ploughs. In demesne [are] 5 hides, and there is
[2] 1 plough, and there could be 4 [more] ploughs. There 16 villans with 6 bordars have 7 ploughs. There are 3 slaves, meadow for 5 ploughs, woodland for 300 pigs, and 2 fisheries [rendering] 2,000 eels. In all it is and was worth £6; TRE £12. Of this manor, Sæwulf, a man of Earl Leofwine, held 6 hides and 3 virgates as 1 manor, and Siward his brother, a man of Earl Harold, 6 hides and 3 virgates; and these men could sell.

IN BURNHAM HUNDRED

● In Boveney Gerard holds of Giles 3 hides. There is land for 2½ ploughs. There is half [a plough], and there could be 2 ploughs [more]. [There is] meadow for 2 ploughs, [and] woodland for 60 pigs. It is and was worth 20*s*.; TRE 60*s*. This manor Siward, a man of Earl Harold, held and could sell.

IN IXHILL HUNDRED

● Alvred of Thame holds of Giles 1 hide and 3 virgates. There is land for 2 ploughs, and there are [2 ploughs], with 2 villans and 1 slave. [There is] meadow for 2 ploughs. It is worth 30*s*.; when received 10*s*.; TRE 40*s*. This manor Sæwulf, a man of Earl Ralph, held and could sell.

## LII. THE LAND OF QUEEN MATILDA

IN DESBOROUGH HUNDRED

M ● Queen MATILDA holds [*sic*] MARLOW [Marlow or Little Marlow]. It is assessed at 15 hides. There is land for 26 ploughs. In demesne [are] 5 hides, and there are 2 ploughs; and 35 villans with 23 bordars have 24 ploughs. There is 1 slave, and 1 mill rendering 20*s*., meadow for 26 ploughs, woodland for 1,000 pigs, and from 1 fishery, 1,000 eels, In all it is worth £25; when received £10; and as much TRE. This manor Earl Ælfgar held.

M ● The queen herself holds [*sic*] HAMBLEDEN. It is assessed at 20 hides. There is land for 30 ploughs. In demesne are 5 [hides], and there are 3 ploughs; and 50 villans with 9 bordars have 27 ploughs. There are 9 slaves, and 1 mill rendering 20*s*., and from 1 fishery, 1,000 eels, meadow for 8 ploughs, [and] woodland for 700 pigs. From all rents, it renders yearly £35 and by tale; when the queen was living £15; TRE £16. This manor Earl Ælfgar held.

## LIII. THE LAND OF COUNTESS JUDITH

IN COTTESLOE HUNDRED

● Countess JUDITH holds in Hollingdon 1 hide and 3½ virgates. Thorkil holds of her. There is land for 2 ploughs. In demesne is 1 [plough]; and 1 villan with 3 bordars has 1 plough. It is and was worth 20*s*.; TRE 30*s*. This man held it TRE and could sell it.

IN BUNSTY HUNDRED

● In Weston Underwood Ansketil holds of Countess Judith 3 virgates. There is land for half a plough, and there is [half a plough]. [There is] meadow for 4 oxen, [and] woodland for 20 pigs. It is and was worth 10*s*.; TRE 20*s*. This land Wulfric, a man of Earl Waltheof, held and could sell.

● In Lavendon Roger holds of the countess 2 hides and 1 virgate and the fourth part of 1 virgate. There is land for 2 ploughs. In demesne is 1 [plough]; and 3 villans with 2 bordars have 1 plough. [There is] meadow for 2 ploughs, [and] woodland for 30 pigs. It is worth 30*s*.; when received 10*s*.; TRE 40*s*. This manor Hunmann, a man of Alli, held and could sell.

● In the same vill Gilbert de Blosseville holds holds [*sic*] of the countess 2 hides and 1 virgate. There is land for 3 ploughs, but there are no ploughs, only 4 bordars. [There is] meadow for 3 ploughs, [and] woodland for 20 pigs. It is and always was worth 20*s*. This manor Alli, a housecarl of King Edward, held and could sell.

● In the same vill Ralph holds of the countess 1 hide. There is land for 1½ ploughs. There is 1 villan and 3 bordars, meadow for 1½ ploughs, [and] woodland for 15 pigs. It is and was worth 10*s*.; TRE 20*s*. This manor Thorbert, a man of Countess Goda, held and could sell.

IN MOULSOE HUNDRED

● In Clifton Reynes Roger of Olney holds 1 hide and half a virgate. There is land for 1 plough, but there is no [plough]. There are 2 bordars, meadow for 1 plough, [and] woodland for 10 pigs. It is and always was worth 10*s*. This land 2 thegns, men of Ælfric son of Goding, held and could sell.

● In the same [vill] Nigel holds of the countess 1½ hides. There is land for 2 ploughs, and there are [2 ploughs], with 2 villans and 4 bordars. There is 1 slave, and half a mill rendering 11*s*., meadow for 2 ploughs, [and] woodland for 20 pigs. From a fishery, 125 eels. It is and was worth 30*s*.; TRE 40*s*. This manor Ælfric, a man of Bishop Wulfwig, held and could sell.

● In Emberton Roger holds of the countess 3 hides as 1 manor. There is land for 3 ploughs. In demesne are 2 [ploughs]; and 6 villans with 3 bordars have 1 plough. [There is] meadow for 2 ploughs, [and] woodland for 60 pigs. It is worth 60*s*.; when received 40*s*.; TRE 60*s*. This manor Alric, a man of Bishop Wulfwig, held.

● In Hardmead Morcar holds 1 hide and 1 virgate of the countess. There is land for 1 plough, and there is [1 plough], with 3 villans and 1 bordar. [There is] meadow for 1 plough, [and] woodland for 50 pigs. It is and was worth 10*s*.; TRE 20*s*. This man held it TRE and could sell it without the leave of his lord.

● In Broughton [near Moulsoe] Morcar holds of the countess 1 hide as 1 manor. There is land for 1 plough, and there is [1 plough], with 1 villan and 1 bordar. [There is] meadow for 1 plough. It is and was worth 10*s*.; TRE 20*s*. This man held it TRE and could sell it.

## LIIII. [THE LAND OF AZELINA, WIFE OF RALPH TAILLEBOIS]

IN COTTESLOE HUNDRED

● AZELINA, wife of Ralph Taillebois, holds of the king half a hide in Soulbury. There is land for 1 plough, and there is [1 plough]. [There is] meadow for 1 plough. It is and always was worth 10*s.* 2 Englishmen hold it, and they themselves held it TRE.

## LV. [THE LAND OF ALRIC THE COOK]

IN 'MOW' HUNDRED

M ● ALRIC the cook holds of the king STEEPLE CLAYDON. It is assessed at 20 hides. There is land for 24 ploughs. In demesne [are] 5 hides, and there are 5 ploughs; and 50 villans with 3 bordars have 19 ploughs. There are 7 slaves, meadow for 4 ploughs, [and] woodland for 100 pigs. In all it is worth £16; when received £11; and as much TRE. This manor Queen Edith held.

## LVI. THE LAND OF ALSIGE

IN BURNHAM HUNDRED

M ● ALSIGE holds of the king in CHESHAM 4 hides. There is land for 9 ploughs. In demesne [are] 1½ hides, and there are 2 ploughs; and 10 villans with 5 bordars have 7 ploughs. There are 6 slaves, and meadow for 2 ploughs, woodland for 800 pigs, and 1 mill rendering 6*s.* 8*d.* It is and was worth £4; TRE 100*s.* This manor Queen Edith held and she herself gave it to the same Alsige after the coming of King William.

IN ASHENDON HUNDRED

● In 'Shortley' [in Quainton] Alsige holds 4 hides as 1 manor. There is land for 6 ploughs. In demesne [are] 2 hides, and there are 2 ploughs; and 5 villans with 4 bordars have 3 ploughs. There are 2 slaves, meadow for 2 ploughs, [and] woodland for 400 pigs. In all it is and always was worth £3. This manor Wulfweard, a man of Queen Edith, held TRE, and she herself gave it to this Alsige with Wulfweard's daughter.

● In Shipton Lee Alsige holds 2 hides of the king. There is land for 1 plough. There is half a plough, and there could be [another] half. [There is] meadow for 1 plough. It is and was worth 10*s.*; TRE 20*s.*; and this land he received with his wife.

## LVII. THE LAND OF LEOFWINE OF NUNEHAM COURTENAY

IN MURSLEY HUNDRED

● LEOFWINE of Nuneham Courtenay holds of the king in Salden 2 hides and 3½ virgates as 1 manor. There is land for 3 ploughs. In demesne [is] 1 plough; and 6 villans with 3 bordars have 2 ploughs. There are 2 slaves, [and] meadow for 3 ploughs. It is and was worth 30*s.*; when received 40*s.* This manor this man held TRE and could sell.

● In Mursley Leofwine holds 4 hides. There is land for 3 ploughs. There are 2 [ploughs], and there could be a third. There are 4 villans with 2 bordars, [and] meadow for 1 plough. It is and was worth 20*s.*; TRE 30*s.* This manor this man held TRE and could sell.

IN 'STOTFOLD' HUNDRED

● In Maids Moreton Leofwine holds 5 hides as 1 manor. There is land for 5 ploughs. In demesne [are] 2 hides, and there is half a plough, and there could be another 1½ [ploughs]. There 3 villans with 2 bordars have 1½ ploughs, and there could be half [a plough] more. There are 5 slaves, and 1 mill rendering 10*s.*, [and] meadow for 2 ploughs. In all it is and always was worth 40*s.* This manor this man held TRE and could sell.

IN 'ROWLEY' HUNDRED

● In Beachampton Leofwine holds 4 hides as 1 manor. There is land for 4 ploughs. In demesne [is] 1 hide, and there are 2 ploughs; and 5 villans with 6 bordars have 2 ploughs. There are 2 slaves, [and] meadow for 3 ploughs. It is and was worth 40*s.*; TRE 50*s.* This manor the same Leofwine held TRE and could sell.

IN MOULSOE HUNDRED

● In Wavendon Godwine the priest holds of Leofwine 1 virgate. There is land for 4 oxen. There are 3 bordars, and meadow for 4 oxen. It is and was worth 2*s.*; TRE 5*s.* This man held it TRE and could sell.

IN 'STOTFOLD' HUNDRED

● A certain bandy-legged man holds in alms of the king Evershaw as 1 hide. There is land for 2 ploughs, and there are [2 ploughs] with 2 villans. It is and always was worth 20*s.* This man held it TRE.

IN 'STOTFOLD' HUNDRED

● HUGH fitzGozhere holds in Dadford of the king 2 hides in alms. There is land for 4 ploughs. There is 1 [plough], and there could be 3 [more]. There are 3 bordars, meadow for 4 ploughs, [and] woodland for 200 pigs. It is and was worth 20*s.*; TRE 40*s.* This land 2 thegns, Rawn and Wulfweard, held and could sell.

IN MOULSOE HUNDRED

● Leofwine Chava holds of the king 1 hide in Wavendon. There is land for 1 plough, and there is [1 plough], with 3 villans and 5 bordars. There is 1 slave, and meadow for 1 plough, [and] woodland for 50 pigs. It is and always was worth 10*s.* This land Leofwine himself, reeve of the king, held and could sell.

IN 'SECKLEY' HUNDRED

● Leofwine Oaura holds of the king 1 hide and 1 virgate in Simpson. There is land for 1 plough, and there is [1 plough], with 2 villans and 2 bordars. [There is] meadow for 1 plough. It is and always was worth 10*s.* This man held it TRE and could sell it.

IN AYLESBURY HUNDRED

● Leofwine holds of the king half a hide in "Wandene". There is land for 1 plough. There is half [a plough], and there could be [another] half. There is 1 bordar, [and] woodland for 30 pigs and rendering 10*s.* It is and always was worth 10*s.* This man held it TRE and could sell it. This land Ralph attached to Wendover but it did not belong to it TRE.

● In Wendover 3 men hold 1 hide of the king. There is land for 1 plough, and there is [1 plough] with 1 bordar. It is and was worth 20*s.*; TRE 40*s.* The same men held it TRE and could sell it. Now they are in the farm of the king in Wendover, in which they were not TRE.

IN BUNSTY HUNDRED

● Ketil holds of the king half a hide in Lavendon. There is land for half a plough, and there is [half a plough] with 1 bordar. [There is] meadow for 1 plough, [and] woodland for 10 pigs. It is and was worth 7*s.*; TRE 10*s.* This man held it TRE and could sell it.

IN MOULSOE HUNDRED

● Godric Cratel holds of the king 8½ hides as 1 manor in Milton Keynes. There is land for 10 ploughs. In demesne [are] 2½ ploughs, and there could be half [a plough more]. There 18 villans with 6 bordars have 8 ploughs. There are 6 slaves, and 1 mill rendering 6*s.* 8*d.*, [and] meadow for 8 ploughs. All together it is and was worth 100*s.*; TRE £8. This manor Queen Edith held.

IN RISBOROUGH HUNDRED

● Hearding holds of the king 1½ hides in Horsenden. There is land for 1 plough, and there is [1 plough] with 2 bordars. It is and was worth 10*s.*; TRE 20*s.* This land Wulfræd held and could sell.

IN DESBOROUGH HUNDRED

● Swærting and Hearding hold of the king Bradenham as 2 hides. There is land for 2 ploughs, and there are [2 ploughs] with 2 villans. It is and always was worth 20*s.* 2 brothers, men of King Edward, held it and could sell it.

IN YARDLEY HUNDRED

● In Cheddington Swærting holds of the king 2 hides and 1 virgate. There is land for 1 plough, and there is [1 plough], with 1 villan and 2 slaves. [There is] meadow for 1 plough. It is and always was worth 20*s.* Fin the Dane held it and could sell it.

IN 'SECKLEY' HUNDRED

● In Caldecote Swærting holds 2½ hides. There is land for 1 plough. There is 1 [plough], and there could be another. In demesne [are] 1½ hides. There are 2 bordars, and meadow for 1 plough. It is and always was worth 20*s.* This land Gunni, a man of Ælfric son of Goding, held and could sell.

IN COTTESLOE HUNDRED

● In Soulbury Godwine the beadle holds of the king half a hide. There is land for 1 plough, and there is [1 plough] with 1 bordar. [There is] meadow for 1 plough. It is and always was worth 7½*s.* Alric Bolest held it TRE, and he who now holds it says this, that after the coming of King William it was forfeit.